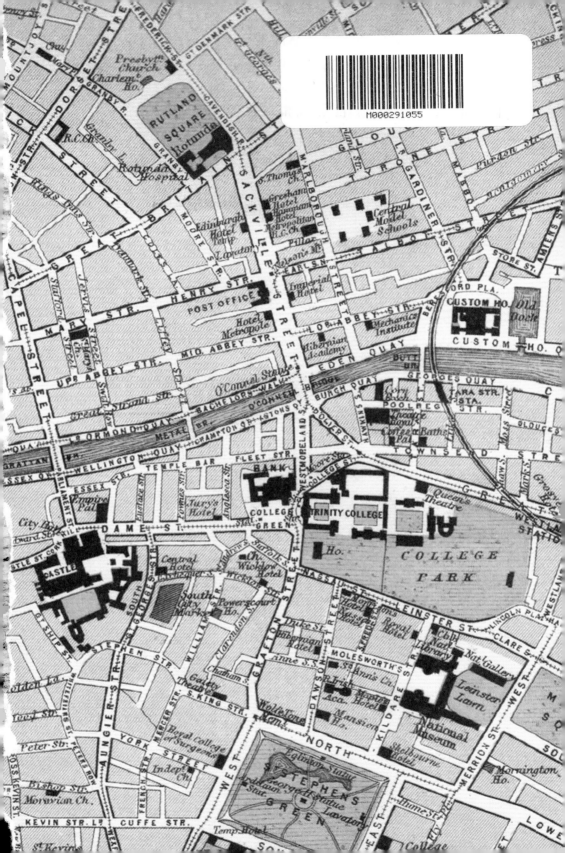

The
Book
About
Everything

About the editors

Declan Kiberd has taught for decades at University College Dublin and at Notre Dame, and been a visiting professor at Cambridge University and the Sorbonne. He is author of *Inventing Ireland* and of *Ulysses and Us*, and has edited *Ulysses* in a student's annotated edition for Penguin Modern Classics.

Enrico Terrinoni holds a chair at the Università per Stranieri di Perugia. His translation of *Ulysses* (published in an inexpensive edition aimed at ordinary readers) won the Prix Napoli. He has recently published a dual-language version of the book, with extensive commentary and notes to assist Italian readers. He has also translated Joyce's *Finnegans Wake*, works by Brendan Behan, Oscar Wilde and the poems and prose of President Michael D. Higgins.

Catherine Wilsdon has written a study of the influence of French social and cultural thought on the playwright J. M. Synge. She has worked for the University of Notre Dame in Ireland where she taught courses on literary representations of the west of Ireland. She now works at the Irish Poetry Reading Archive at University College Dublin.

The
Book
About
Everything

Eighteen Artists,
Writers and Thinkers on
James Joyce's *Ulysses*

Edited by
Declan Kiberd, Enrico Terrinoni
and Catherine Wilsdon

HEAD
ᵗZEUS

An Apollo Book

First published in the UK in 2022 by Head of Zeus Ltd, part of Bloomsbury Publishing Plc

9 7 5 3 1 2 4 6 8

A catalogue record for this book is available from the British Library.

ISBN (HB): 9781801104388
ISBN (XTPB): 9781801104395
ISBN (E): 9781801104401

Typeset by benstudios.co.uk

Printed and bound in Great Britain by CPI Group (UK) Ltd, Croydon CRO 4YY

Head of Zeus Ltd
5–8 Hardwick Street
London EC1R 4RG

WWW.HEADOFZEUS.COM

Contents

Introduction 1

A Note from the Editors 3

Telemachus – Joyce and the Greeks 5
    John Dillon

Nestor – *Ulysses*, Race and the New Bloomusalem 23
    Ronit Lentin

Proteus 45
    Richard Kearney

Calypso 67
    Tim Parks

Lotus-Eaters – Turn on, Tune in, Bloom out 87
    Edoardo Camurri

Hades – Rites of Passage 107
    Lawrence Taylor

Aeolus – Inside 'Aeolus' and *The Irish Times*,
    Everything is Copy 131
    Lara Marlowe

Lestrygonians 153
    Mike Fitzgerald

Scylla & Charybdis – Homer... Shakespeare...
 Joyce... Borges. 183
  Carlos Gamerro

Wandering Rocks – The 'Retrospective Arrangement'
 of Dublin in 'Wandering Rocks' 205
  Shinjini Chattopadhyay

Sirens – Sgt Joyce's Lonely Hearts Club Band 229
  Joseph O'Connor

Cyclops – A Sneer and a Smile 251
  Derek Hand

Nausicaa 269
  Jhumpa Lahiri

Oxen of the Sun – Prescience and Parody. 297
  Rhona Mahony

Circe – Night-Rule in Nighttown. 319
  Caitriona Lally

Eumaeus – Leopold Bloom, Master-Economist. 345
  David McWilliams

Ithaca – Reading as the Police 373
  Eric A. Lewis

Penelope 393
  Marina Carr

Works Cited. 407

Index 412

Introduction

A university classmate of Joyce's, Con Curran, once joked that he made the little he knew go a long way. He was often a lazy student; but whenever he felt frustrated by his ignorance about a given topic, he knew exactly the person whom he should consult to put him right – whether the subject was the dimensions of a house in Eccles Street, the divisions of the police in Sandymount or the passages of Dublin's underwater system. In *Ulysses* he devoted each episode to a particular subject or profession – education; philosophy; shopkeeping; undertaking; drama; music; obstetrics; bartending; and so on.

Joyce became one of the most celebrated authors in the world, and his book influenced writers (and other kinds of artists) on every continent. Commentators have written valuable studies of his style, his pulverizing of the English language and his structuring of *Ulysses* according to scenes from *The Odyssey* of Homer. He raised banal, ordinary events on a single day, 16 June 1904, to the intensity of poetry.

It struck us that the centenary of the publication of *Ulysses* in 1922 could be a good moment at which to invite distinguished professionals and authors, whose expertise often lies elsewhere, to write a short essay on the ways in which

Joyce uses an episode to treat their particular subject in this 'book about everything'. We left each contributor utterly free as to the approach taken. Some had read the book before and kindly returned to it in the context of our invitation; others encountered it for the first time. The result is a medley of voices, all eloquent, with something urgent to say not only about Joyce but about an aspect of his world which they know very well.

Joyce wrote his book to celebrate Everyman and Everywoman. He also believed that Everyman and Everywoman should be able to read it in their own way. In the following pages we get a glimpse of how that might be done. And we thank each essayist for their contribution.

Declan Kiberd
Enrico Terrinoni
Catherine Wilsdon
Bloomsday 2022

A Note from the Editors

In editing *The Book About Everything*, a collection of personal responses to *Ulysses*, we felt that the voices of individual contributors should be foregrounded as much as possible. Therefore, we asked contributors to avoid, where possible, the apparatus of academic writing. Pagination is included for *Ulysses* and *Finnegans Wake* only and we have used Penguin editions of both texts. Where quotes from *Ulysses* appear, the page number is given. For quotes from *Finnegans Wake*, page and line numbers are provided. All other works are referred to by name of author or work only, either in the text or in parentheses. We include a single works cited section at the end of the book including all works mentioned by contributors. We are very grateful to the Keough-Naughton Institute for Irish Studies at the University of Notre Dame for supporting this collection.

Telemachus

Joyce and the Greeks

JOHN DILLON

John Dillon was Regius Chair of Greek at Trinity College Dublin, following a period as Professor of Classics at the University of California, Berkeley. His father knew many of the real-life characters who appear in *Ulysses*. A graduate of Oxford, Professor Dillon is widely regarded as one of the foremost commentators on Plotinus.

My first encounter with the works of Joyce is lost now in the mists of time, but I would have come to a knowledge of him at an early age through my father, Myles Dillon, who had encountered him initially when he was a graduate student in Paris in the 1920s, and was brought round to visit Joyce by Padraic Colum when Colum was in Paris. Joyce, he recalled, on that occasion, while being duly hospitable, gave him a bad time about his father, John Dillon's 'betrayal' of Parnell – Joyce being an inveterate Parnellite, and my grandfather having been a leader of the anti-Parnellite faction. My father did not, I must say, entirely approve of Joyce, though he had picked up in Paris a first edition of *Ulysses*, and liked from time to time to take down *Finnegans Wake* from the shelves, and read passages of it out loud, *con brio*, and much chuckling. He was much more, however, a friend of Oliver Gogarty, who often came to visit us on his lecture tours around America, when I was still a small boy, in Madison, Wisconsin, where my father held the Chair of Celtic and Comparative Philology at the university. As regards the Martello Tower in Sandycove, he always maintained that it was Gogarty, not Joyce, who paid the rent on that!

In later times, my closest encounter with Joyce's works was not in fact with *Ulysses*, much though I have always admired it, but rather with the *Wake*, when in the mid-1970s, in Berkeley, California, I was invited by Brendan O'Hehir, then in the English department of the university, to join him in sing a classical lexicon to that work. This involved us ening after evening, after being fed by my faithful h with our copy of the great work before us, and f Jameson between us, chanting the text out loud, until we came upon something that rang a bell. The results are adverted to at the end of this paper.

However, our business on this occasion is with *Ulysses*, and with the initial 'Telemachus' episode in particular, and Joyce's knowledge of Greek language and culture in relation to that. In that connection, let us first take into account some background data. On 4 October 1906, some months after his arrival in Rome, Joyce wrote, in the course of a letter to his brother Stanislaus: 'I wish I knew something of Latin or Roman History. But it's not worthwhile beginning now. So let the ruins rot.' Much later, in a letter to Harriet Weaver, on 24 June 1921, he says: 'I don't even know Greek, though I am spoken of as erudite. My father wanted me to take Greek as a third language, my mother German, my friends Irish. Result, I took Italian. I speak or used to speak Modern Greek not too badly [...] and have spent a great deal of time with Greeks of all kinds from noblemen down to onionsellers, chiefly the latter. I am superstitious about them. They bring me luck.'

All this adds up to a confession of little Latin and less Greek – or, as he puts it in the *Wake* (FW 25.15), 'some little laughings and some less of cheeks'. But how seriously are we to take it? My intention on this occasion is to explore certain selected passages of the initial, 'Telemachus', episode of *Ulysses*, to demonstrate just how much Joyce had absorbed, over a life of constant enquiry, of Greek language and culture, particularly mythology and history.

So what did Joyce, after all, know of Greek? Firs⟨...⟩ a schoolboy, he had to learn his share of Latin, as d⟨...⟩ everybody else, but he was never introduced to Greek ⟨...⟩

had always a much more restricted clientele, especially in this country, though it was in his day available in both the schools that he attended, Clongowes and Belvedere. Indeed, the only way in which Joyce was introduced to things Greek in either place would have been through the study of Greek mythology and history, and even then only as a background to Roman history and literature. As he testifies himself, he could have taken Greek, and was urged to do so by his father, but, with characteristic self-will, he chose Italian.

I would like to approach the present topic, in fact, by first considering the figure of 'stately, plump' (U 1) Buck Mulligan (representing, of course, Oliver St John Gogarty), who stands forth as an emblem of much that Joyce (in the person of Stephen Dedalus) objects to – specifically, an aggressively British-style Classical education in both Latin and Greek, topped off by a period of polishing in Trinity College Dublin.

Mulligan's elaborate praise of the sea, 'our great sweet mother' (U 3), constitutes the occasion for showing off his command of Greek:

> — God, he said quietly. Isn't the sea what Algy calls it: a grey sweet mother? The snotgreen sea. The scrotumtightening sea. *Epi oinopa ponton.* Ah, Dedalus, the Greeks. I must teach you. You must read them in the original. *Thalatta! Thalatta!* She is our great sweet mother. Come and look. (U 3)

Now those of us of a certain age who studied Greek at school can hardly have escaped the study of Xenophon's *Anabasis*, or *The March Up Country*, which generally constituted the first continuous work of Greek prose with which one was confronted, corresponding to Caesar's *Gallic Wars* in Latin. It is indeed a lively and fascinating work, but one was hardly in a state to appreciate that when one first had to deal with it, and one almost invariably progressed no further than the end of Book I, by which time things had hardly got going. Joyce, of course, did not have this doubtful pleasure himself, but, as co-occupier of the Martello Tower in Sandymount for a season, he was thrust into contact with someone who did, and who was not backward in showing off his knowledge.

One of the most famous passages in Xenophon's *Anabasis* is one from the fourth book, which one did not normally reach in Greek, but which, it seems to me, we all knew about, where the exhausted Greek expeditionary force, after months of slogging through the mountains of eastern Turkey, breast one last ridge, and see before them the expanse of the Black Sea. I let Xenophon tell the story:

> They came to the mountain on the fifth day, the name of the mountain being *Thêkhês*. When the men in front reached the summit and caught sight of the sea there was great shouting. Xenophon and the rearguard heard it and thought that there were some more enemies attacking in front, since there were natives of the country they had ravaged following them behind, and the rearguard had killed some of them and made prisoners of others in an ambush, and captured about twenty rawhide shields, with the hair on. However, when the shouting got louder and drew nearer, and those who were constantly going

forward started running towards the men in front who kept on shouting, and the more there were of them the more shouting there was, it looked as though this was something of considerable importance. So Xenophon mounted his horse, and, taking Lykios and the cavalry with him, rode forward to give support, and quite soon they heard the soldiers shouting out 'The sea! The sea!' (*Thalatta! Thalatta!*), and passing the word down the column. Then indeed they all began to run, the rearguard and all, and drove on the baggage animals and the horses at full speed; and when they had all got to the top, the soldiers, with tears in their eyes, embraced each other and their generals and captains.

Here the key phrase is, of course, *Thalatta! Thalatta!*

This familiarity with Greek, as I say, was one of the things that Joyce tended to dislike about Gogarty, but he did expend a certain amount of effort in later life, in Zurich, Trieste and Paris, in trying to 'read it in the original', though never with much success.* This key phrase, though, *Thalatta! Thalatta!*, keeps popping up later, in *Finnegans Wake*, in various odd, and characteristically Joycean, ways. First of all, we come upon it at FW 93.24 transformed into the incriminating Letter, dug up by the Hen (see also FW 111.30–3):†

---

* Just a little earlier, Mulligan has said to Stephen, 'We must go to Athens. Will you come if I can get the aunt to fork out twenty quid?' Joyce never in fact got to Athens.

† This letter, it should be specified, was sent across the ocean from Boston by Anna Livia Plurabelle, and reveals the sordid truth about HCE. It has been buried, but is dug up from a rubbish heap by a scavenging hen, and is now exposed to the inspection and criticism of the world.

And so it all ended. Artha kama dharma moksa. Ask Kavya for the kay. And so everybody heard their plaint and all listened to their plause. The letter! The litter! And the soother the bitther! (FW 93.22–4)

Just below, at FW 100.02, it becomes 'The latter! The latter!', while much later, at FW 328.29, in a context where a marriage is being arranged,* we find 'tha lassy, tha lassy'. Later again, towards the end of chapter 15, in a passage depicting Earwicker's founding of Dublin, the phrase has become 'Galata! Galata!' (FW 547.32) (with overtones of the nymph Galatea – casting Earwicker, presumably, as Polyphemus).

And finally, in the last chapter of the work, which depicts the resurrection of the hero and a new dawn, we find the phrase again, both in the first paragraph ('The leader, the leader' – FW 593.13), and, in translation, as 'Sea, sea!', near the end, at FW 626.7. The former of these is worth quoting in context, as a nice piece of Joycean composition, hailing the dawn:

Sonne feine, somme feehn avaunt! Guld modning, have youse viewsed Piers' aube? Thane yaars agon we have used yoors up since when we have fused now orther [sc. *orthros*, 'dawn']. Calling all daynes. Calling all daynes to dawn. The old breeding bradsted culminwilth of natures to Foyn MacHooligan. The leader, the leader! Securest jubilends albas Temoram. (FW 593.8–14)

---

* In Earwicker's public house, between a sailor and the daughter of a tailor, to patch up a quarrel between the sailor and the tailor (who represent, in one aspect, the eternal tension of opposites).

The reference to the (resurrected) leader here may be a reminiscence of Parnell as 'the lost leader' – transformed into Finn McCool – who would be viewed by his faithful partisans as enthusiastically as Xenophon's troops once viewed the sea. The use of the phrase, overall, serves as a good example, I think, of the ironic and surrealist manner in which Joyce makes use of material, Greek and otherwise.

But we must turn now, even briefly, to Homer, and the *Odyssey* in particular – Mulligan's *epi oinopa ponton* ('on the wine-dark sea'), after all, is a recurring hexameter line-ending in the poem, as Joyce presumably knew. I don't intend to make any obvious remarks here about the structure of *Ulysses*, but rather to touch on a topic of some significance when we are dealing with Joyce's use of the classics, the question of the particular *secondary* sources to which he had access. One of these was the remarkable Victor Bérard, author of *Les Phéniciens et l'Odyssée* (1902–3) and *Les Navigations d'Ulysse* (1927–9) – this latter composed when he was a member of the French senate, representing the *département* of Jura. I wish I could claim to have read this remarkable book, over the top though it undoubtedly is, but I cannot, though I do hold to a modified form of its thesis, to wit, that the journey of Odysseus to the Western world is loosely inspired by a Semitic, or at least Middle Eastern (originally Sumerian), source, that of the Epic of Gilgamesh – the main significant difference being that Gilgamesh had a definite purpose in undertaking his journey, whereas Odysseus does not: he simply wants to get home, and is driven out of his way by contrary winds. Joyce knew Bérard's work well and greatly admired it (it gave him the underpinning for his decision to make his Ulyssean hero a Jew). Joyce studied Bérard intensively, and took copious notes on him, while he was completing *Ulysses* in Paris in 1919–21, and Bérard also took an interest in Joyce, expressing a desire to meet him in 1928 after reading a French version of the 'Proteus' chapter in the *Nouvelle Révue Française* (a desire of which we do not know whether it was ever consummated). Joyce did, however, go to the scholar-statesman's funeral in November 1931.

His admiration for Bérard, however, does not inhibit him from a nice piece of irony at his expense in the *Wake*, where we find, towards the end of a survey of world literature (all of which is contained in the Letter which has been scratched up by the Hen) a reference to

> the littleknown periplic bestseller popularly associated with the names of the wretched mariner (trianforan deffwedoff our plumsucked pattern shapekeeper) a Punic admiralty report, *From MacPerson's Oshean Round by the Tides of Jason's Cruise*, had been cleverly capsized and saucily republished as a dodecanesian baedeker of the every-tale-a-treat-in-itself variety which could hope satisfactorily to tickle me gander as game your goose. (FW 123.22–9)

The 'periplic bestseller' is a reference to Bérard's postulated Phoenician original of the *Odyssey*, based on accounts of Bronze Age Phoenician voyages in the western Mediterranean and beyond, into the Atlantic. Just below we hear that 'the original document was in what is known as Hanno O'Nonhanno's unbrookable script, that is to say, it showed no sign of punctuation of any sort' – as, of course, an early Semitic document would not.

To return to the 'Telemachus' section, however, I would like to draw attention to a small linguistic detail, very near the beginning of the work which comes across as a bit of Hellenic showing-off, not by Buck Mulligan, but rather by Joyce himself. In describing, with due irony, Mulligan's imposing visage, he comes out with the following:

> He peered sideways up and gave a long low whistle of call, then paused awhile in rapt attention, his even white teeth glistening here and there with gold points. Chrysostomos. Two strong shrill whistles answered through the calm. (U 1)

This epithet, 'golden-mouth', comes across very oddly, as from a young man being portrayed as innocent of Greek, and I would be interested to know just how Joyce picked it up. Two distinguished figures of later Greco-Roman antiquity were graced with this epithet, the orator and essayist Dio of Prusa, from the first century AD, and the noted Christian theologian St John Chrysostom (c. AD 347–407), famous for the eloquence of his sermons, who served as Archbishop of Constantinople from 397 to 403, when he was deposed, largely owing to his quarrel with the Empress Eudoxia. It is probably this latter of whom Joyce knew something, but I find it most significant that he knows what the epithet means – and that he chooses to display his knowledge in this way.

Another, even more baffling, snippet of Greek – baffling because of its almost total lack of context – occurs on page 7, apropos the Englishman Haines, to whom Mulligan is threatening to 'give [...] a ragging' (U 6) if he creates a disturbance, or annoys Stephen. Just following on a passage conjuring up a vigorous ragging from Oxford that Mulligan has alluded to, we have the mysterious line: 'To ourselves... new paganism... omphalos' (U 7).

Now the first two elements of this mysterious sentence might be allusions to Sinn Féin, and to a post-Christian society that Stephen might wish to establish in Ireland (though such would hardly have formed part of the Sinn Féin agenda!), but what are we to make of 'omphalos'? This Greek word, meaning 'navel', has various interesting connotations that could be relevant, but, one asks oneself, how could Joyce have come to know of them?

Specifically, this title was bestowed upon a certain sacred stone that reposed in the Temple of Apollo at Delphi, which was meant to represent the 'navel', or central point, of the earth. This was based upon a rather simple-minded myth, to the effect that Zeus, wishing to ascertain the central point of the earth, released two eagles to fly round the earth in opposite directions, in order to note where they would meet up, since that would mark the mid-point of the earth, and this turned out to be in Delphi. Conceivably, Joyce might have wished to claim this honour for Dublin – but then, as we know, he did not have a very high opinion of Dublin, or of Ireland in general ('the old sow that eats her farrow' – U 692) – or even for the Martello Tower!

Nonetheless, this would seem to be what is going on. *Omphalos* occurs again a little later, when Haines asks Mulligan, 'Do you pay rent for this tower?'

— Twelve quid, Buck Mulligan said.

— To the secretary of state for war, Stephen added over
his shoulder.

They halted while Haines surveyed the tower and said at
last:

— Rather bleak in wintertime, I should say. Martello you
call it?

— Billy Pitt had them built, Buck Mulligan said, when
the French were on the sea. But ours is the *omphalos*.
(U 20)

So there it is. The tower is, after all, in Buck Mulligan's
mind, fortified by his knowledge of Greek culture, in some
sense the centre of the earth – and this is somehow prefigured
by the earlier reference, mysterious and allusive as it is.

However, passing on from these baffling details, I want to
turn in conclusion to some comments on Joyce's knowledge of
Greek philosophy, and the uses to which he puts it, even though
this does not manifest itself in the 'Telemachus' episode. Again,
let us bypass the obvious. Joyce, as all agree, was in philosophy
an Aristotelian rather than a Platonist. Aristotle, filtered
through Thomist scholastic spectacles, was, of course, the
intellectual underpinning of most of his teachers at university
(such as Fr John Darlington, the Dean of Studies and Professor
of English, with whom he had a number of jousts), but the
incisiveness and systematic nature of Aristotle's thought no
doubt appealed to that side of his own personality, while he

shared Aristotle's own impatience with the airy-fairy aspect of Platonism (which Joyce associated with the theosophy of Yeats and A.E.). But the anarchic side of Joyce's personality also could not resist poking fun at the preciseness and pedantry of Aristotelian definitions, and of that tendency I would like to pick out just two contiguous examples from early in *Ulysses*.

Of Aristotle's works, one expects Joyce to have studied fairly closely the *Poetics* and the *Rhetoric*, and even the *De Anima*, but one does not so much expect to find evidence of a detailed interest in logical and physical topics. However, such there certainly is. First of all, in the 'Nestor' episode just following on from 'Telemachus', as Stephen is hearing a boy reciting Milton's *Lycidas* in class, his mind wanders back, first to the problem of the deaths of Pyrrhus and of Julius Caesar, and then to the more abstract question as to whether only that event is possible which is actually the case:

> Time has branded them and fettered they are lodged in the room of the infinite possibilities they have ousted. But can those have been possible seeing that they never were? Or was that only possible which came to pass? Weave, weaver of the wind. (U 30)

This in turn, as the boy starts to recite *Lycidas*, leads him, by association of ideas, to think of Aristotle's definition of movement (*kinêsis*) as 'an actuality of the possible as possible'. He derives this from Aristotle's discussion in Book III, ch. 1, of the *Physics* (*hê tou dynamei ontos entelecheia, hêi toiouton, kinêsis estin*), which we know him to have studied in a French translation. And this in turn leads Stephen to further daydreams about his reading of Aristotle in a Paris library, and to thoughts of the Unmoved Mover of *Metaphysics* XII, and of the discussion of the soul in the *De Anima*:

> Aristotle's phrase formed itself within the gabbled verses [sc. of the boy Talbot reciting *Lycidas*] and floated out into the studious silence of the library of Sainte Genevieve where he had read, sheltered from the sin of Paris, night by night. By his elbow a delicate Siamese conned a handbook of strategy. Fed and feeding brains about me: under glowlamps, impaled, with faintly beating feelers: and in my mind's darkness a sloth of the underworld, reluctant, shy of brightness, shifting her dragon scaly folds. Thought is the thought of thought. Tranquil brightness. The soul is in a manner all that is: the soul is the form of forms. Tranquillity sudden, vast, candescent: form of forms. (U 30–1)

What is delightful here is how Joyce weaves the dry Aristotelian definitions into the fabric of Stephen's reverie, with the aim, presumably, of suggesting how deeply unsuited Stephen is to the banal level of teaching that he is perforce stuck with.

Not long afterwards, as Stephen walks on Sandymount Strand, at the beginning of the 'Proteus' episode, his thoughts turn to the Aristotelian definition of the objects of sensory perception. The issue here is the nature of the visible – what it is that our sense of sight actually apprehends. Joyce has been reading the treatise of Aristotle *On Sense and Sensible Objects* – as we know from a perusal of his notebooks – and in particular the following passage:

Let us deal with colour first. Each of these terms [sc. for objects of the senses – *aisthêta*] is used in two senses: as actual or as potential. We have explained in the treatise *On the Soul* the sense in which actual colour and sound are identical with or different from the actual sensations, that is, seeing or hearing. Now let us explain what each of them must be to produce the sensation in full actuality. In that treatise we have already said of light, that it is, indirectly, the colour of the transparent [*chrôma tou diaphanous kata symbebêkos*] for whenever there is a fiery element in the transparent, its presence is light, while its absence is darkness. What we call 'transparent' is not peculiar to air or water or any other body so described, but a common nature or potency, which is not separable, but resides in these bodies and in all others, to a greater or lesser extent; hence just as every body must have some ultimate surface [*eschaton*], so must this. The nature of light resides in the transparent when undefined; but clearly the transparent which inheres in bodies must have an ultimate surface, and it is plain from the facts that this ultimate surface is colour; for colour either is in the limit [*peras*] or else is the limit itself.

It may seem remarkable that Joyce should have taken such a close interest in Aristotle's theory of sensation, but it plainly answered to something in which he was deeply interested. Let us see what he makes of it:

Ineluctable modality of the visible: at least that if no more, thought through my eyes. Signatures of all things I am here to read, seaspawn and seawrack, the nearing tide, that rusty boot. Snotgreen, bluesilver, rust: coloured signs. Limits of the diaphane. But he adds: in bodies. Then he was aware of them bodies before of them coloured. How? By knocking his sconce against them, sure. Go easy. Bald he was and a millionaire, *maestro di color che sanno*. Limit of the diaphane in. Why in? Diaphane, adiaphane. If you can put your five fingers through it, it is a gate, if not a door. Shut your eyes and see. (U 45)

Stephen now shuts his eyes and begins to explore the sense of sound; but at this point we may leave him.

We have, in truth, only touched here on a few details of Joyce's many-faceted appropriation of things Hellenic, but these will serve, I trust, to show how complex and sophisticated that appropriation was. Of course, the classical world is only one of the aspects of world culture on which Joyce draws, especially in the *Wake* – but it is inevitably a major one – as attested by the 653 pages of the O'Hehir–Dillon *Classical Lexicon for Finnegans Wake*.

Nestor

Ulysses, Race and the New Bloomusalem

RONIT LENTIN

Ronit Lentin is a Palestine-born Jewish Irish political sociologist, and a writer of fiction and non-fiction on themes of race and migration. Among her books are *Racism and Anti-racism in Ireland*, with Robbie McVeigh, *Thinking Palestine*, *Traces of Racial Exception: Racializing Israeli Settler Colonialism* and *Disavowing Asylum: Documenting Ireland's Asylum Industrial Complex*, with Vukašin Nedeljković. She has taught at Trinity College Dublin.

A graffito somewhere on a Dublin brick wall reads, 'Bloom is a cod' (U 616). Modernist literature's most famous Jew is indeed a cod. Joyce's Jew Leopold Bloom – whose father, a Jewish migrant from Hungary named Virag ('flower' in Hungarian, hence Bloom), converted to Protestantism and had his son, born to a non-Jewish mother, converted too – is no Jew in the halachic sense. Joyce took it upon himself to position what the Jewish–British Marxist Isaac Deutscher called a 'non-Jewish Jew' at the centre of *Ulysses*. Deutscher explains a 'non-Jewish Jew' thus: 'If it is not race, what then makes a Jew? Religion? I am an atheist. Jewish nationalism? I am internationalist [...] I am a Jew because I feel the Jewish tragedy as my own tragedy; because I feel the pulse of Jewish history; because I should like to do all I can to assure the real, not spurious, security and self-respect of the Jews.' Today, Joyce would have been questioned by critics of cultural appropriation as to his right, as a non-Jew, to cast a Jew as his protagonist, who, with yet another pinch, could be regarded as Deutscher's heretic Jew who transcends Jewry, yet belongs to a Jewish tradition.

I want to propose that *Ulysses* isn't really about Jews or anti-Semitism at all, but is rather the classic modernist novel about race and white dominion, and that Joyce – no race scholar he – understood race as early as 1907 when he delivered his lecture 'Ireland, Island of Saints and Sages', more of which anon.

So I am thinking about the 'Nestor' episode, and about Mr Deasy's racist sneer about colonized Ireland having never persecuted 'the jews' because 'she never let them in' (U 44, 5) – a blatant expression of institutional racism, particularly in the current brutal global border regime. And I bask in Joyce's prophetic tale of an Ireland already not purely 'Irish' long before the present-day mantra of the post-partition 'migration turning point' when in the 1990s, allegedly for the first time, Ireland received more immigrants than sent emigrants away. And I ponder how to write about *Ulysses* and race from the vantage point of this particular wandering Jew who, when she found herself in the Hibernian metropolis in the late 1960s, used Bloom as her walking guide in navigating her alienation in Christian Dublin. Attempting to not succumb to Joycean obscurities, I want to divide my essay about Ireland as a racial state into three streams of consciousness, the culmination of some thirty years of thinking about race and racism both in Ireland and in my native Palestine (aka the racial colony of Israel).

The first stream circles around Joyce's choice of making Bloom twice the outsider, alienated from Christian society and Jewish community alike, a hybrid flâneur par excellence whose presence in pre-independence Dublin was more a consequence of Jewish wanderings than of Ireland's hundred thousand welcomes, that facile Bord Fáilte slogan shown for all its ugly falsity during the Nazi era. As Louis Lentin writes: 'Although Bloom carries with him bits of his Jewish heritage, Joyce has created in him a man adrift, Irish only by birth, Jewish only by inclination. Yet Bloom belongs only in Dublin, a Jew yet not a Jew; a Christian, of course not. Mulligan calls him the wandering Jew, but in many ways Bloom is more wandering than Jew.'

The second stream exposes Irish exceptionalism dreaming itself as monocultural and racially 'pure' before 'these people' came, and shows that Joyce was committed as early as 1907 to multiplicities of race and culture, in existence long before Anna Livia was plurabelle. And the third reimagines *Ulysses* for our times, and wonders who Joyce's protagonist would have been had it been written today, rethinking the Hibernian metropolis as a newly imagined space of redundant white supremacy, where race continues to construct difference.

I. 'Ever and Always Alien': Anti-Semitism, Race and Racism

'In all countries, in all Christian ages, he has been a usurer and a grinder of the poor [...] The Jew in Ireland is in every respect an economic evil. He produces no wealth himself – he draws it from others – he is the most successful seller of foreign goods, he is an unfair competitor with the ratepaying Irish shopkeeper, and he remains among us, ever and always alien.'

(Arthur Griffin, *United Irishman*, 23 April 1899)

Still a hotly debated topic, anti-Semitism has been described as an ancient, persistent form of racial hatred. However, and despite Catholicism's committed longstanding anti-Jewish ideology, the term anti-Semitism was only coined in 1879 by the German journalist Wilhelm Marr, who argued that the Jews were winning in a battle of the races against the German Aryans and that their dangerous influence could be quashed only if they were vanquished. Marr's concept is totally racial because it regards Jews as Semites – a term without actual meaning

– and as a race apart. Some years after Joyce published *Ulysses* Nazi anti-Semitism employed race and Aryan supremacy in the service of the fascist state, leading to the extermination of a large proportion of Europe's Jews.

In recent years, thanks in no small measure to Israel weaponizing the Nazi genocide to justify its colonization of Palestine, anti-Semitism is again becoming common currency. The International Holocaust Remembrance Alliance's new 'working definition of anti-Semitism' is being employed to silence critics of the Israeli occupation of Palestine as anti-Semitic or, if Jewish like me, as 'self-hating Jews'. One result is masquerading anti-anti-Semitism as anti-racism, while the state of Israel continues to colonize Palestine with impunity. Writing *Ulysses* while political Zionism was emerging in Europe, Joyce has Bloom flirt with Zionist colonialism. An example is the *Agendath Netaim* pamphlet he keeps reflecting on, but there are some other references to Zionist tropes, such as the 'rich fruits, spicy from Jaffa' (U 214) and '*the mirage of the lake of Kinnereth*' (U 590). I cannot help wondering, however, whether Joyce would have joined the campaign against Palestinian, rather than Jewish, oppression had he been writing today, and would he have joined the thousand or so Irish artists in boycotting apartheid Israel.

Although the current elevation of anti-Semitism above other forms of racism occludes the evils of colonialism, slavery, apartheid, Jim Crow and Islamophobia, the racial hostility to Jewish people continues, in Ireland as elsewhere. Sociologist Zygmunt Bauman speaks of allo- rather than anti-Semitism as referring 'to the practice of setting the Jews apart [...] needing separate concepts to describe them'. And I think this is the perfect way of describing Bloom being set apart in his own city, among his own people. Setting Jewish people apart combines with racial tropes and conspiracy theories, as in Mr Deasy's casual anti-Semitism, not so different from Arthur Griffith's blatant anti-Semitism quoted earlier, when he says to Stephen in the 'Nestor' episode: 'England is in the hands of the jews. In all the highest places: her finance, her press. And they are the signs of a nation's decay. Wherever they gather they eat up the nation's vital strength' (U 41).

Though the pre-independence Ireland of *Ulysses* was not the anti-Semitic Catholic dominion it became later, setting the book in 1904 might have had to do not merely with Joyce's meeting Nora Barnacle. Joyce's interest in theology must have made him conscious of Ireland's anti-Semitic tendency, and his anti-racism and rejection of Catholicism, evident throughout his work, overlap with his specific concern about anti-Semitism. Louis Lentin proposes that Joyce must have known about the 1904 virulent and violent outburst of Catholic anti-Semitism that decimated the small Limerick Jewish community of his birth. Joyce returned to Ireland in 1903 while the attacks against Limerick's Jews were in full flight, yet he makes just one oblique reference to the Limerick pogrom when he has Bloom say, in the present tense, 'and I belong to a race too [...] that is hated and persecuted. Also now. This very moment. This very instant [...] sold by auction off in Morocco' (U 431–2). The latter reference, Lentin suggests, via the French term for Morocco – Le Maroc – being a possible, though tenuous, reference to Limerick. And this, I am thinking, might go some way towards explaining Joyce's anti-racist choice of a Jew-ish protagonist.

Bloom the double outsider feels persecuted despite Mr Deasy's refutation. But Deasy is wrong in claiming that Ireland had never let 'the jews' in. The 'My Jewish Learning' website tells me that according to *The Annals of Inisfallen*, Jews first came to Ireland in 1079, when a group of Jewish merchants from Normandy petitioned the British colonizers for admission. During the twelfth and thirteenth centuries there were some Jews on the island, but in 1290 Britain expelled the Jews from both Britain and Ireland, reinstating them only in the fifteenth century as refugees from the Spanish Inquisition. Jews, you see, have always been pawns of racial European regimes, forever moved on the chessboard of racial history. A handful of Jews lived in Ireland during the following 300 years, and though most emigrated due to persecution, a Jewish community was established in Cork in the eighteenth century. The conversion of some Jews to Catholicism caused the closure of the Dublin synagogue in the late 1700s, but in the nineteenth century a small group of Jews from Germany, Poland and England began to rebuild the Jewish community. Ireland's Jewish population grew from 435 in 1881 to about 4,000 in 1901, mostly migrants and pogrom refugees from small townships around the Lithuania–Latvia border. One of them was my grandfather-in-law Kalman Solomon Lentin, who arrived in Ireland as a boy of fourteen, and who today would be called 'an unaccompanied minor'. Like other Jewish migrants he became a travelling pedlar; he made good and remained in Limerick after the pogrom.

Some twenty years after the publication of *Ulysses*, and despite the centuries-long existence of Jewish people in the

British settler colony of Ireland, Deasy's claim became a tragic reality when post-colonial independent Ireland's very poor record of providing asylum to refugees fleeing persecution began with its failure to respond to the plight of Jewish refugees fleeing the Nazi Holocaust. Had he remained in Hungary, Bloom's father would most probably have become a Holocaust victim when, after Germany occupied Hungary as late as March 1944, Hungary's Jews were deported to the death camps. During the Nazi era, between 1933 and 1946, the neutral Irish Free State admitted only sixty Jewish refugees while the Nazis were systematically exterminating millions of Jewish people alongside Roma people, homosexuals, black people and political prisoners.

Irish Jewish population patterns differed greatly from Ireland's general migration trends. Until 1946 the Jewish community continued to grow in contrast with the fall in the Irish population due to emigration, but since then it has been in steady decline. Between 1946 and 1996 the number of Ireland's Jews decreased by more than 70 per cent, though in recent years the 1,500-strong community has seen some increase with the arrival of Jewish professionals. Young Irish Jews, however, continue to emigrate, wishing to experience Jewish communal life, not available in Ireland's dwindling diasporic Jewish community.

The closure characterizing Ireland's migration and asylum policies continues. Though the Republic of Ireland was a reluctant participant in the United Nations refugee programmes, it accepted small groups of invited 'Programme Refugees': Hungarians in 1956, Chileans in 1972, Vietnamese in 1979, Iranian Bahá'is in 1985, Bosnians in 1992, Kosovars in 1999 and Syrians and Iraqis in 2015–17. Many were not successfully integrated into Irish society and left. The closure continues in relation to asylum seekers, mostly African and Asian, who began arriving in the early 1990s as the Irish economy was improving. The number of asylum applications increased from nine in 1991 to 11,634 in 2002, ebbing and flowing ever since. Between 1991 and 2019 Ireland received some 105,000 asylum applications, but it has recognized fewer asylum claims than smaller or similarly sized states, ranking 55th out of 183 states worldwide. It is worth noting that Joyce's Hibernian metropolis has notoriously given its name to the EU's 'Dublin III Regulation' that aims to limit the number of applications by forcing asylum seekers to lodge their applications in the first EU member state they arrive at.

Joyce has Bloom – a migrant's son, but not a migrant himself – wandering freely through his native Dublin. By contrast, asylum seekers and their Irish-born children have since 1999 been incarcerated in 'Direct Provision' centres, where they receive bed and board plus a small weekly allowance, and where they live in overcrowded conditions, often forced to share rooms with total strangers. The DP centres are operated by for-profit companies which were paid 1.6 billion euros between 1999 and 2020 by the state, constituting Ireland's 'asylum industrial complex'.

Returning to Bloom's heritage, in 1956 Hungarian refugees escaping the Soviet invasion – most probably not Jewish – were accommodated in Knockalisheen Camp, a disused army barracks in County Clare still used today to house asylum seekers. In April 1957 they staged a hunger strike to protest their incarceration, and all but sixty-one of the original group left Ireland. After the 2004 EU enlargement a large number of Hungarian nationals, together with other EU accession states' citizens, migrated to Ireland, one of only three EU states to allow them access to the labour market. In 2020 there were 7,000–10,000 Hungarian nationals in Ireland, though precise numbers are difficult to calculate because many have become Irish citizens, replicating Bloom's liminal position as both Irish and 'other'. The story of the Hungarian immigration, since Virag-Bloom's days, sheds a light on the complexities of Irishness and otherness, and on today's Ireland's changing racial landscape.

II. 'Here Comes Everybody':
Race, Racism and Denial

Though a book about everyday life, about Irishness and otherness, about desire and punctured masculinity, and about 'dear dirty Dublin', *Ulysses*, I contend, is above all about race, as is the whole of Joyce's oeuvre. Race and racism, however, have been vigorously denied in colonial and post-colonial Ireland, whose people are fond of claiming they had always been 'monocultural' before 'these people' – migrants – came. I propose that claiming monoculturalism is total nonsense, bearing in mind the revelations in a 2021 RTE docuseries on the Burren that used DNA sequencing to prove that the modern Irish descended from the dark-skinned and blue-eyed Mesolithic hunter-gatherer population.

In *Encounters: How Racism Came to Ireland*, Bill Rolston and Michael Shannon document the existence of people of colour, including African slaves, in the island of Ireland for over a millennium. Moreover, once the Protestant/Catholic difference is recognized, Ireland, from 1169 onwards, cannot but be thought of as 'bi-cultural' rather than 'monocultural'.

Joyce was acutely aware that Ireland had never been that 'monoculture'. In his 1907 lecture, though he did not go as far as the Mesolithic age, he traced the history of various waves of invasion and migration into Ireland, arguing that the three centuries that preceded the English colonization of Ireland included invasions by black (Danish) and white (Norwegian) foreigners. Both groups did not leave but were gradually assimilated, forming what Joyce described as the 'curious character of the modern Irishman'. Joyce was rather contemptuous of what became known as the 'new Celtic race', which, he argued, was actually an amalgam of 'the old Celtic stock and the Scandinavian, Anglo-Saxon, and Norman races'. Irishness, he noted, was also inclusive of Protestant settlers who 'had become *Hibernis Hiberniores*, more Irish than the Irish themselves, urging on the Irish Catholics in their opposition to the Calvinist and Lutheran fanatics from across the sea, and the descendants of the Danish and Norman and Anglo-Saxon settlers championing the cause of the new Irish nation against the British tyranny.' Linking Joyce, race and empire, Vincent Cheng writes about the colonization and racialization of the Irish by the English, ironically citing Britain's *Jewish* Prime Minister Benjamin Disraeli dubbing them a 'wild, reckless, indolent, uncertain and superstitious race', the 'them' who were everything the English 'we' were not. The Irish, Cheng quotes Joyce as writing, are 'a very mixed race', and very much a vision of a complex mix of racial and cultural strains operating within a fluid contact zone. Prophetically, both in *Ulysses* and in *Finnegans Wake*, whose protagonist H. C. Earwicker also stands for 'Here Comes Everybody' – a term of racial inclusion if ever there was one – Joyce self-consciously blurs both the racialized demarcations between a dark other and an imperial self, and the Irish myth of pure racial origins. Consciously rejecting the rigid mirrored racial arguments of both Anglo-Saxonism and Celticism, Joyce, Cheng proposes, attempted to engage in the 'spiritual liberation of my country' and to 'create the uncreated conscience of my race' by representing Ireland in 'my nicely polished looking-glass', a representation definitely not mirrored in the haze of a Celtic twilight.

Joyce clearly knew already in 1907 that if there ever was such a thing as an Irish nation, a 'monoculture' it was certainly not. It is the modern state rather than the nation that must be thought of as racial, as argued by race scholar David Theo Goldberg. Yet when I started teaching race and racism in Trinity College Dublin in the early 1990s, students rejected my description of Ireland as a racial state, claiming that the Irish, formerly colonized by Britain, lack the power to be racist. However, not unlike the British colonizer, the post-colonial Irish racial state, like other modern nation-states, is a state of power, asserting its control over those within the state and excluding others from without the state by using governmental technologies from constitutions, citizenship and migration regimes to invented histories and state memory.

Ireland's racial regime was consolidated by the 2004 passage of the 27th constitutional amendment that replaced the *jus solis* citizenship entitlement to all children born in the island of Ireland with a *jus sanguinis* citizenship entitlement only to the children of Irish citizens.

Before I go any further, I must clarify what I mean by race, and what I mean by Ireland. By race I mean neither biology nor culture, but rather, following race scholar Alana Lentin, a technology for the management of human difference, the main goal of which is the production, reproduction and maintenance of white supremacy. The Australian settler colonialism scholar Patrick Wolfe saw race as colonialism speaking, an idea in search of reassurance that needs to be constantly confirmed and filled with content. As for Ireland: Joyce's Ireland was the whole island, and his work addresses Ireland and Irishness before partition, in his 1907 lecture as in *Ulysses*, set during the twilight years of Britain's colonial rule, and published during the partitionist civil war. However, the racial state of Ireland I write about here is the independent Free State and later Republic – admittedly a partial analysis that does not take on board what Robbie McVeigh calls the northern racial 'statelet'.

With these caveats out of the way, and bearing in mind Joyce's understanding of 'the Irish' – just like 'the Jews', I might add – as anything but a monocultural homogeneous whole, it was not until the arrival of a relatively small number of migrants, mostly in response to the Republic's labour shortages during the 'Celtic Tiger' boom years, that the discourse of the disruption of that alleged 'monoculture' began surfacing. With it came both the awareness and the denial of race and racism, and the disavowal of Ireland's racial plurality.

Denial, according to sociologist Stanley Cohen, is actually a paradox. Using the term 'denial' to describe a person's statement 'I didn't know' means they actually do know about what they claim not to know. The disavowal of race as a technology of state power, and the claim that racism had not existed in post-colonial Ireland before migrants started arriving, were exposed by Robbie McVeigh, the first to outline the specificities of Irish racism along several axes. First, the history of Irish racism is paralleled by the history of racism against Irish people, where, through centuries of colonialism, they experienced attempted genocide, forced emigration, starvation and war. Second, Irish racism was imported from Britain (through the British media, and through Irish emigrants, many of whom travelled between Ireland and Britain, between work and family). Racism was also imported by returning Irish emigrants, one notorious example being the Redemptorist priest John Creagh, a returned emigrant from France, where he was influenced by French anti-Semitism, who led the above-mentioned Limerick pogrom. Third, far from being caused by raised immigration levels in the 1990s, Irish racism had targeted Ireland's own indigenous people – Irish Travellers – as well as Black–Irish people and Irish–Jewish people. Fourth, McVeigh reminds us that Irish racism was imported from the Irish diaspora, for example the United States settler colony, where impoverished Irish famine emigrants 'became white', as documented in Noel Ignatiev's *How the Irish Became White*. The Irish also became white in the settler colonies of Australia and Canada, where they are part of the ruling white elites, and, as McVeigh argued recently, in Ireland too, in the face of its ever-changing racial landscape. Today McVeigh would probably situate the specificity of Irish racism more directly in terms of the complex relationship between Britishness, Irishness and colonialism, as in his 2021 book with Bill Rolston, *Ireland, Colonialism and the Unfinished Revolution*.

I would add to McVeigh's initial specificities of Irish racism the Direct Provision regime mentioned above, which dehumanizes asylum seekers and denies them freedom and dignity. The twenty-first-century Republic of Ireland hides asylum seekers from public view and disavows their existence just as post-colonial Ireland had disavowed the past regimes of coercive incarceration of unwed mothers and their hapless children in Catholic-run Mother and Baby Homes, Magdalene Laundries and Industrial Schools.

Although many Irish people did know about them, Ireland's past institutions of coercive incarceration were hidden from sight and disavowed by state and society. Despite media and artistic narrations of the emotional, physical and sexual abuse and the residue of what was left behind, including the high death rates of babies and children and the sale of children by the nuns for foreign adoptions, and despite public apologies by two taoisigh, commissions of enquiry and redress boards, Irish society continues to disavow today's incarceration of asylum seekers in remote DP centres. Many of these centres are situated in the same buildings used to incarcerate unwed mothers and poor children, as well as refugees, all these years ago.

Disavowal, Sigmund Freud writes, is a 'mode of defence which consists in the subject refusing to recognize the reality of a traumatic perception', and it often leads to repression that keeps out of awareness information that evokes the pains of trauma, guilt and shame. The repressed pain, however, is not really forgotten, and the more profound the wound, the more rigorously it has to be exposed. And the repressed always returns to haunt, and with this the awareness that Ireland is not, and has never been, a racial monolith.

The racism experienced by racialized children in church institutions, I further propose, constitutes the final denial. The 2021 Mother and Baby Homes report acknowledged the evidence by the Association of Mixed Race Irish regarding 'the additional impact' that discrimination had on those 'with different racial heritage'. But race featured only rarely both in the trauma narratives of racialized survivors of incarceration, and in the narration of the experiences of asylum seekers in Direct Provision. Clearly not all black or brown, asylum seekers in DP, like women and children survivors of Mother and Baby Homes, Magdalene Laundries and Industrial Schools, were all racialized through segregation and isolation, coercive incarceration, dehumanization and degradation.

My key argument is that in view of this disavowal, race represents a further layer of denial. The denial of race and the refusal to admit Irish state racism derive from disavowing the role played by Irish people as both colonized and racialized by the British and as involved through service in the British army and colonial administration in the racialization of colonized others. I further argue that denial, and the government's insistence that its immigration and asylum policies have nothing to do with race, constitute racist violence.

This matrix of denial characterizes the racialization of Irishness which is also evident in Joyce positioning Bloom as a double racial outsider in the city of his birth, where Jewish people such as former justice minister Alan Shatter and I are regularly publicly targeted by anti-Semitism, due mostly to our (differently articulated) support for migrants and asylum seekers. Though not rooted in the characteristics of Irishness itself, Irishness and Irish people, as Joyce understood, benefitted from their role within the British empire while also remaining subordinate within imperial structures. I believe that in both *Ulysses* and *Finnegans Wake* Joyce engaged with race as a product of colonial relations and as a wider disputation with nationalism, capitalism and modernity.

III. 'The New Bloomusalem'

Joyce positioned Leopold Bloom as a lone 'other' in the Hibernian metropolis, but in today's Dublin we can no longer ignore the increasing presence of racialized people whose obvious otherness is changing the city's human landscapes.

Though it is not yet possible to describe Dublin as *spatially* racially segregated, the changing city can be read as a-spatially, *socially* racially segregated. Asking how negatively racialized people are effectively excluded from full participation in the Irish 'host' society, allegedly attempting to maximize and monopolize its scarce resources, assumes that racial exclusion is primarily due to a division between immigrants and host societies. This, however, ignores the continuities of both racial segregation and racial pluralities.

I propose that *Ulysses* and *Finnegans Wake* give us a glimpse into what a multi-racial Dublin looks like beyond the double otherness of Jewish people, many of whom were born in Ireland, and beyond the presence of a considerable proportion of 'foreign nationals' who make up over 12 per cent of the Irish population. Poignant Dublin-specific examples of the diminution implied by the commonly used term 'ethnic minorities' are the naming of the Portobello area, home to Jewish migrants at the turn of the twentieth century, 'little Jerusalem', and of Parnell Street, home of African enterprise at the turn of the twenty-first century, 'little Africa'.

This leads me to wondering whether, had *Ulysses* been written in the twenty-first century by another Dubliner, say Roddy Doyle, whose writing acknowledges the presence in Dublin of Eastern Europeans and Africans, Bloom would have been the son of an African, rather than a Jewish, migrant. Doyle's *Guess Who's Coming for the Dinner* is a play about a working-class Dublin family whose daughter brings home a Nigerian refugee for dinner. The girl's father, Larry, prides himself on not being a racist (both racism and its denial being palpably present). He notes wryly that while Nelson Mandela was a hero, (Taoiseach) Bertie Ahern was only a chancer. But dinner is a comically fraught affair, with Larry adopting a tone of white superiority, until all ends in smiles and reconciliation, as the guest explains he is only a friend and has no intention of marrying the daughter.

When challenged about belonging, Bloom insists Ireland is his nation, his birthright. But he is constantly challenged by his fellow citizens, one of whom asks, 'Is he a jew or a gentile or a holy Roman or a swaddler or what the hell is he? [...] Or who is he?', to be answered in just as racially threatening a fashion, 'He's a perverted jew [...] from a place in Hungary and it was he drew up all the plans according to the Hungarian system. We know that in the castle' (U 438).

Just like Bloom, who insists that 'it's no use [...] Force, hatred, all that. That's not life for men and women, insult and hatred. And everybody knows that it's the very opposite of that that is really life [...] Love' (U 432), today's migrants and asylum seekers insist on their right to humanity. As Bulelani Mfaco, spokesperson of the Movement of Asylum Seekers in Ireland (MASI), said plainly during MASI's appearance before the Oireachtas Committee on Justice and Equality in May 2019: 'We are human beings, like everyone, like all of you. All we ask is that we be treated as such. The very fact that people have to ask the government to treat them humanely should shame all of you.'

I have been writing about the Irish racial state for many years now, initially hoping that the awakening to the centrality of race to Ireland's political system that began with the 1997 European Year against Racism might lead to change. As the years went by, my optimism has waned. Yet despite being mocked and pilloried by his fellow citizens, Bloom does not lose his utopian dream of a life without racism:

A new era is about to dawn, I, Bloom, tell you verily it is even now at hand. Yea, on the word of a Bloom, ye shall ere long enter into the golden city which is to be, the new Bloomusalem in the Nova Hibernia of the future. (U 606)

Ultimately, however, just as Moses was only granted a 'Pisgah view of the promised land', so Bloom's dream of the Nova Hibernia, aka Bloomusalem, is not to be, as Travellers continue to be racialized and discriminated against in terms of accommodation, health and education services, and as undocumented migrants and asylum seekers continue to experience the heavy hand of the Irish racial state. Although Joyce surprisingly chose to more or less ignore Ireland's other racialized others (after all, he must have been aware of Synge's *The Tinker's Wedding*), he did carry forward Bloom's raceless visions into *Finnegans Wake*, where the voice of Shem was being sounded, and where 'everybody' came, and was welcome to Anna Livia's plurabelle post-metropolitan Hibernia.

Meanwhile, the racialized – Travellers, migrants, asylum seekers, as well as Ireland's African, Asian, Muslim, Jewish, Hindu and Sikh others – continue to stake their claims as their voices are increasingly being heard, and as the city and its spaces, hospitals, schools and businesses are becoming less homogeneously white. In occupying new racialized spaces outside the state's lip service to racial plurality, spaces that attempt integration from below into Ireland's insistent white dominion while at the same time aiming to subvert it, the racialized are telling 'us' – just like Bloom told his citizen friends – what 'we' already know. Ireland – denial, disavowal and all that jazz notwithstanding – is not, if it ever was, racially 'pure', as new racial (and gendered) landscapes are changing its geographies of exclusion in diverse ways which render the 'we' of today's Dublin as an imagined authentically white 'Irish' space obsolete.

Proteus

RICHARD KEARNEY

Richard Kearney is Professor of Philosophy at Boston College, having taught for many years at University College Dublin. Among his books are *Anatheism*, *Touch* and *The Wake of Imagination*. He has also published two novels.

I've often thought that if Joyce wanted to be a singer more than a writer, it might be also said that he wanted to be a philosopher. His studies of Aristotle and Aquinas in particular – during his Jesuit education in Dublin and his scholastic readings in Paris – led to some of the most philosophically rich ruminations of any novelist in the twentieth century. Up there with Sartre, de Beauvoir, Musil, Mann and Borges. But unlike most other philosophical fiction writers, Joyce's point, I believe, was not to use fiction to communicate metaphysics but rather to show how our speculative ideas ultimately bow to carnal human experience. Having just completed a book on the philosophy of 'touch' when I received the invitation to write for this volume in spring 2021, I was intrigued to review what Joyce might have to say on the subject. Writing during the Covid pandemic, when we were all aware of the importance of touch (because deprived of it), the topic seemed especially vital. Proteus beckoned.

'Proteus' is without doubt the most philosophical episode in *Ulysses*; which is why, I presume, my old friend Declan Kiberd asked me to write about it for this centenary volume. I confess it is a very difficult piece for me or any philosopher to make sense of; and probably even more so for non-philosophers. But at least the non-philosopher may be more easily inclined to abandon the search for coherent argument (which may not be there), opting to flow with the music of Stephen's words.

In Joyce's parodic version, Proteus is not a Greek god with a clear message for his supplicant. Nor a personification of some Platonic idea. Nor a Delphic oracle. Proteus is a deity of the sea whose meaning or identity cannot be grasped as he shifts from one form to another as Stephen strolls along Sandymount

Strand. Stephen encounters no one who articulates the original wise counsel of Homer's Proteus to Menelaus – namely, to offer sacrifice to the gods so he can continue on his way. If anything, in keeping with his name, Joyce portrays Proteus as a flux of multiple phenomena registered by Stephen as he trudges through the sandflats of Dublin Bay. Stephen's so-called interior monologue is in fact a polylogue of voices and sensations. Among the many personae that traverse Stephen's stream of consciousness – which I prefer to call a panconscious – we encounter many of his contemporaries, living and dead: his mother, father, brother, uncle and aunt, friend Kevin Egan, teacher Deasy, flatmates Mulligan and Hynes, erotic ladies of the night, and various local Dubliners who happen to be walking their dogs or harvesting mussels in the mud at 11 a.m. in the morning of 16 June 1904. And we also meet countless Irish ancestors like Columbanus, Scotus and Malachi along with invading Danes and Anglo-Normans, great writers like Shakespeare and Swift, and (most relevant for our purposes) Stephen's favourite philosophers – Aristotle, Berkeley and Aquinas. The list seems endless, and the Protean shape-shifting does not stop with human persons; it extends to all kinds of living things – horses, dogs, molluscs, gulls and algae. Not to mention the elements themselves – wind, waves, silt and mountains – all making up the 'signatures of things' which Stephen, the aspiring writer, struggles to read as he tramps through the flooding sands. He resolves to 'understand with his eyes'. But, it seems, to little avail. The quest for meaning yields not answers but a flux of puzzles and perplexities. What is going on?

Let me begin by trying to read the Protean 'signatures' as a philosopher. The chapter starts with epistemology straight up. Aristotle on the senses. Stephen invokes a basic claim for the primacy of sensory perception – the ineluctable modality of the visible and the audible (U 45). He is operating here on Aristotle's argument that there is nothing in the mind that was not first in the senses (or as Aquinas rendered it, *nihil in intellectu quod non fuerit primus in sensu*). And while Stephen is brimming with abstract ideas from his studies in the *quartier latin* and his visits to Dublin's Marsh's Library, his theories are constantly tested by what lies beneath his feet – the oddities he encounters as he treads the sandbanks of Sandymount Strand. His attempt to give fixed forms to the scattered perceptions of his lived body yields each time to the carnal contingencies of time and space, to the singular events of his finite human corporality. What he calls his 'dogsbody' (U 58) (which stumbles on silt, suffers poor sight and rotting teeth, urinates and deposits nose-mucus on a rock). The whole 'Proteus' passage moves gradually from the upper senses of sight and sound – visibility and audibility – to what Aristotle calls the 'primal sense of touch'. Only the felt body can make sense of Protean change. The sense of tactility is the royal road to lived experience – the only real kind that can serve the art which Stephens seeks.

Who but a philosopher would begin a rumination with a phrase like 'Ineluctable modality of the visible: at least that if no more, thought through my eyes' (U 45)? But from the word go we realize this thoughtful seeing is special. The 'signatures of all things' (U 45) (a phrase from the mystic Jacob Böhme, whose book Joyce kept in his library in Trieste) that Stephen is 'here to read' (U 45), are not celestial signs in the sky but the quotidian flotsam scattered at his feet. '[S] easpawn and seawrack, the nearing tide, that rusty boot' (U 45). In short, it is ordinary tactile things before him here and now. Coloured things. Green, blue and red. 'In bodies', as Aristotle adds, arguing that things can only be visible through the medium of the actual colour which embodies them. These are the 'limits of the diaphane' (U 45) which Stephen rightly attributes to the Aristotelian model of perception. One can really see things by seeing through (*dia*) them, that is, through their given material medium (*metaxu*) as coloured bodies. Visible things are not projections of our subjective mind, as Berkeley and the idealists held, but tactile carnal phenomena. Touch is the primary sensation of flesh – the medium which enables us to touch and be touched. It is the experience of double sensation upon which all other senses are founded. And touch is the most universal of the senses, for Aristotle, in that it connects us to all living beings – including the rusty fungus on a throwaway boot. 'The primary form of sense is touch which belongs to all animals' (*De Anima*, Book II, p. 11). Or, as Stephen riffs: 'He was aware of them bodies [...] How? By knocking his sconce against them' (U 45). If you want to know something exists, knock your skull against it. That's why Aristotle was, in Dante's laudatory words, '*maestro di color che sanno*' (U 45). Stephen cites the master with approval, suggesting that we ultimately see through touch: 'If you can put your five fingers through it, it is a gate, if not a door. Shut your eyes and see' (U 45).

* * *

I have dwelt long on this opening paragraph of 'Proteus' where Joyce provides a map of Stephen's *itinerarium mentis* from the time he sets foot on Sandymount Strand – stepping through 'snotgreen' (U 45) seaweed, rusty boots and the remains of a dead dog's body – to the time he finally departs one hour later. The ultimate message being that there's nothing in our head that wasn't felt by our feet. Thinking begins and ends with touch. Stephen may have the right theory from the outset but he has to walk a littered Dublin beach to feel it in his bones.

'Shut your eyes and see' (U 45). Stephen heeds Aristotle's advice. He closes his eyes in order to experience his surroundings 'nicely in the dark'. He hears and feels 'his boots crush crackling wrack and shells' (U 45). His walking stick ('ash sword') hangs by his side as he taps his way like a blind man along the strand (his weak eyes are failing him). Minutes later he will be ready to abandon his Prospero's wand altogether and embrace the 'thing of darkness' – the carnal Caliban of mortality ('five fathoms down thy father lies').

Opening his eyes again Stephen confirms that the world did not disappear because he stopped seeing it – disproving Berkeley's idealist thesis that 'to be is to be perceived' (*esse est percipi*). It was 'here all the time without you; and ever shall be, world without end' (U 46). But what does he see? First up, Mrs Florence MacCabe, a midwife with 'splayed feet sinking in the silted sand' (U 46) who reminds him of his own earthly birth; 'lugged [...] squealing into life' (U 46). Unlike his first parents in Eden, created out of nothing with no navel, and unlike the god-man Christ who was begotten not made, Stephen acknowledges he was '[w]ombed in sin darkness' (U 46) by 'them', namely, his own parents, who 'clasped and sundered, did the coupler's will' (U 46) in order to conceive him. Unlike Christ, who was 'begotten not made' by God (and a virgin mother), Stephen is decidedly 'made not begotten' (U 46). And here he thinks of the heretic Arius, 'illstarred heresiarch' (U 47), who denied the divinity of Christ and the attendant doctrine that he was 'consubstantial' with the Father who created him. Mortals and gods are not of the same substance. And this basic truth of finitude triggers Stephen's memory of a visit to his aunt Sally and bedridden uncle Richie, where he is offered a bite of herring and told to abandon his haughty ways – 'none of your damned lawdeedaw air here' (U 48). The world is a text full of mortal signatures. Recalling his uncle's home he sighs: 'Houses of decay, mine, his and all' (U 49).

The mixing of the conceptual and the banal in Stephen's thoughts is Joyce's way of reminding us, readers, that this is how we actually think. Not clearly and distinctly, as Descartes speculated, but with fluid involuntary memories and layered carnal associations. No matter how high-flying our ideas, we are radically embodied creatures. Deeply tactile and tangible beings like the many sentient creatures – right down to sea fungi and molluscs – that teem and shimmer through the Sandymount flux.

As he proceeds across the strand 'footpace' (U 49), Stephen rehearses a list of ecclesiastical notions that impressed him when he was an 'awfully holy' (U 49) youth obsessed with saintly things – praying to the 'Blessed Virgin that [he] might not have a red nose' (U 49), reading theology in Marsh's Library and serving Mass for Jesuit 'Jackpriests' (U 49). He recalls the altar bell at the consecration of the Host. 'Dringdring

[...] Dringadring [...] twang in diphthong' (U 49). But where, wonders Stephen, did holiness get Dean Swift of Dublin Cathedral? Running to the wild woods 'horsenostrilled' (U 49) like his fictive Houyhnhnms, 'his mane foaming in the moon' (U 49). Would Stephen, the aspirant writer, do any better than his literary forebear? Such musings on sanctity are followed by ironic thoughts about his literary ambitions. A key moment in Stephen's self-reckoning. 'Books you were going to write with letters for titles. [...] Remember your epiphanies on green oval leaves, deeply deep, copies to be sent if you died to all the great libraries of the world, including Alexandria? Someone was to read them there after a few thousand years' (U 50). Great sacred epics. Mahamanvantara. Renaissance humanist masterpieces like those of Pico della Mirandola. But no. Stephen is called back to his humble carnality on this earth. The soft silt of Sandymount has gone from 'under his feet' as he trudges through the rotting wreckage of grandiose Armadas. 'Unwholesome sandflats waited to suck his treading soles' (U 50). And no matter how warily he walks, the 'cakey sand dough' (U 50) clogs his steps. He cannot escape. All around him, empty '[h]uman shells' (U 50). Signatures of finitude surround him.

Pursuing his self-scrutiny, Stephen recalls his student visit to the Latin Quarter in Paris, where he had highfalutin fantasies of following in the wake of the wild geese (exiled Gaelic gentry) and serving as a 'missionary to Europe' (U 52) like his 'loudlatinlaughing' (U 52) medieval compatriots – Columbanus, Scotus and Fiacre. But reality turned out differently. Instead of great evangelical masterpieces, Stephen settled for cheap Parisian porn mags before receiving a blue telegram bidding him to return: 'Mother dying come home father' (U 52). Once more he was tolled back to his mortality. Reminded that he was his father's son, from his mother's womb. Flesh of their flesh. Mud of their mud. Dust of their dust.

After more idle musings about his pals in Parisian cafes and licentious erotica, new sensations of finitude return as Stephen's feet get further clogged in flooding tidal debris. Joyce repeats his tactile images of material footprints and footfalls. The muddy waters are resisting him, prompting him to renounce his fancied walk to the Kish lightship. The language is elemental, viscous, terrestrial, aquatic. 'He stood suddenly, his feet beginning to sink slowly in the quaking soil. Turn back. Turning [...] his feet sinking again slowly in new sockets [...] slowly ever as my feet are sinking' (U 55). The shift in this passage between third and first person is telling, marking Stephen's firm resolve to leave the literary shenanigans of Mulligan and Hynes in the Martello Tower. 'I will not sleep there when this night comes [...] He lifted his feet up from the suck and turned back by the mole of boulders' (U 55). He will live and write differently from now on, he vows, as he sits on a stool of rock, 'resting his ashplant in a grike'.

And then come the dogs. One dead, one alive. Here we find what I consider to be the most vibrant and sustained passage of the entire Protean chapter. As Stephen ruminates on his writing career, he encounters the 'bloated carcass of a dog' (U 55), lolling on bladderwrack beside the remains of a boat sunk in the sand. He recognizes 'signatures' he must read.

'These heavy sands are language tide and wind have silted here' (U 55). He has no illusions. 'Sands and stones. Heavy of the past' (U 56). The very same past Stephen had sought to flee when he left Ireland for Paris at the end of *A Portrait*, going forth to 'forge in the smithy of his soul the uncreated conscience of his race'. Such youthful Promethean promises are now shattered on the shifting tides of Protean reality. He smells the blood of his ancestors. Feefawfum. 'Bones for [his] steppingstones.' Grounded once again.

Then the 'live dog' appears, running across the strand, filling Stephen with fear and triggering ancient flashbacks. Celtic ancestors fighting invading Vikings over a thousand years ago. Transgenerational traumas. A flood of shame and longing. 'Famine, plague and slaughters. Their blood is in me, their lusts my waves. I moved among them on the frozen Liffey, that I, a changeling, among the spluttering resin fires' (U 56). The weasel word in this surge of ancestral association is, I think, 'changeling'. Why? Because it reminds Stephen of his Protean vocation as shape-shifter. But how to combine this with his Prospero vocation as artist? We will see what 'seachange' (U 63) is in store once the dog has run its course – 'sniffing on all sides [...] Looking for something lost in a past life' (U 57). Once the man's body, drowned ten days ago off Maiden's rock, has been assimilated into Stephen's consciousness. But for now, fear still lingers as Stephen imagines himself being called to save the drowning man and refusing. Until he follows the dog's carry-on once again, as it patrols the lace fringe of the waves and yelps at cockle pickers. Then the moment of truth. The dog sniffs a carcass in the sand. Not the man drowned off Maiden's rock nor anybody's grandmother but another dog. 'Poor dogsbody's body' (U 58). Given that Stephen has been called a dogsbody by Buck Mulligan earlier in the book, the phrase hits home. Touché.

And something strange happens. A shift in space and time. A moment opens to a future image of Leopold Bloom, in the persona of Haroun al-Raschid, eighth-century Caliph of Baghdad, praising Molly's melon-like buttocks. The moment where past-present-future meet in an unconscious epiphany of what is still to come, what must come, if Stephen is ever to embrace the 'mother of memory' he has fled and become a writer of flesh and blood reality. But he is not yet there. Instead he relapses to more 'medieval abstrusiosities' (U 57) of 'morose delectation'. Wearing his Hamlet hat he vacillates and ruminates, still prey to that 'craven scruple of thinking too precisely on the event'. Elsinore guilt at the unmourned parent, the ambiguous mother, the father's voice speaking through him, 'remember me'. But he does try. A stray verse. A quick scribble on the back of Deasy's letter in his pocket. Still sitting on the rock, as the tide mounts, he pens a quick poem. 'Signs on a white field' (U 60) he is not sure anyone will read. A poem about a kiss of death and a kiss of life. A memory of his mother's deathbed as a child bed and bride bed anticipating the love bed of a future lover – 'a woman to her lover clinging' (U 61). But who? The virgin at Hodges Figgis's window? The lady of letters in Leeson Park? Or Molly Bloom herself, 'welcome as the flowers in May' (U 61)? Hat tilted over his eyes, Stephen loses his wits as the poem haltingly emerges.

Stammering. Connecting at last. Words of touch beyond sight. The double sensation of primal tactility. Of hand and mouth. 'Mouth to her mouth's kiss [...] mouth to her womb [...] manshape ineluctable [...] Touch me. Soft eyes. Soft soft soft hand. I am lonely here. O, touch me soon, now. What is that word known to all men? I am quiet here alone. Sad too. Touch, touch me' (U 60).

'And no more turn aside and brood' (U 62).

This is the breakthrough. The carnal epiphany of touch which replaces the pseudo-epiphanies 'on green oval leaves' of Stephen's romantic youth. The moment of momentary truth.

* * *

By my reading, the Protean episode ends here. Certainly the story of Aristotelian sensibility does, as Stephen's poem bookends the wandering passage from the ineluctable modality of sight and sound to the 'manshape ineluctable' of touch – the 'signature' par excellence of our mortal vulnerability. And love. We have passed through the open gate of double sensation which accompanies us from birth to death. Hand touching hand. Mouth touching mouth. The rest of 'Proteus' reads to me like an epilogue; but an important reminder nonetheless that the journey is not over. Stephen's three opening chapters are closing, but he is not yet an artist of the lived body, of real affect. He has learnt his epistemological lesson at the feet of Aristotle and Aquinas, but he is still a neophyte when it comes to real lived experience. For that he must await his encounter with Bloom, and eventually with Molly. For now still promissory notes. Work in progress.

So what, if anything, do we learn from the last pages of 'Proteus'? We learn, I suggest, what Stephen (after Shakespeare) calls 'seachange', what the Greeks call *metempsychosis* and what I call 'anacarnation'. Big words, one might say, for a basic notion that life continues through life, time after time, again and again, *nacheinander, nebeneinander.*

Let's return to the text one last time. Stephen, back to earth, surrounded by the upswelling tide, broods on his 'broadtoed boots' (U 62). He accepts that he is all or nothing. 'As I am. All or not at all' (U 62). Everywhere the waters are rising 'amid seasnakes, rearing horses, rocks' (U 62). The sounds and signatures of animals and sea, of fish and fungi. Wave speech, the four-worded tongue of the elements. 'Seesoo, hrss, rsseeiss, ooos' (U 62). This is the language of the 'Old father Ocean' – Proteus, Mananaan – who watches over 'seachange' and 'seadeath' (U 63). 'Five fathoms out there. Full fathoms five thy father lies' (U 63). And now returns again, 'released forth flowing, wending back' (U 62). Tidal loom of the moon. Like a 'naked woman shining in her courts, she draws a toil of waters' (U 63). The flooding tide slops and slaps through rocks and sandbelts; it brings back the dead. 'A corpse rising saltwhite from the undertow […] Sunk though he be beneath the watery floor' (U 63). And as Stephen envisages this scene of the drowned rising, where bones become coral and eyes become pearls, he, like Prospero before him, is happy to embrace the artistic possibility of a 'seachange into something rich and precious'. The dringdring of the eucharistic bells, which Stephen rang as an altar boy, echoes the 'ding dong, bell' of Shakespeare's Ariel. And he shape-shifts from Prospero – dying to his old magic before a new art of nature – to the dying and rising Christ. 'Come. I thirst' (U 63). He regards the 'crosstrees' of a three-master ship moving on the horizon. But if this be art, as Shakespeare reminds us, it must be an art as lawful as nature. An art that does not renounce flesh but embraces it. An art that celebrates the transformation of all things, through time and space, across species and generations, across all kinds of existence, human, animal and divine. Anacarnating. Soul-body to body-soul. World without end. Metempsychosis made flesh. Stephen gets it. 'God becomes man becomes fish becomes barnacle goose becomes featherbed mountain. Dead breaths I living breathe' (U 63). Accepting his mortal finitude, his carnal embodiment (Stephen's last action is to pick his nose!) is not to deny the endless cycle of anacarnation. The sacramental life of all sentient beings. What Joyce calls 'pantheism' in his account of John Scotus in his Trieste lectures. 'All days makes their end' (U 63), admits Stephen finally, before asking: 'By the way next when is it?' (U 63). *Nacheinander, nebeneinander.*

And sure enough, as we leave Stephen watching the silent ship 'homing, upstream' (U 64) and turn the page to the next chapter, who do we find? Leopold Bloom. The epitome of carnal embodiment preparing breakfast for Molly and frying his favourite kidneys. Stephen, who in the Linati listing for *Ulysses* has not yet acquired a body, yields to Bloom, the master of loving carnality par excellence. We have turned from 'toothless Kinch, the superman' (U 64) – who realizes he is anything but as he beholds the 'urinous offal of all dead' (U 63) – to the surrogate father who will teach us the ways of the body, from a relish for innards to the art of the kiss (with Molly on

Howth Head). We migrate from self-deconstructing superman (Stephen) to full-bodied down-to-earth man (Bloom). *Introibo ad altare dei* with a very carnal twist. Joyce makes no bones about it. The eucharist feasting of Bloom is a relief from the brooding of Stephen. Our mouths water. Here we have it: 'Mr Leopold Bloom ate with relish the inner organs of beasts and fowls. He liked thick giblet soup, nutty gizzards, a stuffed roast heart, liver slices fried with crustcrumbs, fried hencod's roes. Most of all he liked grilled mutton kidneys which gave to his palate a fine tang of faintly scented urine' (U 65).

* * *

A few more thoughts, on a more personal note. Though I have tried to follow the 'Proteus' text closely I confess it is from a particular perspective. I have focused on touch because that is what I am thinking about at the moment, in my life and thought, in the middle of the 2021 Covid pandemic, and in my teaching and writing on 'carnal hermeneutics' over the last decade, culminating in the completion of a book called *Touch: Recovering our Most Vital Sense* in 2021. This is what I am reading into Stephen's thoughts on Sandymount Strand, surmising that it is all about going from high to low, from intellect to sensation, from heady ideas to the tactile experience of hands and feet and water and weeds. I have come across interpretations of this text that offer very different readings – focusing, for example, on Irish cultural history, psychoanalytic working through, Dante's theory of colour or the epistemology of vision (taking the first line about the 'ineluctable modality of the visible' at its word). Brilliant readings have been advanced on these and other motifs in 'Proteus' by scholars ranging from Declan Kiberd and Fran O'Rourke to Emmanuel Alloa and Ernesto Livorni. And each has its place in the hermeneutic river of associations and citations filling Stephen's interior monologue. The 'Proteus' episode shows how consciousness, like life, is a palimpsest of many layers and horizons flowing backwards and forwards in time. A ceaseless interplay of 'intermisunderstanding minds' (FW 118.25 – one of my favourite Joycean terms, connoting the hermeneutic principle that 'all understanding is misunderstanding'). So every reading is invited. And none is original or exhaustive. For Joyce teaches us that we are all ventriloquists. Translators, copyists, impersonators, plagiarists. Magpies, as Joyce's great Paris friend, Maria Jolas, once described him to me. And this is as true of creative literature (as Joyce reminds us in the 'Oxen of the Sun' parody of the genealogy of English writing) as it is of critical and philosophical literature. Every text is a tissue of quotations from beginning to end. It is intertextual even as its reference is ultimately carnal: namely, our concrete lived experience. From life to text to life again. In Stephen's inner soliloquy we move from lived memory to literary citation to relived sensation. Writing and thinking are always, Joyce reminds us, in the service of life. Understanding through the eyes, ears and skin. Body and soul. Flesh and blood. The text as body and the body as text. 'Oh life I go forth...'

I believe that is the real lesson of 'Proteus'. How Stephen's odyssey on Sandymount Strand unfolds. A hermeneutic journey from head to toe – gradually descending from the visual to the aural to the tactile. A promiscuous tumble through serial anacarnations. An eschatology of the everyday where the highest traverses the lowest and all things meet in a snot on a rock.

* * *

So what of irony? Philosophers naturally tend to take 'Proteus' seriously qua philosophy. They love sleuthing the learned sources cited by Stephen as he bounces from one idea to the next. The chapter begins with Aristotle, after all, the master of all who know. And many other major thinkers are invoked by Stephen on the way. Aquinas. Bonaventure. Berkeley. Scotus. But as one reads it's hard not to sometimes ask: is Joyce taking this seriously? Or Stephen, his literary persona? Is not Aristotle referred to by Stephen as a 'bald millionaire' and Aquinas a tunbellied Jackpriest with 'marybeads jabbering on his girdle' (U 59)? Hardly the stuff of scholarly disquisition. Is it perhaps all one big game of random allusion? Free association without rhyme or reason? A ploy to trap philosophers in a game of Jacks and toy with readers avid for meaning? Is Joyce, via Stephen, really exploring philosophy, or parodying the 'loudlatin-laughing' (U 52) of his Irish predecessors – Columbanus, Fiacre and Scotus himself? I suggest Stephen's compound word may offer a comic answer.

The Irish scholars who emigrated to the court of Charles the Bald at Loan in the ninth century were known as 'scotists' (scotus being the Latin for a Gaelic person in the early Middle Ages). Foremost among them was John Scotus Eriugena, who translated major Patristic texts from Greek to Latin (he was

invited by the Carolingian court for this reason) and went on
to pen one of the most extraordinary works of his time, *On
the Division of Nature* (*De Divisione Naturae* or *Periphyseon*)
– a text which Joyce celebrates as a masterpiece of 'pantheism'
(God incarnate in nature). Scotus talked of a *deus currens*
which runs through all things – human, animal, vegetal and
divine. The Irish scholars accompanying Eriugena to Loan –
who included Sedulius Scotus, Martin Hibernensis and Fergus
of Loan – had their own special dwelling called the house of
Hilaritas. This was not only because they laughed constantly
and amused King Charles the Bald but also because their
'panentheist' philosophy spoke of a divine comedy combining
opposed streams of creation and confounding metaphysical
dualisms between spirit and matter, body and soul, created
and uncreated, being and non-being, nature and supernature.
Just think of the interlacing images of the Book of Kells or
The Midnight Court or *Finnegans Wake*. You'll get some idea.
Ezra Pound makes much of this Celtic 'hilarity' in his writings
on Eriugena, something he may have passed on to Joyce. And
Borges celebrates the same divine-human comedy at work in
both Eriugena and Joyce in a conversation he conducted with
Seamus Heaney and myself in Dublin – published in the 1982
issue of *The Crane Bag* celebrating the 100th anniversary of
Joyce's birth. He observed: 'As an outsider looking on successive
Irish thinkers I have been struck by unusual and remarkable
repetitions [...] Wilde, Shaw, Joyce and John Scotus Eriugena
[...] I loved reading his *De Divisione Naturae*, which taught
that God creates himself through the creation of his creatures
in nature [...] Joyce is remarkably akin to Eriugena's system

63

of things coming from the mind of God and returning to him.' I was really struck by Borges's observation and was inspired to go back and reread 'Proteus'.

There is no doubt that Joyce was a great admirer of both John Scotus Eriugena and his Scottish medieval namesake, Duns Scotus. In fact he sometimes mixed them up. While John Scotus spoke of a pantheist deity running through all things, Duns Scotus argued similarly for the univocity of all beings and for the existence of the divine in the singularity of creatures. Duns Scotus called this unique particularity of each being its 'haecceity' (*haecceitas* from *haec* meaning this or that, hence the term *ecce*, meaning behold this or that). Indeed I have long suspected that Joyce named the main character of *Finnegans Wake* HCE (Here Comes Everybody) after '*haec-ecce*'. Moreover the Christic term 'Ecce Homo' is echoed in the title of Joyce's beautiful short poem 'Ecce Puer', about the relationship between father and son. And there is no doubt that a Scotist pantheism of haecceity runs throughout Stephen's river of sensations on the strand. So while I think it is true that Joyce displays ludic irony in his portrayal of Stephen's erudite musings – certainly mocking Stephen's pretension to be a superman (as in 'toothless Kinch the superman') – it is equally true, I suspect, that he is celebrating a culture of *hilaritas* in the mind and body of Stephen himself. If Stephen's internal monologue reeks of irony, it also provokes humour. The two go hand in hand. In fact I am convinced that the best way to read 'Proteus' is with a dictionary in one hand and a fool's cap in the other. If we as readers feel frustrated in our search for clear meanings, we also feel the festive hilarity of it all. There is a logic to the apparent illogicality of semantic slide and slippage, to Stephen's free play of association; but it is a logic of dialectical contradiction, of a mystical coincidence of opposites, of humbling humanity and humour. It is, in fact, a metaphysics of fun – exposing Stephen's scholastic sobriety to the yea-saying playfulness of Molly and Bloom. When I follow Stephen's cerebral wading through the 'flop, slop, slap' (U 62) of rising waves I feel like saying *ecce homo*. Behold a man. Anacarnation. The word is made flesh. Again and again. I celebrate the protean topsy-turvy of life. And heed the Joycean message: I laugh therefore I am.

Calypso

TIM PARKS

Tim Parks is a British novelist, author and translator, who writes from Italy for the *New York Review of Books*. His books include *Europa*, *Italian Life* and *Where I'm Reading From*.

Admiration and ennui, excitement and irritation. Such, from school days on, have been my conflicted reactions to *Ulysses*. This rereading, then, offers a chance to see if anything has changed and, if not, to examine this uneasy response.

Ulysses part two, opening with the 'Calypso' episode, marks a radical change of tone from *Ulysses* part one; thus, invariably, the critics, the cribs. And always with enthusiasm. Everyone welcomes the introduction of Leopold Bloom. Stephen Dedalus is a genius (after all, he's Joyce) but gloomy, resentful and preposterously self-important. With Bloom we have someone we can commend. We like the fact that he's Jewish, that he's a middle-class working man, a homebody, kind to his cat, kind to his unfaithful wife, affectionate and protective towards his daughter. Frequently repeated, the words 'gentle' and 'quiet' meet our approval. We accept his fondness for offal and I have never seen any objections to his voyeuristic sexual fantasies and anal compulsions. We find him charming. He is given depth and gravitas by the loss of a baby son many years before. Above all, we love his busy enquiring mind, his exotic daydreams.

To savour the impact of Bloom, then, one must expose oneself to the earlier episodes first. For Bloom is discovered in relation to Stephen, experienced as a relief from Stephen, and of course – it being impossible to read *Ulysses* these days without being aware of its celebrated trajectory – as a source of hope for Stephen. Despite all Joyce's provocation, it's intriguing how safe and, again, commendable (to schoolchildren and students) that underlying story is: tormented son finds benign father figure; bereaved father discovers wayward child.

Rivalry and hierarchy, winning and losing, are the tensions that dominate the opening episodes. Stephen is obsessed with power relations and prestige, irritated by Buck Mulligan's exuberance and confident physicality, worried that even retrieving his friend's shaving bowl might be construed as an act of subservience. Buck also thinks competitively, setting Stephen's intellect against Haines's, proposing a plan to get money out of him. Haines's Englishness prompts unhappy thoughts of England's dominance over Ireland. Stephen even manages to resent the deference that the milk lady shows to Buck as a medical student.

Anxious not to be a loser, Stephen's resource is to find brilliant words to frame humiliation and loss. Life's affronts must be redeemed in sumptuous language: every barb is parried with a wittily wry remark; Irish art is 'the cracked lookingglass of the servant' (U 18); his mother's death is aestheticized in lugubriously elaborate poetic evocations. Poor Stephen; even those last moments with his mother became a tussle of wills – which he won, of course, but in a way also lost. Her ghost holds him back.

At school, in Episode 2, winning and losing are again in uneasy relation as Stephen chooses the Pyrrhic victory at Tarentum as his subject ('*[a]nother victory like that and we are done for*') (U 28). He scores point after easy point over his mediocre schoolboys yet is afflicted by the thought that they are wealthy and he is not. When they take their 'battling bodies' (U 40) to the hockey field, he shows compassion for one poor loser, but sees no hope for him. The boy is '[u]gly and futile' (U 33), collateral damage; to lose is indeed to lose.

Now Stephen spars with the headmaster, who counts out the coins of his servitude; gainful employment is 'a noose'. Of course he is smarter than the man who tells him that 'Money is power' (U 36–7) but nevertheless feels obliged to run an errand for Mr Deasy in 'his fight' over the response to foot and mouth disease. Imagining Buck dubbing him the 'bullockbefriending bard' (U 44), Stephen acknowledges his humiliation but recovers self-respect by coining the clever phrase. And by creating a little fun: a person having fun is a winner, in a way.

Reaching this point – it's a rapid reading, simply to prepare for part two – I'm suddenly obliged to see how Joyce's conspicuous stylistic mastery and relished irony aligns itself with Stephen's desire to wrest victory from defeat, to convince himself of his superiority. It also explains why these many conflicts – with Buck, with his mother, his students, his employer – are hardly experienced as drama by the reader, who is all but overwhelmed by the plethora of interweaving themes, obscure cultural references, extravagant compound adjectives, boldly foregrounded poetic tropes and teasing Homeric parallels. Rather than drawing us into the 'action', the text invites us to feel intelligent, perhaps to become more intelligent, outside and above these petty clashes, but always in the knowledge that Joyce is more intelligent still. That surely was the drift of the author's claim that he was inventing 'enigmas and puzzles' that would keep 'the professors busy for centuries'. Trying to solve them, the reader is not unlike a young man undertaking errands for his employer. Or a schoolboy trying to answer teacher's questions.

The third episode confirms this dynamic. On his own, Stephen is determined to impress himself with the extraordinary compression and volatility of his thought processes in an orgy of literary and philosophical allusion. Struggling, I take a break to look up something I remember reading twenty years ago: in 'Fragment on Joyce', Jorge Luis Borges imagines a man who never did anything but lie on his bed, then died young, but was nevertheless 'the only lucid man on earth. His perceptions and memory were infallible.' This man 'knew the shapes of the southernmost clouds in the sunrise of April 30, 1882 and he could compare them in his memory to the veins in the stiff marbled binding of a book he once held in his hands during childhood'. Borges then tells us he has conjured up such a prodigy 'because a consecutive, straightforward reading of the four hundred thousand words of *Ulysses* would require similar monsters'. In fact *Ulysses* is only around 265,000 words, but it obviously felt longer, to Borges.

Comically, Stephen laughs at his own adolescent hubris, measuring himself now against his past self – 'Remember your epiphanies written on green oval leaves, deeply deep, copies to be sent if you died to all the great libraries of the world, including Alexandria?' (U 50) – then goes on to show the same over-reaching ambition in every reflection he makes, as Joyce too (who had actually asked his brother Stanislaus to post those epiphanies to the world's libraries should he die on the ferry crossing to France) is showing it in every line of the writing. And the writing is wonderful, above all when it conjures up the physical world. The description of the dog sampling the smells of the seashore is magnificent, and shows once again Stephen's paranoid habit of seeing enemies everywhere: 'is he going to attack me? Respect his liberty. You will not be master of others or their slave. I have my stick' (U 56). In fact it is the dog who is a slave, soon to be treated to a kick from 'his master'. No other relationship seems possible in Stephen's world.

Enter Bloom, introduced with a reassuringly Dickensian flourish. 'Mr Leopold Bloom ate with relish...' (U 65). The reader is grateful for the break. And what does he eat? It's hilarious. Not exactly shit, but 'the inner organs of beasts and fowls' (U 65). Offal. He likes, no, he *savours*, on his palate, its urine tang. The sharp reader will be reminded of a phrase on the previous page where Stephen, riffing on *Hamlet* plus a dead dog, comes up with, 'Dead breaths I living breathe, tread dead dust, devour a urinous offal from all dead' (U 62). For Stephen this is the humiliating human condition. For Bloom it is a tasty breakfast.

Let me pause here and confess that Bloom, in my first readings of *Ulysses*, was a mystery to me and one reason for my feeling suspicious about the book. As I – young and green – saw it, a man who knows his wife is going to betray him, in the marriage bed no less, that very day, would spend hours agonizing over this, not daydreaming about more or less everything under the sun. This apparent discrepancy made it hard for me to take 'the plot' seriously. It was only when, in a splurge of Joyce reading years later, I saw how unremittingly the author's mind revolves around issues of winning and losing, of power and hierarchy, that it all began to make sense. Bloom has learnt to savour the urinary tang of defeat; this is his maturity with respect to Stephen. Though it won't prevent him from wresting little victories from the general debacle. A good cooked breakfast being one.

So although the mood has beautifully softened – 'Gelid light and air were in the kitchen but out of doors gentle summer morning everywhere' (U 65) – we are still in the same world of feeling, the same overarching system of value. Stephen would serve no one, Bloom will serve his cat, his wife, and more or less anyone. And serve them 'curiously, kindly', turning service into a winning card. Certainly he wins our hearts as he chats with the cat and appreciates its cruel, even vindictive nature. Charmingly, just as Stephen measures himself against all and sundry (and fears the dog's attack), Bloom measures himself against his cat. 'Wonder what I look like to her. Height of a tower?' (U 66). And he actually seems pleased to come off the worst. 'No, she can jump me' (U 66).

I put down the book and reflect: but how clever this is! And how clever the reader feels to notice. Though I'm also struck – in the teeth of claims made – by how *unrealistic* it all is. Does Bloom really rehearse, day by day, all these basic, Felines-101 reflections about cats for the benefit of an imaginary reader? Surely not. It's an attractive fictional technique that will soon allow us to know a simply enormous number of things about Bloom, his marriage bed, his wife's background, Dublin streets, and so on. This is much facilitated by the decision to go out to the butcher's to buy breakfast.

After lulling the reader with an entire page free from obscurities or compound adjectives, Joyce begins to deploy his customary mannerisms with the cat's 'shameclosing' (U 66) eyes and the 'warmbubbled' (U 66) milk. Do cats feel shame? The more intensely, precisely and idiosyncratically a writer seeks to describe and interpret ordinary phenomena, the more danger there is that some grumpy reader may resist. Similarly, the more one challenges readers with an encyclopaedic range of reference, the more likely it is that some will just throw in the towel. Joyce courts our rejection. This comes home to me quite forcefully at this point of my reading. He loves to exasperate. For the moment, though, I'm lapping it up. Warmbubbled and all.

Molly Bloom is introduced, off stage, in bed, barely deigning a response to her husband's solicitous enquiry if she would like anything special to eat. Her sleepy 'Mn' (U 67) is clearly meant to be compared, unfavourably, with the cat's more generous 'Mrkrgnao' (U 66). It's all so sweet and smart. And the creaking of the bed as she rolls over (beautifully affording a sense of her physical bulk) sets Bloom thinking money and thinking winning and losing. Her father bought that bed cheap at an auction. A soldier who came up through the ranks. A man who made his fortune trading stamps. A winner. Where Stephen fretted and envied, Bloom admires. We begin to sense that both men are manifestations of the same obsessive mindset, but in different phases of life, different circumstances.

Let's watch Bloom leaving the house:

> His hand took his hat from the peg over his initialled heavy overcoat and his lost property office secondhand waterproof. (U 67)

This is the kind of sentence a copy editor these days will immediately 'sort out' for you. Why do we need so many his's? So many adjectives? And why is intention transferred from Bloom himself to his hand? To suggest the routine nature of the gesture, the automatism of the body's getting through the ordinary stuff? We are given the impression that Bloom is hyperconscious of what belongs to him. To the point that he has had his initials sewn into his overcoat, and likes to remember the fact. But 'initialled heavy overcoat' is heavy indeed, our copy editor would complain. Likewise 'lost property office secondhand waterproof', which of course immediately suggests a comparison with the marriage bed, bought second-hand at the government auction. Getting a good bargain second-hand is another small victory in the general defeat of not being able to buy new.

Unsurprisingly, Bloom's hat is old. With a 'sweated legend', a lovely collocation, hinting as much at the hard work that's going into the writing as the nature of the hat label. And you can't help hearing some borrowing from Italian here, remembering Giacomo Leopardi's *sudate carte* (sweated papers) in the famous poem 'To Silvia'. I'm struggling to think of another occasion in English where 'sweated' is used this way as an adjective, except, significantly, in the standard formula 'sweated labour', the work of the loser, the victim. In passing I reflect that Joyce has an idiolect that endlessly transforms ordinary objects and their humdrum moment-to-moment perception into poetry. It relies heavily on the rhythmic placing of adverbs. The legend in the hat tells him something *'mutely'* (U 67). And then, as he stops to listen in the hallway, 'She turned over *sleepily* that time' (U 67). Here it's wonderful that Bloom not only hears his wife move but interprets the state she's in accordingly. He's an attentive man. Then, not having his key with him, 'He pulled the halldoor to after him very *quietly*, more, till the footleaf dropped *gently* over the threshold' (U 67).

Mutely, sleepily, quietly, gently. Reading these lines brings back so much. First and foremost the old front doors with footleaves (does the word exist?) that I grew up with in northern England. The wood was usually rotting at the point where the rain got in between the door and the 'leaf'. It's a pleasure to be reminded of them. But I'm also reminded of my last year at grammar school when it became the obsession of four or five companions – the kind who listened to Pink Floyd and smoked dope – to present all their English composition homework, both essay and description, in a Joycean stream of consciousness. And the way to do that was to turn every observation into a sort of dreamy poetry by introducing frequent adverbs, preferably between the verb and object, as in the last magnificent reverie of 'The Dead': 'He watched *sleepily* the flakes, silver and dark, falling *obliquely* against the lamplight.' It's interesting how much Joyce loves that 'ee' sound. And I remember how even then my objection was: but this is too flattering; our day-to-day routine simply doesn't have (or am I the only unlucky one?) this perpetually poetic, strangely muffled feel. I would have liked to say this out loud in the classroom, but couldn't, because our English teacher was a huge Joyce enthusiast. Avant-garde had become status quo.

More seriously, I'm aware on this reading that just as Joyce's brilliance aligns with Stephen's need to be smarter than those around him, so his love of detail, his determination to evoke every object however tiny and mundane, aligns with Bloom's attentiveness, his carefulness, his stealth. These two central characters don't just measure themselves against others, they are also made to measure, for Joyce. Every novelist will appreciate how important it is to invent characters who bring out the best in your writing.

But I've overlooked the one major plot development in this getting-out-of-the-house paragraph. Bloom is hiding something in the crown of his hat! A piece of paper. Apparently a secret others mustn't find. This is fun. The stuff of farce. As in any ordinary melodrama we want to know what's going on, and how this is going to play out in a day for which, as we learn a few lines on, Bloom must dress in black for a funeral. Obviously Joyce isn't going to be so incompetent as to let us know at once. We're to be kept on tenterhooks, which is fine. It's good to have something, however corny, to read towards.

Yet almost immediately another order of 'secret' pops up. What on earth is the sense of that Yoda-like formulation, 'Potato I have'? ('On the doorstep he felt in his hip pocket for the latchkey. Not there. In the trousers I left off. Must get it. Potato I have') (U 67). Time and again, even in this 'easy' episode, the reader is faced with the question: do I try to understand this, or do I just read breezily on? Should I think of this as something Joyce is hiding in the crown of *his* hat? It will be the same a long dreamy paragraph later (Bloom conjuring up an oriental street market), when our hero remarks, 'Kind of stuff you read: in the track of the sun' (U 68).

What does it mean to read something 'in the track of the sun'? And what on earth is that colon doing in the sentence?

Inevitably one is tempted to seek help. Our reading experience of any book will depend very largely on what we bring to it; that seems self-evident, and most writers have a shrewd respect for what their readers will know, often playing with the limits of the context available to them. The encyclopaedic *Ulysses*, however, as Borges quickly understood, requires a range of reference no one can have, thus opening an abyss between writer and reader and making the text 'unreadable' (Borges), or perhaps we should say tantalizingly off limits, or even to be read *because* unreadable; the way climbers are most attracted to mountains that look too high and hard to climb. However, modern information technology and modern scholarship (at the service of the great man) can now provide that context swiftly and easily. It takes me only seconds online to discover joyceproject.com, which offers the 'Calypso' episode with multi-coloured hyperlinks to explain everything I have trouble with. This potato, I am told, will get a next mention 130 pages later in 'Lestrygonians' but is only 'explained' in 'Circe' where we learn that it is a talismanic gift from Bloom's dead mother. A rather old potato, then. I wonder what a decades-old potato feels like. *The Track of the Sun*, on the other hand, turns out to be a travel book; Amazon offers a photo-scanned reprint for $19.75; I sampled a page or two and enjoyed what I saw.

But is this the right way for me to read Joyce's work? What would the author have thought? We know from the accounts of his friends that if, on reading *Work in Progress* aloud to them, they understood too easily, he would go away and make it more obscure. So am I cheating, using a crib? Or missing out, perhaps, on the pleasures of masochism? 'Curious mice never squeal,' Bloom thinks of the cat and mouse relationship.

'Seem to like it.' Why doesn't the reader squeal? Very likely the potato was meant to remain buried underground until it sprouted later to my delighted surprise (though I fear I would have forgotten it). Checking in my Kindle edition of *Ulysses*, I see that 'potato' or 'potatoes' occurs twenty-six times throughout the text, though usually not with relation to this shrivelled potato, which, since it eventually becomes part of Bloom's sexless exchanges with a prostitute, begins to take on something of that air of resignation or sad pleasure in defeat that always hangs about him.

I decide to leave any further use of joyceproject.com until a second reading, although simply knowing that it's available somehow alters the experience of the text, puts my mind at rest, as when you know for sure that you can check the answer to the crossword on the back page.

But we'll have to speed up. Bloom goes out, oriental reverie mixes with canny reflections on winners and losers in business and real estate. Meat and Molly and the next-door maid all get mixed up, as sound, sight and smell are frequently confused. She, the maid, has vigorous hips, chapped hands. Did his neighbour hire her, Bloom wonders, standing beside her at the butcher's counter, because his wife is no longer up to scratch? Certainly the girl knows how to whack a carpet on the clothesline. Evidently our hero loves watching her. Now he's anxious to get out of the shop and follow 'her moving hams' (U 71) down the street, but alas, must wait to be served a 'moist tender gland' (U 71) and then place three coins on 'the rubber prickles'.

It's all cheekily allusive, playfully laddish, in a sophisticated sort of way; perhaps the sophistication makes possible the laddishness. It's intriguing to think that when this material was written, many thought it 'smutty', not least Joyce's loyal brother Stanislaus, who dubbed the 'Circe' episode 'the most horrible thing in literature', nothing more than an 'inspection of the stinkpots'. Then, following the author's death and for many post-war decades, everyone felt pleased with themselves for having overcome this Victorian prudishness. But now, in the twenty-first century of Me Too, with our hypersensitivity to power inequality in intimate relationships, a writer once again has to think twice before celebrating the pleasure a man might feel cheerfully sizing up a servant girl as a sex object. Yet power in relationships is very much what Joyce's work is about. Here, in short, is our man Bloom: bold as a voyeur, looking to follow a pair of legs in the street, or later, more famously, masturbating as he spies a crippled teenager's panties, but meek almost to the point of abjection in the presence of his sexually powerful wife. Which again reminds me that I once invited my postgrad translation class, mostly young women, to examine a translation of the Gerty MacDowell scene. It was a serious mistake that I was careful never to repeat.

Meantime I've just realized that the butcher, who was previously 'ferreteyed' (U 70), now has 'foxeyes' (U 72). What am I to make of that? Why does Joyce disdain the hyphen? There are various words I don't know – 'dunam', for example, 'jarvey' (U 81) – and a reference to 'a Norwegian captain' (U 73) that rings no bells. (I remember Jung complained that *Ulysses* made the reader feel stupid.) Then intense gloom when a cloud crosses the sun – I just about recall Stephen's response to the same phenomenon – with Bloom now reflecting learnedly, poetically on the grim fate of the Jews. The Dead Sea is evoked and when 'a bent hag' (U 73) crosses the road clutching another word I don't know – 'a noggin bottle' (U 73) – the sea and she are transformed into 'the grey sunken cunt of the world'.

All this seems over the top and hardly credible. And becomes even less so when we hear: 'Grey horror seared his flesh' (U 73). Surely this is Stephen's territory, not Bloom's. In fact Joyce quickly corrects himself and returns to questions of real estate. But the brief digression on the Jews, wandering from 'captivity to captivity' (U 73), does raise the question of why the writer wanted his character to be Jewish. I can recall no moment in my readings of *Ulysses* when I thought Joyce was seriously interested in the Jewish community or Jewish issues, though of course there are any number of erudite references. Certainly none of the essential drama hinges on Jewishness nor are we ever invited to share in the spirit of a Jewish family, since Bloom himself is hardly a synagogue-goer. The only thing that occurs to me is Joyce's fascination with the figure who is at once both inside and outside the community, part and not part. That is true of Stephen at every stage of his development and of course of Joyce himself, living far away from Dublin but always seeking to possess it and share in its life through his writing. The overwhelming Irishness of voice and reference in *Ulysses* is the product of the author's distance from the Irish scene. Bloom, as even these opening pages show, is very much a family man, yet strangely detached from those around him, living in his own mental space. In all these cases – Stephen, Joyce, Bloom – it is the apartness, the separate mental world, that guarantees special status.

No sooner is Bloom home than we have bedroom farce: a lover's letter hidden under a pillow (but peeping out!), a husband spying his wife's treachery over his shoulders (and describing her breasts as 'goat's udders'), mention of that supreme song of sexual betrayal *La ci darem la mano* (wonderful here how Bloom ignores the humiliation the song insinuates but asserts his superiority by wondering whether his unfaithful wife will pronounce *voglio* properly). And the lovely moment when, asked to bend down and pick up her book, which has fallen beside the chamber pot (another chance to enjoy a tang of urine), Bloom shows off his knowledge by explaining to his wife what 'metempsychosis' (U 77) means.

Here I could not resist. Would *Ruby: The Pride of the Ring* – the novel that Molly is reading (and insists isn't 'smutty') – really include the word metempsychosis (so useful of course for the novel's mythic connections)? In seconds joyceproject.com gave me the exact title of the book and showed me the illustration that Bloom contemplates as he stands up from the chamber pot: a man with a whip leaning over a half-naked woman – *'The monster Maffei desisted and flung his victim from him with an oath'* (U 77–8). Again domination, humiliation. Google Books then allowed me to run a full text search on the novel and, no, the word 'metempsychosis' *does not occur* in this once popular book!

Got him! Triumph.

At once I felt shocked. I can think of no other author who would have drawn me into such an infantile spirit of competition. Is it because no other author attempts to lord it over me quite like this? Or did Joyce foresee my little victory? Is it like the expert gambler who loses one hand on purpose to draw the beginner deeper into the game? Or was the game precisely to challenge the reader to find the mistakes deliberately scattered through the book? Whatever the case, like any fine writer, Joyce has brought me into the world he moves in, one of intense rivalry, of submerged power struggles (think of the crazy plot of *Exiles*!), and I seem to be positioning myself there more like Stephen than Bloom.

Chastened, but without shameclosing eyes, I now notice the extraordinary expression 'all the beef to the heels were in' in Milly's – Bloom's daughter's – rather extravagantly fey letter. This time I decide not to check what it means. Suffice it to say there is an awful lot of meat in this episode, 'toothsome pliant meat' (U 79), which Bloom eats 'with discernment' (U 79) and whose physicality Joyce loves to savour in the mental space of language.

There remains the famous trip to the 'jakes' (another new word for me) to loosen our bowels. Here the measuring of the two protagonists against each other – Stephen and Bloom, that is – is complete. 'Asquat on the cuckstool' (U 83) – yet another new word – Bloom slows his bowel movements to match his reading of 'Matcham's Masterstroke' in *Titbits*. Even defecating is a question of mastery (reading about mastery), getting it right (as Bloom was so careful to set his wife's breakfast tray right). Story completed at exactly the moment his turd satisfactorily drops in the can, our hero now measures himself with the story's author, Mr Philip Beaufoy, feeling he could easily compete (like Stephen, like Joyce) at this writing game. What Bloom then envies – and it's my favourite sentence in the whole episode – is not Beaufoy's writerly skill, but the money he earned on publication: he 'glanced back through what he had read and, while feeling his water flow quietly, he envied kindly Mr Beaufoy who had written it and received payment of three pounds, thirteen and six' (U 84).

Verb adverb object. Oh to be able to envy *kindly* Mr Joyce!

After this first enjoyable, but also disquieting reading – as when one meets an old acquaintance who is entertaining, but not necessarily friendly – I went back through the whole chapter checking all the explanatory links in joyceproject.com and was struck by how similar the experience was to visiting a museum where some items attract one's fascinated gaze while others pass one by or seem merely clutter. That mysterious 'orangekeyed chamberpot' (U 77), for example. Could it really be, as Hugh Kenner surmised, the 'continuous labyrinthine pattern often called a meander, Greek fret, or Greek key', thus 'connecting the Blooms' bodily needs to ancient Greek times'? It's hard to care. And in general it's hard to think of anything less like Ulysses's seven-year sojourn with the immortal Calypso than Bloom's ménage with Molly. But perhaps again it's a question of the Joycean cat playing with the readerly mouse. 'Cruel. Her nature' (U66).

Fortunately there's no crime in leaving a museum before you've looked at everything. Pressing duties eventually freed me from Calypso's clutches. I must reread proofs of my translation of Pavese's *The Moon and the Bonfires*. This novel too can be difficult and is intensely aware of myth and ritual. Non sequiturs and ellipses abound. You're never quite sure where a paragraph is going, let alone a chapter. Yet for all Pavese's meandering, one soon becomes aware one is being told a powerful, even harrowing story. Sketched in with a few words, the many characters take on an urgent reality. You feel you must know their destinies. The book is thankfully short but the experience huge. And reading those proofs I realize how little I am able to care about Joyce's characters, perhaps precisely because he is determined to tell me so much about them, and in a way that foregrounds manner at the expense of matter. When reading *Ulysses* you think about the Joyce experience, the Joyce experiment; it is that you engage with, not the story, or the people. And I remember that Pavese, who in his twenties translated *A Portrait of the Artist*, later refused to translate *Ulysses*. 'In confidence,' he wrote to the publisher, 'all of Joyce irritates me.'

Lotus–Eaters

Turn on, Tune in, Bloom out

EDOARDO CAMURRI

Edoardo Camurri is a famous broadcaster, author and TV anchor in Italy. He writes a column for *Il Foglio* and has edited the partial translation of Joyce's *Finnegans Wake*.

1

Leopold Bloom comes from the future, he is a hyperstition, a self-fulfilling prophecy. Before Leopold appeared, humanity had not yet received instructions on how to proceed, and the utter mobilization of the First World War was evidence of such a bewilderment. In a sense, even the Great War came from the future, as an alienating and eradicating horizon (scrap iron, gas, trenches, lightnings, explosions, planning, mass schizophrenia, metallic hallucination) fallen as a devastating asteroid from a dimension unthinkable for us. With Bloom's appearance, we glimpse a road to take, we grasp how to face our interesting and devastating times, an age which still features a war – now a mainly spiritual and neurologic one: a war between the powers of openness and those of closedness, between those who fight for liberation and for the blooming of the Human beyond Itself, and the digital and algorithmic structure capable, in watching us, of turning our bodies and our desires into fetishes on which it can perform its digital voodoo.

Let us look at the 'Lotus-Eaters' episode from this perspective; let us imagine that James Joyce wrote it while being linked up to a 100th-generation supercomputer, beyond the usual unfolding of time, and that he gave it to us in order to change, *hic et nunc*, the course of events, to save us from destruction, in a fight in which the sweetest human being of all times, Leopold Bloom, has become the democratic example we can all follow.

Before all this, though, we need to understand what the stakes are, in which sense we can speak of digital voodoo, and why the First World War is still on, albeit carried on with different means, in an unprecedented attack on our spirit and our nervous system. We will also see how Leopold's invitation to access a technically psychedelic dimension – which, to be sure, happens in this episode for the first time – can be the great Joycean Yes to be set against the powers of closedness and control which since time immemorial wish to cut off the bloom we all are.

2

Algorithms gather immense information about us. In this sense, our data, the traces of our digital life, feed the algorithm as in an upward motion. Our data's updraught allows the algorithm to progressively form *an idea* of us. The algorithm wishes to know everything about us; its natural tendency is to look more and more like us so as to anticipate us.

Anticipating us is important, for only in this way can it reach its economic and political scope.

In order to become us, the algorithm darkly performs some magical and sapiential practices: the updraught reaches us from below and at the same time sends a descensional draught of data from above.

This initially reveals itself in the dimension of our digital life, in the continuous flux of information and images dooming us to a more and more personalized profiling, its aim being to limit our unpredictability for the aforementioned reasons.

Thus, the algorithm hands back to us a bubble of information and emotions, knowing that we will identify with it so it can play the cat-and-mouse game with us (Elias Canetti used the image of the cat enjoying itself in delaying the mouse's death as the paradigmatic example of Power).

Here is when we experience an interruption in the data's ascensional and descensional circulation which characterizes the symbiotic relationship between human beings and the algorithm. And here is why: by becoming more and more like us for the very reason that the algorithm gives us back data capable of confirming our own world, we will begin feeding it less and less new data which are of interest to it. Here is when the updraught starts diminishing, while the descensional draught grows in intensity.

Thus, human beings progressively become the very field on which the algorithm can practise its own magic. From such a perspective, there are two conclusions we can draw. *First*: if human beings have been wholly transferred into the algorithm, our only existential changes can occur on a digital level: the human mind is in the hands of computer programmers. *Second*: the huge quantity of data and their management cannot be left to human programmers, for as human beings themselves, they are victims of the same spell they have triggered. Thus, such a mass of data can only be managed by a super artificial intelligence. This technological entity will then be capable of programming the soul of human beings. We have a God, at last, endowed with all the characteristics of the God of theology. All but one: it is omnipotent and omniscient, but not endlessly merciful (however, the question of goodness will obviously not concern us, for, being anticipated and anticipatable, we will not be preoccupied with the moral question anymore).

3

The reader of *Ulysses* is in the position to see the world from the point of view of the algorithm. When we follow Leopold Bloom on his day in Dublin, we gather endless data on his person; the whole book is constructed on hundreds of coincidences which intertwine according to a synchronicity logic, in a thick and marvellously inextricable net of connections.

We follow Bloom's GPS, we monitor him metre by metre in his movements, we know all of his thoughts, the way in which they are born and how they come to an end; and yet we sense that we have no power whatsoever over him; we cannot anticipate him, despite the many elements we draw from his behaviour. We get to know Bloom probably better than he knows himself, we grasp his coherence as an individual, but at the same time we feel that it is Leopold Bloom who holds us in his hands; this is because Leopold Bloom is in fact trying to hack the algorithm.

Bloom is telling the algorithm (or God) to leave him alone, once and for all.

In the fifth episode of *Ulysses*, Bloom keeps bumping into the oppressive order of the world, its religious, military, economic and mediatic structure, in order to wreck it in a state of lethargy and psychedelic awakening; he practises a counter-ritual in which power is weakened until it can no longer have a grip on his mind – just as happens with martial arts, when the opponent's force is first 'received' and then returned, minimizing the effort and maximizing the result.

In the post office Bloom sees military recruitment posters, but they don't have any effect on him. They vanish like shadows, a game of representation, a deceitful illusion, a Vedic maya. On the portal of All Hallows he reads a note about a sermon preached by the most Reverend John Conmee, whose surname – which belongs to a real person who played a role in Joyce's schooldays – incorporates the verb *to con*, meaning 'to deceive' but also, algorithmically, 'to govern, to pilot'.

Bloom has a newspaper with him, but he only looks at it passively, in passing: he prefers to use it as a baton, a third leg, a folded penis, a protuberance attracting the attention of sad horse-race betters, who in their craving for money and competition, prove to be unaware of the phallic symbolism.

The eucharist is a sexual ritual (a lollipop), an almost digestive mechanism of the needs of the human flesh; and the host is a Hockypocky, which reminds one of the ice cream sold by street vendors, but also of hocus-pocus, a deceit, a fraud. It comes from *hoc est corpus*, 'this is the body', in a process of progressive and psychedelic revelation of the subliminal meanings the act implies.

Leopold Bloom, with his own peculiar sweetness, and always respectful of the golden and magic rule that one should never directly oppose the allure of power so as not to fall victim of its own black charm, repeats, albeit in a context here illuminating in unpredictable terms, the Marxist motto about religion being the opiate of the masses.

This statement could easily be reversed, in the name of the ongoing spiritual and neurologic war, so turning into its programmatic opposite: the opiate *will be* the masses' religion.

4

In 1953 Aldous Huxley tried mescaline and narrated his experiences in a book entitled *The Doors of Perception*. Here is what happens during a psychedelic vision according to Huxley: it is as if we, whose brains are designed to perceive and conceive reality on the basis of biologic usefulness, thanks to psychedelics could loosen its meshes and cognitive filters so as to be open to the contemplation of the thing in itself. Huxley wrote that mescaline delivered him from the world of selves, time, moral judgements and utilitarian considerations. It was a world full of self-assertion and of words and notions that had been overvalued and worshipped. Thus, he longed to be left alone with Eternity as in a flower, to experience the Absolute in the folds of a pair of his flannel trousers! Abolishing space and time, dissolving the slogging and hateful Ego, reuniting with an archetypical universe whose traces we can still perceive in the nostalgia of the lost ecstasy and its neuroses, the possibility to enter a realm of light where we can try to build an alternative to the totalitarian world of atomic threats and the mass narcotization by psychopharmacology. This is why for Huxley psychedelic substances are like Raphael's Madonna of a new possible humanism. This is why, after Huxley, the psychedelic revolution has attempted to turn, with different and controversial results, into political practice for a spiritual war against the powers of closedness and the instincts of death. It is the same war which was fought by Parmenides to overcome the illusion of reality; it is the war of Spinoza and Giordano Bruno against a type of superstition which becomes a system of violence; it is the war of Freud and Jung for the acknowledgement of the unconscious. This is the war of artistic and musical avant-gardes, the struggle for the liberation of the body, the war of the poets and the underdogs, the war of scientists who do not renounce the freedom of research. It is the war of lovers and free-thinkers, the war of the crazies and the Don Quixotes.

This was the struggle, lived through with desperation until his suicide in 2017, of the English philosopher Mark Fisher, while he was working on a book whose title would have been *Acid Communism*.

Acid Communism was an attempt to oppose the powers of closedness Fisher calls 'capitalist realism'. What he meant was that the structure of power had created conditions which made it impossible to find and practise a real alternative outside of themselves.

In the few pages of the book he managed to write, there is a hint to the possibility of a counter-ritual capable of breaking the spell of closedness.

Fisher writes that acid communism refers to actual historical developments but also to a virtual confluence not yet manifested. This is because potentials exert influence even when they are not actualized. The actualization of potential formations is impeded by actual social formations, and it is the very structures of a capitalist realist world that make freedom impossible.

These are crucial words: Fisher thinks we need to *identify* a still unexpressed possibility within the cultural, political and social forms which already 'occurred' in history, and *reactivate* it against the working powers of closedness.

Potentials, then, are capable of exerting an influence without being actualized. This hallmark, these 'potentials', are for Fisher the great psychedelic counterculture of the Sixties, for the defining feature of the psychedelic is indeed the question of consciousness, and how it is related to what is experienced as reality. If our sense of space and time, that is, the fundamentals of our experience, are subject to alteration, it means that the very categories by which we live are changeable. A crucial feature of the psychedelic culture of the Sixties was its ability to 'mainstream' those metaphysical questions, as experiments with consciousness promised a democratization of neurology itself, leading possibly to a new awareness of the brain's role in the production of what we experienced as reality.

5

In 'Lotus-Eaters' we see Bloom fighting the same struggle and accepting, in this somnolent and drugged episode, some of the principles I tried to sum up. But, he also bumps into coincidences and prophecies which are rather astonishing (and we know only too well that such prophecies, such hyperstitions, are very common in Joyce, just as they are in the psychedelic experience when, by a suspension of the brain's organizing filter, space and time are reorganized according to different orders and modalities, beyond the linear flow of past, present and future).

In 'Lotus-Eaters' Bloom is a disciple of Dionysus, the liberator, the god of inebriation and metamorphosis, whose characteristics are here rendered more popular and simple, more at hand, through a great sense of goodness and accepting life beyond good and evil, beyond any normative order imposed in the name of democracy and sharing. It is an episode in which every aspect of reality blooms and manifests itself (the very meaning of psychedelia is 'the mind that reveals itself').

Bloom's first feeling is of compassion for a young boy rummaging about in the rubbish; then he starts thinking of the Orient, of teas, prefiguring an India similar to that which will be 'seen' by the counterculture hippies: 'cactuses, flowery meads, snaky lianas' and then again 'Sensitive plants' (U 87), that is, intelligent, spiritual, psychedelic.

Dublin functions just like a *theatrum mundi*, a machine for thinking and creating associations and neuronal connections the system of control cannot predict. Dublin and Bloom *bloom* and manifest themselves in a higher dimension of reality. Meeting a horse instantly becomes a shamanic, Amazonian experience, in which Leopold imagines the animistic and Dionysian possibility of interspecies communication; his pen-lover's letter is a flowery game which abounds with desires, bodies, perfumes; life itself becomes a flux ('Always passing, the stream of life, which in the stream of life we trace is dearer than them all') (U 107), and in this flux Bloom foresees his own forthcoming androgenic metamorphosis: already a queer change, already a gender-fluid type of free love ('free leaves for everybadies', we will read in *Finnegans Wake*, a splendid psychedelic pun-phrase blending marijuana leaves, love and bad boys).

The powers of closedness are dissolved and dismembered in a wider vision. 'Eunuch. One way out of it' (U 101) is a Buddhist thought against the tyranny of desire, against the survival instinct which replicates and strengthens the fear of dying; and Molly's betrayal, of whose imminent occurrence Bloom is fully aware, starts turning slowly into a nuisance, into a gradually weakening atavism later to be overcome by a bigger love and a bigger Yes.

The mind's unidentifiability and its unfolding in every direction, becoming every direction, is the first antidote against control. Bloom does not dissolve, he blooms, becoming everything. What a magnificent hint, what a splendid psyche-delic coincidence the very fact that in this episode he will fantasize a swim in the Dead Sea: 'Couldn't sink if you tried: so thick with salt' (U 87).

Bloom and the Dead Sea. The experience of floating without resistance, in a negation of sensory experience, allows the mind, freed from the stimuli of the external world, and therefore protected by the digital voodoo, to manifest itself. A nice coincidence, for aside from being one of Leopold's intuitions, it is also the story of one of the great exponents of psychedelia in the years of American counterculture: John C. Lilly.

6

In the 1950s, Lilly graduated from the California Institute of Technology and became an important member of the National Institutes of Health in the US. There he studied the connections between the mind and the brain. When the Pentagon asked him to work on controlling the human mind through cerebral electro stimulation, Lilly abandoned the NIH. His refusal to collaborate with the powers of closedness inevitably opened him to those of openness. He dedicated himself to LSD and ketamine, and just like Bloom with his horses, he worked on interspecies communication, choosing dolphins. At the same time he invented the Dead Sea, a flotation tank for sensory deprivation intended to simulate, just like Bloom, a total abandonment of the senses in order to access Vision. But this is not the end of the story. During those prolonged sessions with LSD and ketamine in the tank, Lilly could access a universe similar to a cosmic computer, full of programmers and automatons organized according to a sort of archontic hierarchy; he came back from that trip convinced that everybody could similarly reprogram themselves, and therefore external reality, by partaking in this ultimate dimension of psychedelic revelation.

Lilly says that he was caught in the grips of a paranoid cosmic conspiracy just like a small program in the big computer. Knowing where he was, he was able to recentre himself by accepting his role as part of the cosmos, realizing then that he *was* one of the programmers of the big computer. This led him to state that we run the universe even if not yet awake. We program it, we are the controllers, we are in communion with their network.

It was a profound experience. Lilly had access to the algorithmic machine of digital voodoo and knew how to hack it.

7

There is a sentence in 'Lotus-Eaters' which is of paramount importance: 'Every word is so deep' (U 93). We can accelerate this expression in the direction of Mark Fisher's discourse: just as every historical age has not exhausted all its possibilities in the moment in which it was actualized (leaving then to humans the revolutionary task of trying to 'shamanically' awaken the future from a buried past), so every word preserves yet unexplored meanings and depths, and Joyce teaches us how to unleash them in our own world; a bit like psychedelics, which show us how to expand reality beyond cognitive principles.

'Every word is so deep' is also the manifesto of *Finnegans Wake*, Joyce's last work, a book literally worshipped by psychedelic counterculture. Marshall McLuhan held, for example, that the *Wake* was more powerful than LSD; Terence McKenna read it as an oracle; libertarian psychoanalyst Norman O. Brown considered it a treasure recovered at the end of his own process of radicalization of Freud's ideas; and Robert Anton Wilson loved to recite to his friend Timothy Leary a passage which seemed to prophesy him, for his very name was transfigured becoming a great king with an ardent marijuana head full of psychedelic colours: 'High Thats Hight Uberking Leary his fiery grassbelonghead all show colour of sorrelwood herbgreen' (FW 611.33–4).

Philip K. Dick, perhaps while visiting similar interior regions as those of Lilly, viewed *Finnegans Wake* as a pool of information which was based on computer memory systems yet to come, in Joyce's lifetime, convinced as he was that Joyce was also plugged into a sort of cosmic consciousness which was the very source of inspiration for his entire work.

The *Wake* narrates in the most complex way possible a very simple story: the sleep and dreams in the night of its protagonist, the publican H. C. Earwicker, whose premises are in a Dublin suburb. His name is crucial: Earwicker points to the insect which, according to various legends, penetrates the ears while one is sleeping. Readers of *Finnegans Wake* are thus always in movement, their brains are constantly changing, run through by the zigzagging electric earwig connecting their synapses and inducing unthought-of associations. The earwig, just like LSD, is a cerebral reprogrammer capable of blowing up every fixed scheme, including the book itself. The book still baffles critics wishing to tell us what happens in it, for every time we open it, its contents change. It was published in book form in 1939, and yet we find email in it ('Speak to us of Emailia') (FW 410.23); we come across Google ('One chap googling the holyboy's thingabib') (FW 620.22), we even find Nike shoes ('Nike with your kickshoes') (FW 270.24), golf champion Tiger Woods ('tigerwood') (FW 35.7) and soccer legend Francesco Totti ('Totty go') (FW 327.7). And, when we encounter the coronavirus ('And the corollas he so has saved gainsts the virus he has thus injected') (FW 321.5–6), we cannot but go back to the middle of the book where an allusion to 'a mushroom' (FW 315.18) and a mention of Nagasaki ('Nogeysokey') (FW 315.22) are juxtaposed in less than five lines.

Examples are endless, and to say so isn't just rhetoric. They are so many. Technically, they are infinite, for *Finnegans Wake* is a book whose end and beginning coincide, and whose composition, not an exercise in puzzle composing, but a free game of analogies, continuously changes in time and space, according to who the reader is, to the age in which we read it and to the setting conditions in which we experience it.

101

Finnegans Wake brings one to think the unthinkable: just like LSD, it switches on the brain by connecting neurons which were not communicating before; just like a libertarian Internet, the open original net, it connects peoples, concepts and ideas which would not have met otherwise. An example? At some stage Joyce mentions the prophet Mohammed, writing 'Moyhammlet' (FW 417.18). Here we have the French *moi* of the Cartesian I; we have Hamlet and in it we find *ham*, but also the biblical *Ham*, one of the sons of Noah. We instantly laugh on spotting the presence of a pig in Mohammed's new semantic body, and thus we start thinking the unthinkable: what is the new relationship between two heroes of doubt like Descartes and Hamlet and the founder of a religion of certainty and absolute submission? And what is their rapport with Ham, cursed after seeing his naked father? What are the connections there? Connection, analogy, strong emotions, unrecognizableness, freedom, new communities. They seem to be the political characteristics Fisher tried to evoke in order to fight and eliminate once and for all the powers of capitalist realism. They are the libertarian and socialistic values of Leopold Bloom. They are the hallmarks of the powers of openness.

8

'Every word is so deep', Bloom says to himself. Joyce repeats as much a few years later by hinting at the fact that *Finnegans Wake* speaks the language of the future. The *Wake*, and Leopold Bloom, are showing us how to use the freed imagination of psychedelia in order to actualize the possibilities contained in the potency of ordinary language. Against all powers of closedness.

9

Thanks to Bloom's morning walk, we can understand how the digital voodoo can be faced through a counter-ritual capable of tuning the mind to unpredictability and unicity.

From this perspective, Leopold is telling us how necessary it is to access new visions in order to recover a new discipline of imagination. In fact – and here's the rub, it seems – a war is being fought eminently within the domain of imagination, a domain we cannot define or see anymore, and one which, despite everything, keeps existing and acting.

To reconquer imagination was the philosophical task of Henry Corbin, the great French scholar of the Islamic mystical tradition who in the 1960s warned that the disappearance of it in the Western world could lead to a catastrophe of the spirit. He simply used the word 'catastrophe'. Imagination was the space of the spirit, between sensory perceptions and intellectual abstractions. This middle-world makes it possible for the material external reality, which our senses encounter every day, to become spiritual and, at the same time, to shape abstract concepts and the intelligible forms we think out, providing them with a dimension. Imagination is not made of fanciful or oneiric vagaries; according to Corbin, it is a real world we are no longer used to inhabiting and cultivating. It is the very world through which man accesses vision, the world in which meanings 'occur', the world where they become possible. Without imagination, catastrophe can proceed and manifest itself with us unaware of its meaning and of what it actually is. Imagination is a schema, a matrix, a net, a smaragdine tablet where the bodily becomes spiritual, and the spiritual bodily; it is the axis uniting heaven and earth.

The algorithmic structure, with its capability to elaborate and circulate meanings and images, is the plainest possible parodic representation of what imagination is.

The algorithmic machine, as we have seen, functions in order to replicate the human; it works for the construction of a puppet made of data on which it can cast its digital jinx.

Imagination is thus externalized. And the Paracelsian crucible where the above and the below meet is replaced by a perverse imitation of it. Now, here's the new rub for us all: imagination is also the space in which magic is possible, and this is why it is also the most obvious ground on which the war between closedness and openness takes place. If in imagination the bodily becomes spiritual, and the spiritual bodily, then imagination is the meeting point between those two opposite domains in the world: it is the place where matter and spirit meet and burn together for an instant. It is the old dream of magic: to do things with words. Words denote objects in the external world, and the magicians of old tried to use those words to change, according to their desires, and through sortileges and formulae, the surrounding reality. It is the ancient principle, already hinted at by Aristotle, according to which letters are like atoms making up the matter: you change one letter and the matter is changed accordingly. 'Every word is so deep' is Bloom's discovery.

In the word we see the embrace of heaven and earth: they couple in a cosmic coitus, which is pregnant with possibilities only a magician can cause to bloom.

10

Bloom is a flower, and 'Lotus-Eaters' ends with the greatest possible flowery expression, the epiphany of a world of imagination.

What was for India – so present in this episode – the *lingam*, the cosmic phallus, is here embodied in a floating Leopold in a Turkish bath, the portal of the Orient, which is a tank of sensory deprivation. Leopold contemplates himself from the above, away from himself, in a psychedelic ecstasy; and he does so with words which christen him a magus – a womb of heat, soaped with the perfumed soap which, dissolving, cleanse him softly: 'He saw his trunk and limbs riprippled over and sustained, buoyed lightly upward, lemonyellow: his navel, bud of flesh: and saw the dark tangled curls of his bush floating, floating hair of the stream around the limp father of thousands, a languid floating flower' (U 107).

Turn on, tune in, Bloom out.

Hades

Rites of Passage

LAWRENCE TAYLOR

Lawrence Taylor is Emeritus Professor of Anthropology at National University of Ireland, Maynooth. His ethnographic works explore life, death and religion in Ireland and along the US/Mexico border. More recently, he has been writing fiction and memoir.

I stood shivering over Neasa's grave in Carrick churchyard, surrounded by the familiar dead. Neither she, nor any of them, were among 'my people', yet I knew more souls in that Donegal burial ground than anywhere in the wide world. I came there first half a century before and kept returning, for months or weeks, down through the years, the way I witnessed the passing of some and joined in remembering many others. And there I was again, Neasa's grave the end of a journey that had begun – allowing for the distortions of time and memory, of the contractions and expansions of meaningful moments and durations – with the death of another woman. My mother, Harriet. Her passing in the bleak January of 2013, just months short of her ninety-seventh birthday, provoked my immediate return to Ireland, and eventually, to that remote corner.

There would be nothing strange about such a 'return' if my mother had been from Donegal. Or even Irish and living anywhere on this Island. But Harriet died, as she had lived, in New York. She was neither Irish, nor had ever been to Ireland. As for me, I have long held a passport affirming my identity with the authority of the state. Éireannach. Irish. By adoption. And while none of my friends here would likely describe me as 'Irish', after so many years on the Island, when I am away, they do ask 'when are you coming home?' So, I suppose it is fair to say that the death of my mother in the city to which all my ancestors had come only a generation earlier from the other end of Europe, in which both she and I were born, and from whose larger environs she hardly ever ventured in all those years of life, sent me reeling back 'home' to Ireland.

* * *

The story of that return came back to me when asked to join Bloom on his meander across Dublin to the funeral of Paddy Dignam in Glasnevin. Although happy to find myself along for the ride, I could not escape the sense that, like A. J. Leventhal at the first 'Bloomsday' re-enactment of the same carriage ride, I had been invited aboard as much for my Jewishness as my writing on Irish Catholicism and death. So, I ride alongside Bloom, each of us 'imagined' Jews, 'strangers' at home in Ireland, belonging to and observing the death customs of this Western tribe.

For people like us there is nothing unusual about that, of course. We wander. And if we come to rest one place or another, even for a millennium, we remain strange. My mother's people lived in what is now called Poland for about a thousand years. Far longer than the Navaho and Apache have dwelt in the American Southwest. But, unlike those 'natives', the Grynbergs and Zwikielskis were never indigenous. There are no sacred Jewish mountains near Lodz or Krakow. Nor did they do what all those Fitzes famously did on this Island, making their bloody way into the lands and beds of the locals until no one could tell them apart. No one ever accused the Jews of being more Polish than the Poles themselves. So, we always remain, for the others about us, and for ourselves as well, 'strangers'. Of the sort about which Simmel mused, 'who come today and stay tomorrow…' It is an alienation that naturally foments questions of identity, an awareness (often born of necessity) of the strange ways of both Ourselves and Others, the habit of observation, grasping at a largely illusory sense of knowledge, and hence control, of an unpredictable, always potentially hostile world, within and without. Perhaps psychoanalysis and ethnography are Jewish folk arts, like Polish Mazurkas or Bavarian Scherenschnitte.

* * *

So, back to my journey to the Donegal churchyard, which began, like my mother's death, in the darkest days of winter, but evoked, as will any such movement over important and familiar ground, my very first passage into that *iargúlta* end of Ireland, in an unusually splendid summer.

A very young man, I walked and hitched into a place of majestic sea cliffs and greened bog cut through by effervescent, Guinness-black streams. Late sun lighting soft evening strolls alongside the rocky stream as it widened into the sheltered bay from whose high, reedy meadow corncrakes – a bird now rare everywhere on the Island – croaked their well-being into the night. A welcoming world peopled by attractively eccentric and amusing souls. There was even a new family with whom to lodge: a brood of interesting children near enough my own age, a father happy with a new audience for language lessons, and, in firm command, Neasa, a red-headed mother whose formidable self-assurance in all things was leavened by a lively wit and ready appreciation of humour wherever she met it. A family in every way an improvement on my own. An unrequited fantasy, of course. Aren't we often enough playing only bit parts, walk-ons, in the lives of those who, unbeknownst to themselves, are characters central to our own plots?

So I mused as I alit from the bus, only to be slapped awake by a chill wind. As if to remind me that winter was real and such idyllic summers nostalgic dreams. Only 'a pet day'. Meant to allure and deceive.

I was in Largymore, just west of Killybegs, where the yellowy meadows and low drumlin hills of the east of the county meet the wild, granitic, boggy west. I would walk the remaining miles from there, always wary of the wet ditches that banked the road. 'In through,' they say, denoting both place and people. An ancient, North Atlantic version of an Old Testament landscape, trod by irascible saints, each as moody as Moses, whose tearful confrontations with a testing deity left 'holy wells' all about the place. A separate, western world reached by way of windy roads that follow the land's contours along the wild coast or inland.

I took that shorter, steeper way through rough gorse meadows and recent spruce plantation, my knees feeling every rise and fall. The pale sun had begun its retreat behind Cró na Roda – and the deepening gloom of the mountain shadows oozed like spilt oil over the flowerless heather. The high streaks of grey-white snow did nothing to soften the land, harrowed by the last glacier, its soil flayed off a bristling schist skeleton.

Coming finally down into the lightly peopled glen, a first sprinkling of cottages and bungalows, my spirits should have been lifted by the beckoning promise of warm fires and human company. Yet those human outposts seemed as cold and dark as the hills that framed them. Nothing offered comfort against the damp, whose relentless assault had already numbed my thinly clad feet, spreading up through me as it does the walls of any home here when the last fire dies out of the grate.

Uaigneach. Lonely. A word often heard in these parts to describe a piece of the landscape as often as a person. Haunted. A road, a bog, a field, where other-worldly forces were at play and might be encountered.

Thus did the inchoate sadness that had grown in me since the death of my mother take material form in the landscape as I came into the village. Maybe I should have been wary of giving way to such feeling and free rein to the concatenation of remembering, a weakening of ordered time that might in turn threaten the integrity of the space about me, which at first glance down the street looked very little changed. An impression that would be given the lie when I entered the old hotel, where I was to spend the night.

I knew I would miss Morrissey, at rest with all the others down the road. But I was not prepared for the transformation of his dark and homely bar and lounge, against whose wet walls I had so often leant with pints and whiskies among my neighbours, waiting for the intermittent wise and witty comment to rise audibly from mumbled conversations. As if we were all trapped in an uncut, first draft of an interminable play.

The place had been totally redone, a well-heated, but cavernous emptiness that mocked ambition in tourist-free February. Upstairs was also remade, into a row of simple but comfortable en-suite rooms, with another, smaller, unmanned bar in the hallway for special occasions. There, on the highest shelf, well out of any casual reach, was Morrissey's material legacy – a row of obscure whiskies and exotic liqueurs. I managed to hoist myself up on the rungs of a stool to retrieve the bottle of *Bruidstranen*, 'bride's tears' – a wondrous concoction spiced with cardamon, cinnamon, cloves and anise – happy to hold and roll it, to watch the 'tears', flakes of 24-carat gold, whirl slowly about, as they had when Morrissey poured a toast to my new wife a lifetime ago.

Released like a genie from his own dusty bottle, Morrissey was back from the dead, leaning over the old bar in his sagging jumper, a shock of sooty silver hair veiling the same sardonic eye that always took us all sharply in, stranger and local alike. And behind him gathered more conjured shades, every one of them delighted to be back in his old 'haunt'. As on any Sunday after Mass, they streamed in to take their accustomed seats.

Among them 'the Nodder', as I remembered him, in his trademark rakish beret, who slid into the seat next to me, fixing me with expectant eyes, as he would at my every return after months or years away. To catch me up.

'You know Kelly?' His eyes happy with the assurance that of course I did and would remember what a great pleasure was to be had in Kelly's company. When I had smiled assent, he would close his eyes and let his face sink slowly into his hands, miming poor Kelly's passing. And then on to the next, leaving me as sad to hear of each loss as he was glad for the chance to remember them.

And now that he had joined them, I wondered, did another have his job?

'Oh, aye,' Morrissey remarked, sliding a pint before the Nodder. 'Always happy enough to recall their passing. But Maggie Ann? Now, there, as you might say, was the true Death Messenger.'

He pointed a sharp chin towards the doorway, where Maggie Ann stood, as she always did, a toe or two inside, a grimace-y sort of grin playing at one end of her mouth. Ready to speak what she knew – what everyone knew – were important lines in the ongoing play in which all were actors and audience.

'Johnny beyond in Letterkenny is failing... (long pause) ... sure, they say he won't last the night.' Her gift of the latest update a prelude to the final report she would file in due course. Death. The only news, and no news at all.

'So, you might worry,' Morrissey observed, 'as Maggie Ann stood always on the threshold of death, that you might see your own passing in her eyes, if you dared look. But, as we like to say, 'Death comes to us all'. As if, in saying it, you might get Death to abandon the idea of surprising you, seeing as you are calm and ready. But wouldn't Old Death see through that easy enough? Hasn't he seen every kind of sad dodge? But we say it all the same. As if it made sense of the very thing that made a nonsense of everything else.'

He let his newly coined aphorism sink in, as if he were talking to a faithful secretary, before continuing.

'But wasn't Maggie Ann well matched with her husband, Hugh?' I followed his eyes to a familiar figure, a short man hiding beneath his tweed cap, work-gnarled mitts gripping a steaming mug of milky tea, slumped on his own in a dark corner. Morrissey continued in a respectful whisper, 'A man as careful about death in his own way. Never one to miss a wake, always among the first to arrive, content in himself to pass many hours with his neighbours and kin, taking cigarettes and crustless sandwiches of butter dressed up with scraps of ham from the trays passed about. And endless cups of tea. At the right hand of the priest for the midnight rosary, and always among the last to leave, fortified with a good dram against the weather, of course. If Maggie Ann foretold and announced the death, you might say that Hugh presided in the *teach tórraimh*, the house of the wake, leaving Father McDyer, in all his priestly glory, to lead the rites next day in the *teach Dé*, the house of God.'

Happy with that formulation, Morrissey resumed the narrative.

'To be fair, Hugh was in every way diligent. His few rocky acres and sorry beasts were as well looked after as the hours God gave him would allow. And good man himself, didn't he somehow find time to see to the needs of his neighbour, Francie Con Joe? An old man bent with the arthritis the way the smallest chore was an agony, but Hugh was there for him, fetching this, mending that. Bringing in his hay and turf.

'Now, as you well know, old bachelor farmers are far from scarce around here, but this old lad had a nice stretch of flat land on which to grow a better class of silage for his cossetted beasts and – so people believed – a great lump of cash socked away as well. So, Hugh was up and down the road to your one regular, catering to him as if he were his own kin. As there were none of the same anywhere about, nor even in the country, as far as Hugh could find out, he felt it was only the decent neighbourly thing to do. And if the old man passed and left him something, maybe even the farm itself? Well, there would be nothing wrong with that, to reward the very goodness that God requires.

'Maggie Ann knew better – sure, didn't we all? "There's no way anything will go to you. In the end, nothing matters, only kin," she'd tell Hugh, who of course never spoke of it directly, but couldn't she read his thoughts plain enough? Anyway, up and down he went to the old fellow until one fine dry morning, didn't he come into the house only to find your one slumped there in his favourite chair. Poor Francie gone to his reward.

'Now, Hugh would have been worrying, all those years, that the old man wasn't getting around to making up his will, do you see? And if he died that way, they'd be off scouring the wide world for third cousins and the like while the fine house collapsed into wet ruins and the fields choked with thistle, as they always do when there's no "writing" to be found. But a will there was, so Hugh heard from Philomena in the post office who had taken the call from a solicitor in Donegal town. And so Hugh waited patiently for word from the same man, in the way perhaps of a letter telling him he was named and needed to meet for signings and the like.

'The call did not come, but some sort of a nephew did – from the great state of New Jersey – and with the help and advice of Sean Phat James of the pub there across the way, the nephew put on the wake in the very house in which poor Hugh had spent so many hours tending to the old one's wants and needs. And everyone went of course, spinning all manner of yarn for the Yank, all the time casting sideways glances at poor Hugh, who couldn't bring himself to tell your man – Tony, I think his name was – the mother an Italian lady, I believe – about all his service to a relation the American had never met in his life. And I suppose, whether out of shyness or divilment – a disposition to see the point about kin driven deeply home – none of the others there saw fit to say anything to the American lad about Hugh, and all he did for the great uncle.

'Now, the American, who was happy to hear all the amusing stories anyone could offer about the poor, dour departed, took no notice of Hugh, who was left brooding there in the corner without so much as a cup of tea in his fist. And so, when the priest had come and gone, didn't Hugh slip out and make his way home to Maggie Ann, who had the sense not to say, "I told you so," or at least not that night. But Hugh found no consolation and said, when she asked him next morning about the wake, that he wasn't offered so much as a cup of tea. That the Yank hadn't any more sense or manners on him than Bran, the hound there by their fire. And he said no more about it to her, but he couldn't shake it from his mind do you see, and so his nights were haunted by that wake until the old man finally came to him, in a dream, and weeping for the sin of his ignorant kin, apologized for the rudeness, and held out a great steaming mug to him. Which he took and forgave, though neither of them made mention of anything else.'

I couldn't help smiling up at Morrissey, acknowledging both the wisdom of the story, and the artistry of form and delivery. And, of course, my mind turned to other deaths and wakes, like the passing of Mickey, whose mocking smile I could just make out in the shadows where he was sitting, by the door, his whiskey glass pushed to the very edge of the table. The way any unsuspecting visitor might bang open the door and upset the glass – and atone for his sin by the offer of a double whiskey. Mickey had never missed a session in the pubs or beyond and so the musicians had returned the favour, coming one or more to his hospital bedside, playing if the staff allowed. And when it was time for the wake, when, in the words of his brother, 'they put the jam on him', the musicians entertained us all again, and all of us, even I, having my own stories of Mickey, rehearsed for the hundredth time his exploits here and abroad. But there was no such carry-on at the funeral or burial. No way. The priest took firm charge of all that and it was Michael, not Mickey, whose soul was committed to the Lord, with words and rites like those of any other.

'All changed now,' Morrissey reminded me, 'now it's a football jersey, hurley, or maybe a tin whistle brought up to the altar and a lot of talking from all quarters. Make it personal, do you see? Buyers' market. Just so.'

So went the evening, and the night beyond. Time, like Mickey's squeeze box, moved to its own rhythm, so when I rose with the late winter sun, I could not say which of those memories or characters came to me awake or asleep, in the bar or the bed. But it was another day, and I made my way through the frosty morning down the road to the churchyard, with those neat rows of stone monuments so inadequate to the peculiarities of whoever lay beneath, the rogues and gentle souls who will be known only by the stories worth telling. Among them, Neasa. The mother I found and quickly lost. Now a cold stone streaked with melting snowflakes, recalling a much earlier winter passage 'in through'.

* * *

It was a few years after that first, idyllic summer, when awed and daunted by the harsh beauty of rocks and ruins, I had made my way down the riverside, hoping for a confirmation of memories. Of a happy time and place. Of a *bean a tí* presiding with such stern cheerfulness over all she surveyed.

But the woman who opened the door to me was transformed, her bright, handsome face now a greyed winter landscape. The flesh had shrunk back around the sharp bones, throwing shadows over those penetrating grey eyes. Eyes from which your failings and sins could no more escape than a poor mouse running between rocks could those of a hungry falcon. They were now opaque, calmed but empty, looking inward, as if seeking something to explain the severity of fate, or patiently waiting for her God to divulge the otherwise obscure meaning of her loss. For loss, insouciant young man though I was, I knew there was. She told me the story over tea, of a young daughter's tragic, sudden death far from home. The fact that she was one of many children did not seem to allay the pain in any way.

It was a death that, even then, I could feel. Not an ethnographic fact. I had known the girl in that summer of my first visit and, like everyone, was much taken by her open heart and easy, earthy wit. Unlike the rest of the family, she was at ease with the locals, indeed happily at home among them. In all those respects, she was the very opposite of the mother but in that way may have offered her a vicarious window. A window now shut.

We may all be headed for the grave, but Neasa came to hers by purposeful stages. We have all seen it, the way the very religious person, the one who feels as well as follows, when upended by the unacceptable death of a child, reels off in one direction or another. A wild fury in the face of betrayal, or a deeper, desperate, clinging embrace. For her it was the latter, and it was Death Himself she pulled to her bosom, as she began a quiet withdrawing descent into her faith, from which she seemed to look out at the world, even on her family, from an ever-increasing distance.

Outside her quietening core, there was no lapse in her usual, habitual care and competence. She looked after her children as before, organizing and financing their lives like so many start-ups. Sending them off one by one, well launched. And if she missed them, she seemed happy enough to consecrate the newly free hours to increased devotion, until, finally freed by the death of her husband, she moved into a small bungalow in the village, from which she could effortlessly shuttle back and forth to the church. All the time withdrawing further and further into herself and her faith, preparing for one more move, one more 'downsizing', into that grave alongside her husband's and daughter's.

But what do I know of the forces within herself or her family that may have resisted her embrace of death and steady progress to the grave? Looked at from the height of time, Neasa's path, like that of 'history', seems clear, as if at every point irrevocable. From that same vantage, Harriet appears to have marched resolutely in the opposite direction, shunning the very possibility of death – of others as well as herself. No wakes, no *shiva*, no funerals, graves, or tombstones. Not her own sister's, mother's, husband's, or son's.

We followed her down this path, hewing always to life, but in the inevitable end, wasn't it a march to oblivion? A march that took me to Riverbank Park to recite a bit of Kaddish and pour my allotted portion of her ashes into the Hudson River. Only to have a sudden breeze whip a burning bit of them back into my eyes.

We couldn't even manage that together. Couples may break up over the death of a child because they cannot bear the shape of each other's grief. For siblings, the death of a parent may not only remove the linchpin of 'family', but also leave them struggling for control of the lasting memory of the deceased. And hence of themselves. Afraid of a difference that might threaten each one's coherence. Did Harriet see this coming?

'You shouldn't be so hard on your mother.'

Another spectre had joined me graveside, this time from further afield. Fabian Grynberg, my mother's much older cousin, stood beside me in the best suit he could afford, deep brown eyes beneath silvered black brows, carrying a bulging, travel-worn black satchel, like the sample case of a wayworn salesman. He put a hand gently on my shoulder, though I couldn't feel any weight.

'When I met her, in the summer of 1939, she was a beautiful young woman – all life and hope – engaged to your father – so blissfully unaware of the world I had left only months before, fleeing with my family from the horror to come.'

He squinted and shrugged, seeming to recall his own ambivalence, and sat himself down on a nearby, low gravestone, settling the satchel on his lap, absent-mindedly caressing it, as if the worn old thing carried things dear and precious.

'It's true, at first, I wasn't so charmed... I had left Zgierz a man of substance, a man of business and of letters, a community leader with four languages. But none of them was English and so – I could read this in your mother's eyes – I stood there in that grand American room of Cousin David's there in Long Beach, as bereft as a naked castaway washed up on their shore. At forty-six, I was already an old-fashioned old man from the old country. As you know, nothing old ever interested her. Of course, I resented her for that.

'Yet I was also very attracted, not just to her beauty, but to her very "newness", her easy movement about that modern American home, unburdened by any past. Her father, your grandfather, Abraham, and his older brothers had come to America decades before, as young men, but still they stood or walked with a slight stoop, the past, what they had endured, gained and lost in both countries, a visible weight on their shoulders. But your mother, and I suppose the other young ones as well, they were a different breed. That our family could come to such a point was disappointing, but also very hopeful. Like the ocean breeze there, it seemed to offer relief from the descent into night underway in the "old country". A different path, the path I had been on, would have led me to Israel, but "Affa-David", as he was nicknamed for his efforts, clerical and financial, to snatch us all from the devouring flames, was there in New York, where his success was our salvation. So, a new path, leading perhaps inevitably to the world of your mother, where history doesn't survive a generation.'

Fabian looked around him, taking in his foreign surroundings for the first time.

'And don't go all teary over such as Maggie Ann. I remember Fishel the *shammash* passing through the centre of the street every morning before dawn banging his wooden hammer on the gates of the Jewish homes. He would bang three times on each gate. If only twice, the residents of the street would know that someone passed away in the city that day, may G–d save us, and that one must prepare for the funeral. And we had our burial societies, and our cemetery. We were trying to preserve all that without going the way of the Hasidim. To be both Jews and Europeans, weren't we after all a part of that story as well? Why shouldn't we be at the centre of it? Of course, your mother and her friends were convinced *they* were the story, now unfolding in New York, clearly the centre of the world.

'And all my father's brothers must have believed that as well, but perhaps thought that they could keep what they wanted of the old ways, but in a new form? The Zgierzer Benevolent Society, just like all the committees in the old town, to help the poor, to bury their dead. But those did not last, dear boy. Oh no. By the time I died there was no Society left, no one to assign the plots, and my children buried me somewhere in California.'

A lonely grave, *uaigneach*. So different here, I thought, looking about me at the churchyard, where locals found fellowship. And theatre. The drama and power of those graveside moments, the last churchyard scenes in the Catholic rite. There was Paddy Sean, led sobbing away from the edge of his mother's grave. There the sober, stiffened stagger of Paddy, alone after a lifetime at his brother Mickey's side.

And it was easy enough to picture poor Bloom among the tombs as well, taking mental notes, ticking off the ways in which things resembled or differed from grand Glasnevin. 'Preoccupation with corpse' indeed, but displayed at home for days, centrepiece for their own carry-on. Monuments less fanciful. Modest send-off, no plumed horses or the modern equivalent, but with great crowd in attendance, everyone happy in his food and drink. Stories of the deceased told and retold.

Born in Ireland, only Bloom's immigrant father was one of the Tribe, and he a 'convert' to the Protestant faith, with a change of name into the bargain. Then young Bloom comes along and switches creeds again, this time to Catholicism. Yet for the others, he was still a Jew and a stranger. And to me, he seems a *landsmann*. As for names – they are, for us, always provisional. Cloaks bestowed by strangers and enemies, easily changed to suit the weather. And conversion? Well, we've a long history of that as well, another life-saving adaptation. Not that anything like 'sincere' conversion is ever possible. Too late to plant unconscious tremor and trauma, to develop inchoate childhood memories and forgettings.

So, free of the comforts and constraints, unburdened by the beliefs and habits of the faith – of any faith – Bloom was the ethnographer, watching from a place of intimate distance. Rational to the point of macabre, he saw through all the elaborate Catholic and civil ritual to the worm-bound corpse in the box, past the robes and aspergillum to the distastefully corporeal, bullying priest. Near as he was, he watched all this from afar. Perhaps from Trieste, where his author could safely release his half-Jewish avatar, now bereft of competing beliefs and delusions (save a stray wish for interment with 'a bit of soil from the Holy Land') to report on the strange customs he grew up with and which will no doubt claim him and his own in due time. The secular Jew, released by enlightenment from the confines of belief and habit, wanders into a liminal cosmopolitan space, where he meets the Gentile who, having arrived there from another direction, has acquired the stranger's alienation as well. Together, they look into, and see, other worlds. And, ultimately, their own.

But such creative alienation comes at a price. Life brings pain and confusion. And death, as Morrissey reminded me, 'comes to us all'. What do we do when consolation, the comforting form – the priest (I knew some who, whether through wisdom or innocence, were no empty 'Father Coffeys') at the deathbed and all that follows – drifts beyond reach? And no analysis can offer relief or release?

'[T]he worst of all', says Power, 'is the man who takes his own life.' 'A coward,' adds Simon D. Leaving poor Bloom alone with his secret shame and pain, always lurking just behind his *constats objectifs*. 'They have no mercy [...] drive a stake [...] through his heart' (U 120).

I felt the hand of Fabian, no allegorical Jew, on my shoulder. He seemed resigned to his fate but bemused by his lost cousin. Bringing his face close to mine, he whispered, 'Anyway, all cemeteries – even this one, I'm sure – are lies. They pretend the souls named on the stones were as neatly arranged in life as they are in death. A community. A community that has always been, and would always be, there. But the neat stones and the wall that encloses them are as ephemeral as the bones within. A few generations are not forever! And the final lie, that everyone, all the people come to this orderly, dignified end.'

I thought of the letters from the bishop to the local priest back a mere century and a half ago, urging them to ensure that their parishioners forsook the unfortunate custom of burying their dead among the ruins of the medieval church, where the Protestants had built theirs, so that the dead of both faiths lay 'promiscuously' mixed. Make sure, the prelate demanded, that they bring them instead to the newly constructed Catholic chapel, to be laid to rest within its walls and dominion. Walls meant to exclude as well as include, leaving out not only the Protestants but the unbaptized, the suicides, the unwelcomed mothers and babies and children of industrial homes whose death was as shameful as their lives, to be hidden in death as in life. Not to mention long-lost, long-forgotten (but for their use in establishing national blame and innocence) famine dead.

'Yes, of course,' Fabian remarked, having the same ability as Morrissey to pass in and out of my thoughts as easily as through any material object. 'In Poland too the snow falls on the unmarked graves of millions but to make it more personal... I will tell you a story. When I first met you, a little boy at your mother's side, I had just returned from a visit to Zgierz. 1959.'

He opened the satchel as he spoke, and pulled out a bundle of papers, holding it up as he continued. 'I wrote an account which you should read, but one small part you can hear now and remember in my voice. It follows my discovery of a document recording the 2,000 silver rubles the burial society had received from my grandfather, your great-grandfather, Benyamin Bendyt Grynberg. I was at first very proud to read that, not only for the gift from our family, but for the ways in which we looked after our own, no less the Maskils (like nearly all our family – worldly ones that spent more time with Hegel or Marx than the Talmud) than the Hasidim. But every building in which those committees, working groups, debating societies met, along with the shtiebels and the Synagogue, were gone. Burnt to the ground.'

His eyes dropped to the page, and he read.

'Thinking about the burnt holy buildings, I walked along the alley upon which my father, still a young man, was carried to his eternal rest. His son has now come from a faraway land to visit the graves of his ancestors. I found a few broken monuments in the cemetery. This ground upon which the barbarian enemies uprooted our holiness has become a wasteland – very fresh green grass for cattle grows here.'

The reading reminded him of something else. 'Here,' he said, handing me more paper pulled from that bottomless satchel. I unfolded four pieces taped together with a handwritten genealogy signed in the corner by another cousin, who had spent the war in Uzbekistan and then taken up residence in Paris. It began with my great-great-grandparents, but most space was taken up by the eleven children of that same Benjamin Bendyt Grynberg. Fabian's father, Gedalia, was one of the eldest and the youngest was Abraham, the father of my mother. Descending from the marriages of those siblings were many dozens of men and women. From those who came to America, there were children and grandchildren, great-grandchildren, and even a few beyond. But from those who remained, no issue. They were the last of the line there, every name underlined in heavy black ink, explained in a neat key at the bottom: *morts en deportation*.

Does history, even when so heavy, obliterate or mock the personal, the private, in our paltry, continuing lives? What do any of those tragic, horrific deaths have to do with my mother, whose name appeared there on the tree, under Abraham's?

'Wasn't your mother right to turn away from it? Maybe she saw beyond the pretence...'

But as he spoke, he was again rifling in the satchel and withdrawing a great ream of paper. Many hundreds of pages.

'And yet we can't stop writing. This is our Yizkor book. The memorial book of Zgierz. In place of gravestones, we wrote lists of those who perished. But were we satisfied with that? Of course not, because we needed a stone for the town itself, to remember not only the lives but the way of life. The sons and daughters of hundreds of towns, from Bialystok to Szombathely, those who escaped like I, thank G-d, and those precious few who survived, met in Tel Aviv, New York, London, Buenos Aires... talked, remembered, wrote...' He paused, holding aloft the ream of papers.

'Is paper stronger than stone? That we've always believed.'

* * *

So do they here, I thought, as we walked together out of the churchyard, remembering a day many years before when, after a job interview, I wandered the Dublin streets wondering what life might be like there and in a rare moment of practicality walked into a bank to discuss mortgages with a woman wearing a business suit and smile.

Having finished apprising me of the possibilities, the rates and so on, the banker's eyes fell upon a volume projecting from my coat pocket. 'Are you reading John McGahern?' She said, her face taking on an altogether different aspect, alight with the curiosity of a friend leaning over a table in a pub, but then changing again, darkening and darkening second by second. 'Do you know "The Country Funeral"' – indeed I had read it that very morning – her face now fully disfigured by a black twist of loss – 'I'm from a place like that myself, do you see...' and suddenly what was so Dublin, so bank and mortgage and city job, was not at all that and even the clothes she wore seemed to coarsen about her. 'My father died not long ago and I was down for the funeral. By God, it was just like that...'

Aeolus

Inside 'Aeolus' and *The Irish Times*,
Everything is Copy

LARA MARLOWE

Lara Marlowe is *The Irish Times* correspondent in Paris. She has written extensively on the Middle East and her recent book is *Love in a Time of War: My Years with Robert Fisk*.

S ome time before the Covid pandemic started, the editors of this book invited me to participate in a symposium on *Ulysses* that was to have taken place at the Irish College in Paris in June 2020. They wanted my reaction to the 'Aeolus' episode because it is set in newspaper offices in Dublin, and because I have worked for *The Irish Times* for the last quarter-century. It is always easier to say yes to such proposals when they are made far in advance. My attempts to read *Ulysses* had proved futile. I thought the project would enable me to comprehend a literary masterpiece that had hitherto eluded me.

The symposium was cancelled because of the lockdown, so its organizers asked me to contribute to this book instead. As the deadline approached, I read and reread 'Aeolus' with growing frustration bordering on despair. I cursed myself for having accepted. Then something clicked. I began to understand, even enjoy it. I opened myself to its flashes of poetry, emotion and humour. I allowed myself to be sidetracked by mental associations. Anne Kearns's use of Lourdes water for her lumbago reminded me of the Irish neighbour who dabbed Lourdes water on me to guarantee my safety in the Middle East (U 184). Kearns's Lourdes water came 'from a passionist father', so I remembered President Mary McAleese calling on passionist fathers at St Joseph's Church in the Avenue Hoche when I covered her visit to Paris. As a fan of Alexander Korda's *Lady Hamilton*, I too was tickled by Stephen Dedalus's depiction of Nelson as 'the onehandled adulterer' (U 187).

Most of all, 'Aeolus' immersed me in memories of journalism. Joyce's descriptions of printing presses made the strongest impression, and reminded me how much my profession – and

Ireland – have changed since I started working for *The Irish Times*.

Having struggled for decades to write clear, straightforward prose, I still find *Ulysses* difficult. But I was reassured by this sentence in Professor Declan Kiberd's *Ulysses and Us*: 'The need now is for readers who will challenge the bloodless, technocratic explication of texts: amateur readers who will come up with what may appear to be naive, even innocent, interpretations.'

THE MACHINES CLANKED IN THREE–FOUR TIME. THUMP, THUMP, THUMP

My first good job in journalism was in television, as an associate producer for CBS News's *60 Minutes* programme in the early 1980s. I travelled with a television crew to Nicaragua to film a documentary about the still young Sandinista revolution. The Chamorro family – whose matriarch Violeta would become president of Nicaragua from 1990 to 1996 – owned the opposition newspaper, *La Prensa*. We interviewed the paper's editor, Violeta's son Pedro Joaquin. Producer Barry Lando wanted to shoot 'wallpaper' footage of the printing presses on the ground floor of the newspaper.

Paper spooling off giant reels, twisting through the printing process, being cut into pages, assembled and sent in bundles to waiting vans. Joyce described it better than I could, with sound effects: 'Sllt. The nethermost deck of the first machine jogged forwards its flyboard with sllt the first batch of quirefolded papers. Sllt. Almost human the way it sllt to call attention. Doing its level best to speak' (U 154).

While Barry and the crew filmed, I watched from the sidelines with *60 Minutes* anchor Mike Wallace. 'You want to be a print journalist,' Mike shouted over the din. *Yes*, I thought to myself, not unlike one of Joyce's characters in silent monologue. *Yes, I would like to be a newspaper journalist.* In that instant, I found my vocation. The power and mesmerizing rhythm of the machinery. The smell of newspaper ink. The fact that tens of thousands of newspapers were about to fan out through the city.

'Machines,' Joyce wrote. 'Smash a man to atoms if they got him caught. Rule the world today' (U 150). A century later, it is not machines but digital technology that crushes us. When there's a glitch in the presses at *The Irish Times*'s state-of-the-art plant at Citywest, on the south-western periphery of Dublin, staff call an electronics technician, not a mechanic or a fitter.

'His machineries are pegging away too. [...] Working away, tearing away. And that old grey rat tearing to get in,' Joyce continued (U 150). Could 'his machineries' refer to God or some higher power? Am I right in thinking the 'old grey rat' is death? I stopped worrying about whether my interpretation was correct. Didn't Joyce say that he 'put in so many enigmas and puzzles that it will keep the professors busy for centuries arguing over what I meant'?

When I joined *The Irish Times* in 1996, the paper was known as 'The Old Lady of D'Olier Street'. She had been domiciled in a triangular block between Westmoreland Street, D'Olier Street and Fleet Street in central Dublin for more than a century. The official entrance was in D'Olier Street, but journalists and printers used the shabby back entrance in Fleet Street. Fleet Street; like newspaper offices in London.

I am an American citizen, born in California. The centrality of what Dedalus called his two masters, the imperial British state and the Roman Catholic Church, has been a constant feature of my experience at *The Irish Times*, and more generally in Ireland. One no longer sees 'vermilion mailcars, bearing on their sides the royal initials, E.R.' (U 148), but Britain is ever present in our pages, through the antics of Boris Johnson, Brexit, the Northern Ireland protocol, the legacy of the Troubles.

Joyce compares the Irish to the children of Israel, particularly in Professor MacHugh's rendition of a speech by John F. Taylor, whose plea for the revival of the Irish language culminates with his assertion that if Moses had '*bowed his will and bowed his spirit*' before the arrogance of the Egyptians, '*he would never have brought the chosen people out of their house of bondage*' (U 181). Joyce could not have known that the 1917 Balfour Declaration would lead to the creation of the State of Israel and the dispossession of the Palestinians. Were he alive today, I suspect he would have compared the Irish to the Palestinians, not Israel.

There was a little glass booth with a security guard inside the Fleet Street entrance to *The Irish Times*. Behind the guard one could hear and see the printing presses, sometimes sleeping, sometimes roaring. They had to be on the ground floor, because of their weight. The caseroom, so called because typeface was kept in large wooden cases resembling bedroom dressers, was on the first floor. In 'Aeolus', Bloom traverses the caseroom on his mission to renew an advertisement from Alexander Keyes, merchant of tea, wine and spirits.

HOW A GREAT DAILY ORGAN IS TURNED OUT

I used to laugh when a British colleague referred to his newspaper with mischievous, naughty innuendo as 'my organ'; surely a joke that Joyce would have appreciated. While working on this project, I consulted Colm FitzPatrick, who started as a messenger boy in the *Irish Times* newsroom in 1977. Colm retired in the summer of 2021 as general print manager at Citywest. The newspaper he and I joined in the 1970s and 90s, respectively, had not changed all that much since Joyce wrote *Ulysses*.

In those days, the *Irish Times* offices resembled those described by Joyce: rambling, labyrinthine, filled with nooks and crannies in which one encountered eccentric, erudite, sometimes incomprehensible characters. The newsroom, foreign desk and editorial offices were on the second floor, above the caseroom.

Journalists typed their articles in duplicate on guillotine-cut newsprint, two sheets with carbon paper between them, on heavy old manual typewriters. One copy went to the subeditor, the other to compositors in the caseroom. Subeditors used scissors and paste, like Red Murray in 'Aeolus', to make dummy copies of the paper. When the compositor finished retyping the story on the keyboard of the linotype machine, he activated a lever which sent the text into a carriage. Molten metal poured into the carriage, creating typeface.

'There were open pots of metal. There was a smell off it. A lead type of material,' Colm FitzPatrick recalls. He concurs with Joyce's description of 'a heavy, greasy smell'. Once the paper was printed, the metal was dumped down a chute to a Hades-like furnace room in the basement, where the metal was melted in a crucible over flames. It was made into bars that were sent back up to the caseroom for reuse. 'It was very visual. Absolutely fantastic to see,' says FitzPatrick.

The typeface was a mirror image of the newspaper page. 'You were reading it upside down and backwards,' FitzPatrick recalls. Bloom pauses in his walk through the caseroom to observe and describe this process: 'Reads it backwards first. Quickly he does it. Must require some practice that' (U 155). The image prompts Bloom's memory of his Jewish father reading the Passover book Haggadah. He digresses about bondage in Egypt, twelve brothers, Jacob's sons, the lamb, the cat, the dog. 'Sounds a bit silly till you come to look into it well,' he concludes. Bloom, we realize, is no more comfortable with his Jewish heritage than he is with Catholic liturgy. His mind returns abruptly to the typesetter. 'How quickly he does that job. Practice makes perfect. Seems to see with his fingers' (U 156). The best compositors at *The Irish Times* could read text upside down and backwards 'as well as you could read a normal newspaper', FitzPatrick says.

In 1981, *The Irish Times* acquired visual display units; big mainframe computers with monitors the size of television sets. This leap in technology was to newspaper production what *Ulysses* was to the nineteenth-century novel. For years, journalists nonetheless continued to type stories in duplicate. One copy still went to the compositor in the caseroom, who keyed it in. So two people were still doing the same work.

There was something sad about separating journalism and the

production of the paper when *The Irish Times* moved its printing facility to Citywest in 2002. Before the move, FitzPatrick says, 'If you were in the office late at night, you would hear a shudder all the way through the building when we started printing the paper between 11 and 11.30 p.m. There was a romance about the printing press and the size of the building and the way it was all shoehorned into the basement and ground floor. You had a room called the dispatch department where they parcelled up newspapers, wrapped them with bailing twine, stuck labels on them with wallpaper paste and threw them in a van. There was huge nostalgia for the press down in the basement. I don't think people thought about it too much because it was always there. Then it was gone, and they thought, "Where is the shudder in the building?"'

As a young journalist, I typed articles on rickety telex machines and dictated text to copytakers over scratchy phone lines. Every technological innovation – the IBM golf ball typewriter, the first word processors with floppy disks, the fax machine and ultimately the Internet – was a revolution. Technology changed everything. Today Bloom would not go to the National Library for the graphic for his House of Keyes advertisement. He would find it on the Internet. Nor would he slip into the editor's office to telephone the client. He would send a text message on his mobile phone.

I remember with nostalgia the days when *The Irish Times* was a noisy, rambunctious place, more like the building housing the *Freeman's Journal* and *Evening Telegraph* in *Ulysses*. The journalistic side of the paper moved 300 metres from Fleet Street to Tara Street in 2006. The foreign desk shrank from six editors to two. The newsroom became as quiet as a library, with every journalist focused on his or her keyboard and computer screen, sending emails to colleagues a few metres away rather than break the silence. 'Time is money', Professor MacHugh laments in 'Aeolus' (U 169).

Where have all the colourful characters gone? Today's journalists in Tara Street are talented, hard-working, good people. But I miss the jokes and banter and caustic humour. With his white hair, glasses and modest all-knowingness, Dr David Nowlan, theatre critic and medical correspond-ent, played the role of Joyce's professor MacHugh. On the newsdesk, the names of Colm Boland, Willy Clingan and Eugene McEldowney had a Joycean ring to them. These edit-ors were as witty and intimidating as Bloom's colleagues. McEldowney sang Republican ballads in the newsroom.

I never had an editor like the alcoholic Myles Crawford, with his 'scarlet beaked face, crested by a comb of feathery hair' and 'bold blue eyes', but I might have (U 160–1). When Crawford repeats reassuringly, 'That'll be all right'(U 170), I hear an echo of the foreman in 'Aeolus', saying a few pages earlier: 'We can do that' (U 153).

'I want you to write something for me. Something with a bite in it. You can do it. I see it in your face,' Crawford says to young Dedalus when he tries to recruit him 'for the pressgang' (U 171). In the late 1990s, Conor Brady, then editor of *The Irish Times*, sent me off to Afghanistan and the Gaza Strip, saying 'I want to know how it looks and smells and sounds and feels.' Myles Crawford tells Dedalus virtually the same thing: 'You can do it.'

A certain reverence surrounds every newspaper editor. Staff refer to him or her not by name but as 'The Editor' in conversation. When 'the coast is clear', Bloom slips in to use the editor's telephone (U 162). At *The Irish Times*, Cerberus-like secretaries control access to the editor's office, which Joyce calls 'the sanctum' (U 159).

A large dark oil portrait of the hulking, legendary editor Bertie Smyllie, who led *The Irish Times* from 1934 until 1954, still hangs in the editor's office. It reminds me of Ingres's portrait of the nineteenth-century French newspaper editor Louis-François Bertin, which inspired Picasso's portrait of Gertrude Stein. At the Versailles peace talks after the First World War, Smyllie bagged an exclusive interview with the British Prime Minister David Lloyd George. He obtained one of his biggest scoops – the revelation of a Fianna Fáil–Labour pact for government in 1927 – by piecing together torn paper scraps from a wastebin. Smyllie was known for singing parts of his editorials, and for holding court in the Palace Bar. He dressed in a green sombrero and cape, and strode rapidly into his office every afternoon, dodging hangers-on and supplicants who came seeking favours, like J.J. O'Molloy seeking a loan from Myles Crawford in 'Aeolus'.

Professor MacHugh refers to 'our watchful friend *The Skibbereen Eagle* (U 176)', another legend in Irish journalism. At the end of the nineteenth century, Fred Potter, editor of *The Skibbereen Eagle* began writing editorials about global affairs, in the hope of staunching the haemorrhage of readers to the rival *Southern Star*. On 5 September 1899, Potter warned the expansionist Czar Nicolas II in an editorial that

The Skibbereen Eagle was 'keeping an eye on the Emperor of Russia'. Potter and his newspaper became famous.

'But can he save the circulation?' (U 150) Bloom asks himself, referring to the Archbishop of Dublin, who has telephoned twice, presumably regarding the publication of his letter in the *Evening Telegraph*. Douglas Gageby is still revered at *The Irish Times* for having doubled our circulation in his first stint as editor, from 1963 until 1974. He was brought back to resuscitate circulation after a slump in 1977. Circulation figures remain the holy grail of every newspaper editor, especially since readers have abandoned newspapers in droves for free news on radio, television and the Internet. Today, an individual journalist's value is also gauged by the number of clicks on their articles.

Stephen Dedalus shows up at the *Evening Telegraph* with a letter from his boss, the unionist school headmaster Garrett Deasy. Again, Joyce writes about a real issue, but transposed in time, since the foot and mouth outbreak occurred in 1912, eight years after the day described in *Ulysses*. Deasy read excerpts from his letter to Dedalus in the earlier 'Nestor' episode. Cutting through Deasy's verbosity, one understands that he fears the economic threat of an embargo on Irish cattle. I covered a very similar issue in Paris at the beginning of the 2000s, when France continued its embargo on British and Irish beef out of fear of mad cow disease, after the EU lifted its ban.

Like many an old-timer, the editor, Myles Crawford thinks everything was better before. He harks back to Ignatius Gallaher – the reporter Fred Gallaher in real life. 'That was a pressman for you,' he says. 'That was a pen' (U 172). The French call a talented writing journalist *une plume*, a pen. I had never before come across it in English.

'You know how he made his mark?' Crawford continues. 'I'll tell you. That was the smartest piece of journalism ever known [...] Where do you find a pressman like that now, eh?' (U 172). Following the 1882 Phoenix Park murders, Gallaher used a code to telegraph a map of the killers' escape route to *The New York World*.

A subeditor on the *Irish Times* foreign desk used to say that if Conor O'Clery designed a rocket and wanted to make a reporting trip to Mars, the paper would finance his mission. Conor had a knack for being at the right place at the right time. When the paper sent him to Moscow, Mikhail Gorbachev invented glasnost and the Soviet Union collapsed. The paper sent him to Manhattan. Conor rented an apartment facing the World Trade Center, and delivered an eyewitness account of al-Qaeda's destruction of the Twin Towers on 11 September 2001.

Bloom watched the 'stately figure' of William Brayden, editor of *The Freeman's Journal*, pass solemnly up the staircase (U 149). I recalled glimpses of Thomas Bleakley McDowell, who was chief executive of *The Irish Times* for thirty-five years. McDowell was a Protestant born in Belfast in 1923, the year after *Ulysses* was published, and a veteran of the Royal Ulster Rifles. 'The Major', as he was known to all, was like Joyce's Brayden a silent authority whose presence was more felt than seen. His oak-panelled office overlooking D'Olier Street was known as 'the Bunker' because it was removed from the noise and bustle of the rest of the newspaper.

The real *Freeman's Journal* was published continuously in Dublin from 1763 until 1924. *The Irish Times* surpassed the *Journal*'s longevity in 2021, when we reached our 162nd year. Joyce drew his descriptions of the newspaper office from visits to *The Freeman's Journal* in 1909. His method in 'Aeolus' is almost journalistic, since he describes a real newspaper building, and real men, including the opera singer Mario and William Brayden. (How, I wonder, did anyone make sense of *Ulysses* before the Google search engine?) The Phoenix Park murders mentioned above, in which a radical group that broke away from the Irish Republican Brotherhood and called itself the Invincibles assassinated two high-ranking officials, really took place. So did John F. Taylor's speech to the Trinity College Dublin Law Students' Debating Society. Joyce strengthened his pastiche of journalism by inserting newspaper-style headlines in boldface capital letters on every page of 'Aeolus', a method he used in no other section of *Ulysses*.

When Professor MacHugh mocks Myles Crawford as 'the sham squire himself', he alludes to a much earlier real-life owner of *The Freeman's Journal*, Francis Higgins, who steered the newspaper away from nationalism and towards accommodation with Britain at the end of the eighteenth century. Higgins is believed to have spied on Irish nationalists for the British. Crawford's retort to MacHugh – 'Getououthat, you bloody old pedagogue!' – seems to be more teasing than hostile (U 161).

My initiation to Irish unionism and nationalism, Protestantism and Catholicism – so prominent in *Ulysses* – came late. Like a blundering American, I asked my colleagues at an *Irish*

Times foreign desk dinner in a Dublin restaurant in 1996 if they were Protestant or Catholic. We went round the table and all but one confessed to being Protestant. 'Didn't you know you work for a Protestant newspaper, Lara?' the sole Catholic asked me, only half-joking. When dinner was over, I shared a cab with a subeditor. 'That was the most extraordinary conversation,' he said. 'I've been decades on *The Irish Times*, and I never heard anything like it.'

I remember hearing President Mary Robinson, a Catholic who married a Protestant, telling a radio interviewer that when she was growing up, *The Irish Times* was banned from her parents' household because it was 'a Protestant newspaper'. Looking back into the archives, I read that Bertie Smyllie shifted the paper's emphasis from British interests to broader Irish questions as early as the 1930s. Though a Protestant, Douglas Gageby was a convinced Republican and was considered by some to have 'turned', a term used by Joyce. Conor Brady, the editor who hired me, became *The Irish Times*'s first Catholic editor in 1986. Yet the perception of a 'West Brit' newspaper lingered for a long time.

Bloom walks through the caseroom, past Old Monks, the dayfather or father of the chapel – the trade union representative. Monks's name alludes to the time when monks were involved in printing. 'Queer lot of stuff he must have put through his hands in his time: obituary notices, pubs' ads, speeches, divorce suits, found drowned,' Bloom thinks of Old Monks (U 155). It is a reminder of the all-encompassing nature of newspaper journalism. A newspaper is a self-contained, disposable snapshot, if not of *the* world, of *a* world, every day. 'All the talents, law, the classics…' Myles Crawford says of his entourage. 'The turf,' Lenehan adds. 'Literature, the press,' says another (U 171). Professor MacHugh mockingly adds Bloom and 'the gentle art of advertisement' to the list of the newspaper's competencies (U 171). There is even an off-colour allusion to Molly Bloom as 'Dublin's prime favourite' (U 171).

As Bloom watches the printing presses in action, he wonders, 'What becomes of it after? O, wrap up meat, parcels: various uses, thousand and one things' (U 152). A French colleague used to deflate perceived signs of pretension in me with the reminder that 'newspapers are used to wrap fish the next morning'.

To the amusement of his colleagues, Ned Lambert mocks a purple prose speech made by 'Doughy Dan' Dawson the previous evening and published in the *Evening Telegraph*. Simon Dedalus qualifies it scatalogically as 'shite and onions' (U 160). I daresay there is not a journalist alive who has not encountered the challenge of writing about empty political rhetoric. The two most severe cases I've known were the former French foreign minister Dominique de Villepin, and the former Irish Taoiseach Brian Cowen. With both men, I tape-recorded what sounded like plausible interviews, only to find that all substance or meaning evaporated between the spoken word and its transcription.

Even Bloom dismisses Dawson's speech as 'High falutin stuff. Bladderbags' (U 157). Yet he has learnt a great deal about newspapers and understands the need to publish it. 'All very fine to jeer at it now in cold print but it goes down like hot cake that stuff,' he thinks to himself (U 160). Earlier, Bloom muses that 'It's the ads and side features sell a weekly not the stale news in the official gazette' (U 150). He enumerates sections of the paper, from Nature Notes and Cartoons to Letters to the Editor. He is amused by a letter enquiring about 'a good cure for flatulence' (U 151).

Recent titles from *The Irish Times* would not be out of place in Bloom's litany: 'Do we love Ireland enough to care for it?'; 'I spend my week wondering what my therapist thinks of me'; 'I have to say, it's a boost to the old ego to see how well I look compared to some of the other yokes here'; 'Am I happy? I want more, I suppose'; 'My partner's depression is affecting our sex life' and 'The art of being tipsy all the time'.

Drink and journalism were for many years indissociable. Ned Lambert's performance of Doughy Daw's speech serves as a pretext for a trip to the pub. 'I must get a drink after that,' Simon Dedalus says, ignoring the editor's injunction not to drink before mass (U 161). Dedalus proposes rhetorically 'that the house do now adjourn' so they can all head to what Mr O'Madden Burke calls 'Ye ancient hostelry' (U 182). 'To which particular boosing shed?' Lenehan asks, casting his vote for Mooney's (U 182). 'We will sternly refuse to partake of strong waters, will we not?' He continues with an oxymoron: 'Yes, we will not. By no manner of means' (U 182). 'Aeolus' ends with the whole group heading for Mooney's (U 188).

When Crawford and Professor MacHugh set off for the pub, Crawford walks 'jerkily' and MacHugh observes that he is 'pretty well on' (U 165). One of my colleagues at *Time* magazine, where I worked from 1989 until 1996, had covered the Vietnam War. In the old days, he told me, editors kept whiskey bottles in their desk drawers in Manhattan. By 2 or 3 a.m. on the night the weekly went to bed they were all completely sloshed.

No one kept bottles in desk drawers in my time. But when *The Irish Times* moved from D'Olier Street to Tara Street in 2006, an article by Hugh Oram about the history of the paper stated that Bertie Smyllie used to whip out a brandy bottle after filing his copy, while his deputy, Alec Newman, kept a bottle of Powers. In the late 1990s, journalists and printers would still wander across the street to Bowes, Doyle's or the Fleet for a few drinks. In those years, if you could walk a six-foot straight line, you were considered safe to drive.

Drinking journalists have gone the way of the linotype machine. 'It's not acceptable now,' Colm FitzPatrick says. 'It was acceptable in journalism then. The newspaper industry tolerated a lot of people's failings, whether it was alcohol or other issues. It allowed for people to make mistakes. It carried people in a way, which was a nice thing to do. Maybe it had to do with the creative gene required in newspapers. Time has moved on. Things have become much more homogenised. We are all part of the same society obeying all the same rules.'

When the *Irish Times* printing presses moved to Citywest in 2002, the printers called the new plant 'the Betty Ford clinic'. All had to drive to and from work, and there wasn't a pub within miles. At editorial headquarters in Tara Street too, a drink after work has become a rare thing, at most 'a pint rather than a skinful'.

In the section of 'Aeolus' entitled THE CALUMET OF PEACE (U 165), J. J. O'Molloy offers cigarettes all around.

When I started in journalism, nearly everyone smoked. At *The Irish Times*, the stench of cigarette smoke wafting from under the door of the smokers' room made me glad I had quit before joining the paper. If you crossed the street to Bowes, Doyle's or the Fleet, the air in the pubs was thick with smoke. All that changed – for the better – with the smoking ban.

Joyce describes barefoot newsboys waiting in the hall of the newspaper building, squatting on the doorstep, scampering and capering in Bloom's wake when he leaves for Bachelors Walk to search for his advertising client. Crawford and MacHugh throw a newsboy out of the office. These urchins used to cry out headlines in the street to hawk papers. Though they disappeared before my time, they remained as a folk memory, shouting 'Extra, extra, read all about it' in old Hollywood movies.

The Irish Times observes what it calls 'separation of church and state', meaning that the commercial and journalistic sides of the paper are not meant to influence one another. A common gripe among journalists is that the 'commercial side' think our job is merely to fill in the blank spaces between advertisements. So I was a little surprised to find in 'Aeolus' that Myles Crawford becomes involved in negotiations about advertising. It is possible, says Colm FitzPatrick, who remembers tales from 'old codgers' who had worked at *The Irish Times* before the Emergency (the Second World War). 'Back in those days,' he said, 'they would not have had a commercial department. A newspaper would have been all in the mind of the editor. Everything went through him, and he'd be happy to raise a few bob.'

Bloom is trying to organize the renewal of an advertisement for Alexander Keyes, tea, wine and spirit merchant. He construes the graphic of two crossed keys in a circle as 'political innuendo', since the lower branch of Tynwald, the house of parliament on the Isle of Man – which unlike Ireland is already independent – is called the House of Keys. Contemporary advertisements are far more blatant in their politics. Hungary's populist nationalist Prime Minister Viktor Orbán purchased advertising space in some European newspapers in June 2021 to justify his law censoring mention of homosexuality in content destined for children. China's ambassador to Dublin took out a full-page advertisement in *The Irish Times* on 1 July 2021, to mark the hundredth anniversary of the Chinese Communist Party. The ambassador likened the Chinese event to Ireland's War of Independence.

In Homer's *Odyssey*, Ulysses is blown off course after his followers foolishly open the bag which Aeolus, the keeper of the winds, gave to him. This episode is filled with setbacks and frustrations. Bloom is told his client must renew the advertisement for three months; the client will commit to only two. Lenehan's jokes fall flat. J. J. O'Molloy does not get his loan from the editor. Myles Crawford plays the role of Aeolus, first encouraging Bloom, only to tell him later that his client 'can kiss my royal Irish arse' (U 186).

The newspapermen ignore Bloom, and do not include him in their jokes and camaraderie. Joyce successfully portrays the cruel edges of a newspaper office. But there is also the sense of a newspaper as a daily miracle of technology and teamwork. Regardless of Myles Crawford's drinking and brusqueness and politics, he is still excited about the story.

The title of a documentary about the American journalist and screenwriter Nora Ephron summed up what could be a universal motto for our profession: *Everything Is Copy*. On hearing Dedalus's tale about two old Dublin women climbing Nelson's pillar, Crawford utters the quintessential newspaperman's assessment: 'That's new. That's copy' (U 187).

Lestrygonians

MIKE FITZGERALD

Mike Fitzgerald founded and ran the Michelin-starred Commons Restaurant located in Newman House from 1991 to 2003. He established and operated The Commons Cafe in the National Concert Hall. He is a founding member of the Jack and Jill Children's Foundation and also of the Friends of Joyce Tower which was established to protect and preserve the tower and its collection.

MIKE: How'ya-head, how's it going? My name is Mike, and I'm an alcoholic. Welcome to my thoughts.

I'm also a Dub, a moniker which empowers me for this exercise.

Looking back on my life now, I feel that I was always destined to have a connection with Jimmy, better known to you as the greatest writer of the twentieth century, Mr James Joyce.

Sure, Jimmy and I even went to the same school on North Richmond Street, the O'Connell School for boys run by the Christian Brothers. Jesuits me arse!

I was born in 1952 over a now famous pub called The Temple Bar beside the River Liffey, Joyce's Anna Livia.

I experienced my formative years living over, and working in, another famous boozer, Fitzgerald's pub in Sandycove, the nearest watering hole to the James Joyce Tower and Museum.

I founded and operated The Commons Restaurant in the magnificent Newman House – the birthplace of UCD, currently home to Museum of Literature Ireland and, of course, Joyce's alma mater.

Now, I'm living in an apartment overlooking Killiney Bay on the grounds of a Victorian villa designed by the renowned architect Sir Thomas Deane, a character mentioned in this very episode of Joyce's *Ulysses*.

As a relatively uneducated Dub, I often feel that I won the Jimmy Joyce jackpot because, whether by destiny or default, I've bumped into and befriended numerous Joyce hobbyists and scholars. I've listened to and learnt from these jovial Joyceans and I like to think that I have even managed to soak up some scholarly snippets. They encourage me to experience Joyce's exceptional understanding of humanity and its behaviour. They expose and explain his extraordinary power of description and brilliant sense of humour, and his ability to constantly and continuously engage and challenge us in our own personal interpretation of his art.

In other words, I feel very privileged and to be completely honest, it's bleedin' great craic!

In this eighth episode of *Ulysses*, 'Lestrygonians', we experience the everyday atmosphere and ambience of 1904 Dublin. Put in the context of the lives of Dubliners, even tasting and digesting the food and drink of the day, we will share Bloom's gustatory experiences, which will help us gain a visceral understanding of the character and personality of our Leopold. In addition to eating and drinking with him, we share his thoughts, look through his eyes, and walk the main streets of Dublin undergoing a virtual vibrant documentary-style tour of the city and its citizens.

I'll be digesting, discussing and deliberating, so pay attention and try to keep up.

OK, let's begin with some 'talking heads and simple minds' – Leo's and mine.

MIKE: How's it going, Leo? Did you hear my introduction to our readers?

LEO: I did, and may I say it's a pleasure to meet you, Mike. What year is it with you?

MIKE: 2022.

LEO: Fascinating. Unfortunately I can't engage with you about that now. Just between us, I have a very difficult task ahead of me today and I'm feeling quite stressed.

MIKE: How's that, Leo?

LEO: Your hero and my creator, Mr Joyce, has written a very challenging role for me over the next few hours. It's now 1 p.m., and at 4 p.m. today, herself, my missus, Molly, will be entertaining Blazes Boylan, and I know that they will be – how shall I put this? 'At it', if you know what I mean. So I must, as they will no doubt say in the future, 'live in the now', and attempt to keep my anxieties suppressed and my mind in the moment.

MIKE: Well, good luck with that, Leo!

LEO: Actually I'm quite good at it, and over the years I've found a great peace of mind, and also a certain contentment in my heart. Come with me and I'll show you. You seem like a decent, thoughtful, perceptive person and I suspect you'll understand.

MIKE: I can't argue with that, Leo, and I commend your wisdom. So, where are we now and where are we going?

LEO: We're outside Graham Lemon's sweet shop on O'Connell Street, between Abbey Street and the River Liffey, and we're heading south to the National Library on Kildare Street.

MIKE: Will we be buying some sweets for our journey? I'd love a lick of that luscious-looking lemon platt... Yummy!

LEO: No. Too much sugar and very addictive, and anyway, you're supposed to be in my mind, not in my mouth.

MIKE: Gobstopper! Okey dokey. I'm in.

LEO: Like you I'm a Dub, but being of Jewish descent, and despite having been baptized in the Protestant faith and later converting to Catholicism, I have no chance of ever being accepted in my home city.

MIKE: I know how you feel, I'm a Munster rugby fan.

LEO: Well, you are about to experience a part of Dublin 1904 in its authentic state. When I enter my own private headspace, it's like entering a womb with a view. I feel protected, inaccessible, removed and indifferent to everything and everyone outside. My self-confidence emerges and feeds my imagination. More-over, my personal talent as an advertising agent enables me to see things in a more creative and visionary way.

MIKE: Now you're talking.

LEO: Look over there to your right, on Bachelors Walk. That's Simon Dedalus's daughter, Dilly, outside Dillon's auction rooms. Her mother is dead and her father isn't capable of taking on the mother's role. She has to step up. Fifteen children produced in that household. I suspect she's selling off some old furniture to get money for food.

> Good Lord, that poor child's dress is in flitters. Underfed she looks too. Potatoes and marge, marge and potatoes. It's after they feel it. Proof of the pudding. Undermines the constitution. (U 191)

MIKE: Great stuff, Leo. The genius of Joyce enables us to feel the impact of unjust societal structures on the poor and marginalized during this period.

LEO: All very true. The population of Dublin has grown to over 400,000, but the gap between the wealthy and the poor is enormous, and despite its status as the second city of the British empire, the living conditions of the poor are deplorable.

MIKE: What about the change in the custom of dividing up property within the family and giving it all to the eldest son? That must have contributed greatly to the movement of the very poor into the cities.

LEO: Yes, it did. Most of the wealthy and upper middle class have now moved out to the suburbs. But they left their city properties divided into a myriad of rooms in order to cram in as many poor souls as possible. The unsanitary conditions in these neglected properties result in the spread of contagious diseases like tuberculosis and dysentery.

MIKE: Well, it's no wonder that the average life expectancy is only forty-seven years. Ironically, after the Great Hunger, the diet in rural areas improved with more availability of potatoes, vegetables, fish, milk and 'stirabout' – the poorer version of porridge.

LEO: True, but in the cities it was more likely to be bread and dripping.

MIKE: Surely the diet improved for those who had managed to get better opportunities and stability at work?

LEO: Yes. The fruit and veg market opened in 1892, and the fish market in 1897. However, there just isn't enough work for the thousands of unskilled workers in the city. Those who are fortunate enough to get work have absolutely no security or protection from their apathetic, covetous bosses.

MIKE: Speaking of work, tell me about your job.

LEO: OK, but let's cross over O'Connell Bridge. Advertising is not always based on truth or common sense, you know. Look at the Guinness Brewery barge swaying down the Liffey carrying export stout bound for England. It's a public perception that rats get into the vats.

> Drink themselves bloated as big as a collie floating. Dead drunk on the porter. Drink till they puke again like christians. (U 191)

Now who in their right mind would want to drink that?

MIKE: And then they advertise, 'Guinness is good for you!' Well Leo, after eight centuries of oppression, the rats might do us a favour. Don't the Brits deserve it? Maybe the advert is right, Guinness is good for us.

LEO: You're beginning to think just like me Mike. Now, let's walk on towards Westmoreland Street.

I believe that advertising is fundamental in society. You can advertise for particular products or, in this case, treatments in the strangest of places. There was a certain quack doctor, Dr Hyman Franks, who crept around the city at night putting up his advertisements for treating venereal disease in all the greenhouses, or 'public urinals' as you would probably call them. Just imagine, you have a dose, you're feeling vulnerable standing there in the greenhouse with your poor patient in your hand and he's burning up. Don't tell me that advert wouldn't arouse your interest and soothe your mind!

MIKE: A clever man.

LEO: 'Fly by night' (U 193).

But wait, oh no, what if Boylan has the clap?... No, no can't go there.

MIKE: OK, let's keep moving.

LEO: Oh look, here comes a walking advertisement.

He read the scarlet letters on their five tall white hats: H.E.L.Y.S. (U 194)

Wisdom Hely's, the professional stationeries supply shop in Dame Street, and their six sandwich board walkers with their big tall white hats traipsing through the main streets of the city for a few bob a day. Not enough to live on but just enough to keep you there. I used to work for that firm. Got the job in 1888, the year Molly and I got married. My daughter Milly was born in '89. Ah, great happy memories!

Those tall white hats remind me of the night of the musical director James Goodwin's last concert in the Oakroom at the Mansion House.

Remember when we got home raking up the fire and frying up those pieces of lap of mutton for her supper with the Chutney sauce she liked. And the mulled rum. Could see her in the bedroom from the hearth unclamping the busk of her stays. White.

Swish and soft flop her stays made on the bed. Always warm from her. Always liked to let herself out. Sitting there after till nearly two, taking out her hairpins. Milly tucked up in beddyhouse. Happy. Happy. That was the night... (U 197)

My son Rudy was born in 1893 but only survived eleven days. Never the same again. Molly and I just stopped doing it. You know what I mean?

MIKE: Sadly I do. And I have to say, Leo, Joyce created, in that last quote and in a most unconventional way, an extraordinary love scene which helps us to begin to understand your complex, adoring and thoughtfully controlled love for Molly.

LEO: Well thank you, Mike.
But now, on a somewhat humorous note, another brilliant walking self-advertisement is that colourful character, the dashing, dazzling dance instructor, Professor, Denis J. Maginni.

Everyone knew his costume of tailcoat and dark grey trousers, silk hat, immaculate high collar wings, gardenia in buttonhole, spats on mincing feet, and a silver-mounted silk umbrella in hand (Ellmann)

MIKE: Now, that's a perfect description of my brother Tom, who'll gussy up for any occasion at the drop of a hat.

LEO: Speaking of which...

O, how do you do, Mrs Breen? (U 197)

I fancied this one before I met Molly. She used to be a snappy dresser. Sadly, not anymore. She married an eccentric, Mr Denis Breen, who is now off his chump she tells me. She says he saw the ace of spades climbing up the stairs last night!

MIKE: Well either he's some joker or he's not playing with the full deck.

LEO: She's upset. I'm going to comfort her. I'll look her in the eye and listen intently. Then I will change the subject by asking her about a mutual friend, Mina Purefoy, who she now tells me was admitted to the lying-in-hospital in Holles Street by the master, a Dr Horne no less. She's been in labour now for three days and a rake of chisellers at home, God love her.

'Oh careful Mrs Breen, let this man pass.' (U 201)

He always walks outside the lampposts. (U 201)

His name is Cashel Boyle O'Connor Fitzmaurice Tisdall Farrell. (U 201)

These eccentrics are generally harmless and curiously are often more content with life than we are ourselves.

MIKE: You're right there Leo. I remember in the 1950s and 60s we had our share of eccentrics – Fortycoats, Mouse the paper vendor. Oh, and the famous Bang Bang who...

LEO: Mike, this is 1904. Stay in the now. You're not supposed to be thinking. These are my thoughts.

MIKE: Sorry, Leo. You're right.

Leo: 'Mrs Breen, there's your husband. Good bye now Mrs B. I'll remember you to Molly.'

That's the offices of *The Irish Times* on your left-hand side. I placed an advertisement in there recently and I, eh, no no, I can't tell you about that now, maybe some other time.

Mike: Pity, that sounds interesting.

Leo: Recently, I bought a copy of another paper, the weekly *Irish Field*, which is devoted to the interests of country gentlemen and comfortable ladies. It's a different world altogether for the privileged classes. Some of those horsey ladies are stronger than their men, must be all the time they spend in the saddle. Want to be in the whole of your health to satisfy them. Down a glass of brandy quicker than any man.

Mike: Oh, the grandeur of the gentry and the poverty of the people.

Leo: I remember the park ranger, Mr Stubbs, got me into a party at the Viceregal Lodge up in the Phoenix Park – a high tea no less.

> Mayonnaise I poured on my plums thinking it was custard. (U 203)

I still ate them.

Mike: That's not a recipe I'll be trying. Why has that kid over there no shoes on?

Leo: Family can't afford them, fairly common sight these days. Terrible poverty in some parts of the city. They give out free breakfasts every Sunday in the Christian Union Building on Abbey Street. Penny and halfpenny dinners during the winter months. The poor divils who can't afford this pittance have to stand and eat off a plate which is literally chained to the counter to prevent them from stealing it.

MIKE: Shamefully, the meals are still needed due to the indifference of thirty-two successive Irish governments. Thank God for Brother Kevin in the Capuchin Day Centre.

LEO: Now, it's my lunchtime and for those of us who can afford to eat out we have a reasonably good choice of cafes, restaurants and bars. I could have a light snack, a saffron bun and milk in the educational dairy, or maybe a sixpenny option at Rowe's on George's Street. No, better still, something more substantial, an eight penny at the Burton on Duke Street. It's on our way to the National Library. I want to check that keys advertisement.

MIKE: Sounds like a plan.

LEO: That's Bolton's tea shop there. Fine selection of teas. I can't get Mina Purefoy off my mind. Three days! Imagine her...

groaning on a bed with a vinegared handkerchief round her forehead, her belly swollen out. Phew! Dreadful simply! Child's head too big: forceps. Doubled up inside her trying to butt its way out blindly, groping for the way out. Kill me that would. (U 204)

Life with hard labour. (U 204)

MIKE: Ha ha, very witty Leo and disturbingly descriptive. But does anyone ever take the time to remember the unborn babies that don't survive their journey?

LEO: 'Not the stillborn of course. They are not even registered. Trouble for nothing' (U 204).

MIKE: Disingenuous discussions about life beginning at conception. We think it's easier to forget and move on but the consequences stay with us.

LEO: I can relate to that. But now, speaking of moving on – over to your right is the Irish House of Parliament and on your left Trinity College. But look, up there, at that flock of pigeons – probably just finished a meal and debating about who they will drop their digested defecation on. It must be shamelessly satisfying to be able to pick out your victim from the air and then release it on the unfortunate and unprepared soul.

MIKE: I kinda like that idea.

LEO: I'm beginning to worry about you! But look, over to your left, a stream of constables coming from and going to lunch, one lot stuffed to the gills and the other lot sharpening their teeth. No scarcity of food there. You wouldn't want to get on the wrong side of them. End up in the Bridewell.

MIKE: The purporters of justice, law and order while their allegiance is to the corrupt system of a domineering perpetrator. Hypocritical hardshaws.

LEO: Too true! There's Tommy Moore wagging his roguish

anatomy over the College Green greenhouse. There are no facilities for ladies.

MIKE: There's been some progress in the move towards equality but it's shamefully slow. We're all prejudiced in some way and we tolerate inequality and racism as a part of life that we're unable to challenge or change. This perilous paralysis of thinking is morally unacceptable.

LEO: I must say that I'm not surprised.

MIKE: A sad reflection on society! But tell me, what are your thoughts on education?

LEO: They say education is crucial and can be the answer to all our problems. But take a look over there at those naive, so-called highly educated Trinity students passionately protesting. There is nothing surer than they too will soon be part of the very same privileged and unjust system that they're objecting to now.

> Few years' time half of them magistrates and civil servants.' (U 206)

MIKE: What changes in their minds and attitudes so quickly? Is it just human weakness?

LEO: No. Human weakness will always prevail if the system is wrong.

The so-called upper class have more than they could ever need, the middle class have just enough to survive and the unfortunate lower class have less than enough to live on. It's all just luck. Wherever you're born determines your destination.

MIKE: Accident of birth.

LEO: The British government, who allowed millions to die during the Great Hunger, have established their unequal, unjust policies and structures in our society. This has created the environment to force people against each other. Just look at the G-men, for example.

MIKE: Who?

LEO: The G-men, the intelligence division of the Dublin Metropolitan Police. They are a bunch of dangerous deviants whose primary purpose is to infiltrate and destroy the self-worth and feelings of any individuals that they prey on by bribing, beating and bullying. Ultimately they divide vulnerable families and destroy friendships.

MIKE: It's a shocking reflection on humanity when the so-called authorities put pressure on individuals to rat on their friends by threatening their families.

LEO: Yes it is. The working-class struggle day to day with minimum pay and no security, and yet they are the very ones to stand up to the authorities while the middle class and the aristocrats turn a blind eye.

MIKE: Nothing changes.

LEO: Then we have the passionate rebels on the other side. They are the Irish Republican Brotherhood, who have a fair and arguably just cause. They are also driven to evil when they have to deal with the sad result of the G-men's unrelenting pressure on some poor unfortunate 'rat'. Their response is swift, usually with a sharp silencing knife. Imagine having to kill our own people. What sort of species are we?

> James Stephens' idea was the best. He knew them. Circles of ten so that a fellow couldn't round on more than his own ring. Sinn Féin. Back out you get the knife. Hidden hand. Stay in. The firing squad. Turnkey's daughter got him out of Richmond. (U 207)

James Stephens was ratted on by a Republican rat and then escaped with the aid of an Imperialist rat!

MIKE: Rat-a-tat-tat.

LEO: We also have the pacifist patriots who go to Phoenix Park for the annual patriot's banquet. These are Irish nationalists who gather to eat oranges symbolizing Orangemen being swallowed up in a United Independent Ireland.

MIKE: Vegetarian vigilantes swallowing bitter, sectarian mandarins.

LEO: You're learning fast.

MIKE: It's never too late. But tell me this Leo, did you know that Joyce himself grew up in a very complex and challenging household? He experienced and understood what it was like to go without money or food. Despite having a university education, he, and even more so his family, lived from day to day because of their father's alcoholism.

LEO: But how did he manage to succeed?

MIKE: He knew he had a gift. However, he could not fulfil his mission in life in this sad, stifling environment. He needed to break away from the superficial Catholic tribalism that permeated and controlled Irish society. He made a selfish, but in reality brave and correct, decision to leave Ireland.

LEO: I can understand that.

Coming events cast their shadows before. (U 210)

MIKE: He feeds us his words, encouraging us to digest and process his thoughts, until, with a peristaltic movement, we release ourselves from the shackles of a paralysed and demoralized society in order to heal the sickness of our country's soul. He is a prophet in many ways, highlighting inequality and injustice in society and the shameful neglect by church and state of those most in need. His message is challenging but honest. His knowledge and comprehension of the consciousness of humankind is truly extraordinary. He is the consummate analyst of human nature. Through his characters, and most notably through you, Leo, he encourages us to question our own objectivity and our real purpose in life.

LEO: I might end up liking him yet, despite my current predicament.

She was humming. The young May moon she's beaming, love. He other side of her. Elbow, arm. He. Glowworm's la-amp is gleaming love. Touch. fingers. Asking. Answer. Yes.

Stop. Stop. If it was it was. Must. (U 212)

But look, over there, passing Walter Sexton's silverware shop. That's the chief's brother, John Howard Parnell. Two brothers, the image of each other. One brilliant and one dull. Our City Marshal and registrar of pawnbrokers, no less. Chief used men as pawns. The brother plays chess in a teashop. He's a real introvert. Looks like he's sleepwalking.

Poached eyes on ghost. (U 209)

MIKE: You are getting peckish.

LEO: Did you see who just passed us? That's the eminent poet, A.E., George Russell.

Beard and bicycle. (U 210)

MIKE: My sister, Anne, is a powerful and profound poet.

LEO: Your brother is a dazzling entertainer and your sister an eminent poet... what happened to you?

MIKE: Me? I'm only beginning to bloom!

LEO: Ha, can't wait for that. Now, did you know that A.E. is a vegetarian?

Don't eat a beefsteak. If you do the eyes of that cow will pursue you through all eternity. (U 210)

Maybe vegetables are good for the creative side of the brain. I mean, look at that hefty policeman over there, after his feed of Irish stew.

You couldn't squeeze a line of poetry out of him. (U 210)

MIKE: Interesting visual. But tell me this, do the religious institutions do much to alleviate the suffering of the poor?

LEO: No, and it's hard to accept or understand the blatant hypocrisy of all the religious institutions. They've consistently bribed, brainwashed and bargained with food to maintain control over extremely vulnerable people. Imagine, during the Great Hunger the Protestant clergy gave soup to anyone who converted from Catholicism and was willing to change their name. For example, from O'Connor to Connor. Even now the Salvation Army continue this shameful conditional feeding practice.

Halffed enthusiasts. Penny roll and a walk with the band. (U 207–8)

MIKE: What about the Catholic Church?

LEO: They are even worse, with their pious cycloptic outlook. They tell their flock, who haven't enough to feed the children they already have, that they should increase and multiply. This is unacceptable ignorance and indifference to their responsibilities, while they themselves are living off the fat of the land with their housekeepers and three meals a day.

MIKE: Amen. Get off the fence, Leo! I believe that Joyce was a man of deep faith who analysed all religions meticulously and objectively. He concluded that they had all lost their way and he chose to maintain his own personal relationship with God. I have to admit that I too often wonder what interpretation of the truly great news of the Gospel these so-called educated but morally corrupted people have swallowed.

LEO: Amen to you too, Mike.

But now we are on the smartest and most fashionable street, Grafton Street. Number 4 here is La Maison Claire, the court dressmaker, no less!

There's Bob Doran and he's swaying like he's on his annual bender. I'd say he's heading for the Empire Bar in Adam Court on our left-hand side.

MIKE: That's where there was an entrance to the famous French restaurant Jammet's and also, in my day, the legendary Lillie's Bordello.

LEO: Men seem to need alcohol to confide in each other. Bloody hypocrites! They accuse women of idle gossip but after a few jars they rend and destroy the character and reputation of their fellow citizens.

MIKE: I agree. It may seem naive to continue swallowing lies and liquor to fool ourselves into repeating the same old mistakes but, unless you have personal experience of the complexity and dire consequences of alcoholism, it's practically impossible to understand its perilous attraction. No turning back once you start. Abstention or addiction, not a great choice.

LEO: Very true. But now an alluring distraction – we are passing the rather attractive windows of Brown Thomas, who are famous for the best quality of Irish laces and linens. You would probably feel at home here Mike.

Cascades of ribbons. Flimsy China silks. (U 213)

Gleaming silks, petticoats on slim brass rails, rays of flat silk stockings. (U 214)

MIKE: Now you're getting to know me.

LEO: That brings my Molly to mind. Memories of sexual, sensual intimacy are taunting my brain. Her perfume, her flesh I crave to adore. Can't think like this, must eat now, feel better then.

MIKE: I think you need a cold shower. But just listen to these wonderful words:

A warm human plumpness settled down on his brain. His brain yielded. Perfume of embraces all him assailed. With hungered flesh obscurely, he mutely craved to adore. (U 214)

That is just superb. If I could write like that, I wouldn't talk to anyone but myself.

LEO: Now that might be a very good idea.
We're going left into Duke Street and the Burton is a bit further up on our right.
In we go… Whoa!… Oh dear God… The smelly, stifling stink of overcooked food. Yuck! It's nauseating and repulsive. Men, men and even more men. They're like animals feeding!

MIKE: I didn't realize you were bringing me to the Zoo!

Perched on high stools by the bar, hats shoved back, at the tables calling for more bread no charge, swilling, wolfing gobfuls of sloppy food, their eyes bulging, wiping wetted moustaches. (U 215)

LEO: I need to get out of here.

— Roast beef and cabbage.
— One stew.
Smells of men. His gorge rose. Spaton sawdust, sweetish warmish cigarette smoke, reek of plug, spilt beer, men's beery piss, the stale of ferment.

Couldn't eat a morsel here. (U 215)

MIKE: Are we leaving or what?

LEO: OK, I'll pretend to be looking for someone. 'No he's not here, I'll be back some other time. Thank you.'

Out. I hate dirty eaters. (U 216)

MIKE: Men should not be left alone.

LEO: I couldn't agree more. A.E.'s vegetarian choice seems more appropriate now!

After all there's a lot in that vegetarian fine flavour of things from the earth garlic, of course, it stinks after Italian organgrinders crisp of onions, mushrooms truffles. (U 217)

Pain to the animal too. Pluck and draw fowl. Wretched brutes there at the cattlemarket waiting for the poleaxe to split their skulls open. Moo. (U 217)

Hot fresh blood they prescribe for decline. Blood always needed. Insidious. Lick it up smoking hot, thick sugary. Famished ghosts. (U 217)

Ah, I'm hungry. (U 217)

MIKE: You're making me sick!

LEO: Shall we adjourn to see Davy Byrne?

MIKE: What's keeping you?

LEO: The fellow who owns this pub is a decent enough chap. The type that stands you a drink every year. No sorry, I mean every leap year.

MIKE: I have a friend like that!

LEO: Now, I could do with a drink, what will I have? I know, I'll have a glass of Burgundy.

MIKE: Bonne santé.

LEO: Don't look now but there's a gossipy old codger called Nosey Flynn at the bar trying to get my attention.

'Oh, hello Flynn. All tip top, thank you.'

MIKE: Our Mr Joyce describes perfectly the atmosphere and ambience of a Dublin middle-class pub and captures precisely the nature of this proud publican, Mr Davy Byrne. There's a Nosey Flynn-type character in every bar but, unlike the cycloptic Citizen in Barney Kiernan's boozer, his opinion is more likely to switch sides to whoever is forking out for the next round.

LEO: You can bet your bacon on that. Now, what will I eat?

Those customers in the Burton reminded me of cannibals. Can you imagine cannibals eating their captives?

Expect the chief consumes the parts of honour. Ought to be tough from exercise. His wives in a row to watch the effect. (U 218)

MIKE: Vegetarianism is becoming more appealing by the minute. Now, have you decided on what you are going to eat?

LEO: I'll have a Gorgonzola cheese sandwich with some olives, please.

Oh, here come some more personal questions now from Nosey about my Molly. 'Yes, she's engaged in a big tour at the end of the month, and yes, Blazes Boylan is organizing it.'

MIKE: Nosey by name. Nosey by nature.

LEO: 'Ah, my sandwich, how much? Seven d, thank you.'

MIKE: Nosey is sniffling and snuffling his nose while scratching his groin.

Flea having a good square meal. (U 220)

LEO: Here comes the owner, Davy Byrne. Nosey is straight in to engage him, asking him if he has a tip for the Ascot Gold Cup. The righteous Mr Byrne says he doesn't approve of gambling – that it has ruined many a man. This is true but hypocritical. Take the plank out of your own eye, Mr Byrne. What about the drink and all the lives that it ruins?

The Vintner's Sweepstake [...] Heads I win, tails you lose.
(U 221)

Flynn is not capable of taking that in, he's still nattering on
about tips and people in the know.

Nosey numskull. (U 221)

Fool and his money. (U 221)

MIKE: I remember when I was working in The Commons I used
to visit each table to ensure that their gastronomic experience
had lived up to expectation. Happy then. Happy now.
How's your lunch?

LEO: Tasty sandwich. I needed that glass of wine to ease my
anxiety. He should be gone by six o'clock. I can go home then.
Champagne and oysters supposed to stimulate the sensual.
I wonder, was Boylan swallowing oysters this morning? Ohh,
can't go there.

Oysters? Unsightly like a clot of phlegm. Filthy shells.
Devil to open them too. Who found them out? Garbage,
sewage they feed on. (U 222)

MIKE: But tell me, do you think it's right to force-feed geese
to enlarge their livers, or for lobsters to be boiled alive, and all
this for the delicate palates of the privileged elite in our society?

LEO: No, but...

Wouldn't mind being a waiter in a swell hotel. Tips,
evening dress, halfnaked ladies. May I tempt you to a

little more filleted sole, Ms Dubedat? Yes, do bedad. And she did bedad. (U 223)

Still it's the same fish, perhaps old Micky Hanlon of Moore street ripped the guts out of. (U 223)

That wine is definitely helping me to relax. Look at the two flies on the window stuck to each other. Reminds me of the day Molly and I were lying down in the wild ferns on Howth Head.

Stuck on the pane two flies buzzed, stuck. (U 223)

MIKE: I'm absolutely dumbfounded by the diverse nature of your imagination.

LEO: There was nothing, only the sweet sound of nature around us. Both of us enjoying each other. Our private sensual soundings in tune. I was getting ready to make my move. She was finishing off a piece of seed-cake when she kissed me and passed it into my mouth.

Warm and chewed. (U 224)

Joy: I ate it: joy. Young life, her lips that gave me pouting. Soft, warm, sticky gumjelly lips. (U 224)

Flowers her eyes were, take me, willing eyes. (U 224)

There was no going back. When suddenly our passionate performance was interrupted by a wandering nosey nannygoat. Well, we leapt and laughed and loved and left, if you know what I mean? Oh, such exotic and exciting memories.

Me. And me now. (U 224)

What would life be like if we could predict our future?

MIKE: Pointless. Everyone, whatever their circumstances may be, has the ability to cope with and find peace in life. You are living proof.

Now tell me, did the goat stay?

LEO: No. But now it's time to go. 'Good day and thank you Mr Byrne.'

Mike, look over there. Are you hungry?

At Duke Lane a ravenous terrier choked up a sick knuckley cud on the cobble stones and lapped it up with new zest. Surfeit. (U 238)

MIKE: Thanks for that. I'm glad I haven't eaten.

LEO: And look again, another opportunity for a job advertisement.

Against John Long's a drowsing loafer lounged in heavy thought, gnawing a crusted knuckle. Handy man wants job. Small wages. Will eat anything. (U 230)

MIKE: That glass of burgundy has contaminated your creativity.

LEO: We are now passing Katherine Grey's confectionery shop, and we'll turn right onto Dawson Street. Then we pass the Reverend Thomas Connellan's bookstore where they specialize in Protestant propaganda. Across the road on the corner of Molesworth Street we have the Church of Ireland Auxiliary to the London Society for Promoting Christianity Among the Jews which, incidentally, my dear departed father attended.

MIKE: Rest in peace, Rudolph.

LEO: Thank you, Mike.

I wonder should I offer to help this poor blind young man to cross the street? It's hard to imagine what life is like for him. We feel awkward in their company. Imagine walking around the city in complete darkness. Other senses possibly stronger. Probably make a great lover or a piano tuner.

Bloodless pious face like a fellow going in to be a priest. (U 231)

MIKE: The perfect pilgrim for the priesthood, the blind leading the blind.

LEO: There goes Sir Frederick Faulkner entering the Freemasons' Hall after his fine lunch. He'd turn up his nose to the glass of Burgundy that I had to accompany my sandwich.

Crusty old topers in wigs. (U 233)

MIKE: It would have to be a full-bodied red wine for him in order to lubricate the lordly larynx of himself and his legal cronies.

LEO: Yes, those legal eagles like to keep their wine like their defendants – locked up!

MIKE: Very good, Leo!

LEO: Now let's cross over Kildare Street and into the National Library. But wait. Oh no. It is. Well I think it is. Is it? Yes it is. It's that bloody Boylan.

MIKE: Don't panic, get your head down, and veer right into the National Museum.

Handsome building. Sir Thomas Deane designed. (U 234)

LEO: OK. I'll keep walking. Pretend to be looking for something. Hand in jacket. Now trousers. Heart pumping. Pounding. Through gate. Oh God. Yes. Phew!

MIKE: Now Leo, cool your heels, and take a deep breath!

I must insist on having the last word because I know it's SAFE.

Scylla & Charybdis

Homer... Shakespeare... Joyce... Borges[*]

CARLOS GAMERRO

Carlos Gamerro is a leading Argentinian novelist and critic. His books include *The Islands* (which he has reconstituted for theatre) and *An Open Secret*. He has translated Shakespeare and W. H. Auden into Spanish.*

*   Many thanks to Ian Barnett for revising this text into its present, much-improved version!

'Ah, there's only one man he's got to get the better of now, and that's that Shakespeare!' Nora Joyce once declared, according to Richard Ellmann's *Ulysses on the Liffey*. Had Harold Bloom's *The Anxiety of Influence* been published at the time, you might almost believe she'd been reading him on the sly – unlikely as that may be – so neatly does her remark tally with the late American scholar's critical fable about the new poet or ephebe inevitably engaged in a life-or-death struggle to overcome a great father poet or precursor in his writing.

It was more likely to have been Harold Bloom who read Nora, expanding her remark into the twenty-odd pages of his 'Joyce's Agon with Shakespeare', which features in *The Western Canon*. Bloom understood literary agon solely in individual terms, as a one-to-one duel, but in the 'Scylla and Charybdis' episode of *Ulysses*, Joyce stages a more populous engagement. The scene is the librarian's office at the National Library of Ireland; the characters, in order of appearance, chief librarian Mr Lyster, Stephen Dedalus, assistant librarian John Eglinton, the poet A.E. (George W. Russell), assistant director Richard Best and Buck Mulligan, who joins them later; the topic under discussion, whether it's acceptable to identify Prince Hamlet with Shakespeare; the form, a Platonic dialogue in which Stephen plays the part of Socrates and Eglinton that of the main antagonist. Haines, already reluctant to commit himself when invited by Mulligan in Episode 1, is conspicuously absent: 'I couldn't bring him in to hear the discussion,' remarks a crestfallen Mr Best (U 238).

The conversation opens, for us, with Mr Lyster, author – in his life beyond *Ulysses* – of a *Life of Goethe*, quoting this 'great poet on a great brother poet' who sees in Hamlet 'a hesitating soul taking arms against a sea of troubles', 'the beautiful ineffectual dreamer who comes to grief against hard facts' (U 235). This is promptly sneered away by Stephen, as the standard Romantic Hamlet was, by 1904, a spent force and need not engage his dialectic verve. But no words are ever wasted in a Platonic dialogue: in the course of this chapter, other non-British authors, such as Stéphane Mallarmé, George Brandes, Edward Dowden, Ernest Renan, George Bernard Shaw, Frank Harris and Oscar Wilde, are quoted on Shakespeare, whereas of the standard English commentators only Coleridge is mentioned, as if to remind the English that the Bard is not their exclusive property. This would also account for Haines's absence. We can almost hear his thoughts – which Joyce mercifully keeps from us: never in *Ulysses* do we access his interior monologue – when invited by Mulligan to listen in: 'What can these paddies tell *me*, an Englishman and Oxonian, about *Shakespeare*, for Christ's sake? I'm here to study *them*, imagine the presumption of their trying to study *us*.' Haines is so sure of owning Shakespeare that he can speak of *Hamlet* with studied nonchalance ('a wonderful tale', U 21); rather than listen to Stephen, he has gone to buy Hyde's *Love Songs of Connacht*: he will only put up with an Ireland that behaves itself in a properly Celtic manner. One of the distinguishing features of the colonizer's mind is that it considers it not only a right but a duty to define the colonized culture, to articulate some or many kinds of discourse about it. Put in simpler terms, when the English talk about the Irish, the Irish must listen; the English in turn might lend an ear to what the Irish have to say about the Irish, but never on any account will they allow the Irish the right to utter words of knowledge about the English. (During my own stay at Cambridge as a visiting fellow, I would find the lecturers and dons surrounding me when I held forth on Borges, for example, or Peronism, but if I dared to move on to Shakespeare, or Joyce for that matter – writers I humbly specialize in in my home culture – they would suddenly vanish in a swirl of black gowns, and I'd find myself talking to the air.)

Eglinton, speaking 'with elder's gall' (U 235) – the dividing line, at this early stage, appears to be age – attempts to put the young Stephen in his place by reminding him of his project of enlisting six medical students to write *Paradise Lost*, taking it for granted that Stephen will have a go at *Hamlet* as well: 'I feel you would need one more for *Hamlet*. [...] The shining seven W.B. calls them' (U 235–6). This reference to Yeats isn't expanded explicitly, but the poet's views, set out in his essay 'At Stratford-on-Avon', in which he expresses a 'Celtic' preference for the beautiful ineffectual dreamers Hamlet and Richard II over the power-driven 'Saxon' Fortinbras and Bolingbroke, are strewn across the chapter. Like Professor Dowden, John Eglinton is a 'West Briton', one who hides his ostensibly Irish name, William Kirkpatrick Magee, under this ultra-English pseudonym and whom, later in the chapter, Stephen envisions as shielding behind 'his Wordsworth' (like a vampire-slayer behind their crucifix) when being visited by his father, a 'rugged rough rugheaded kern' (U 265). As if to confirm Joyce's diagnosis, he would resign his position in 1922 in protest at the founding of the Irish Free State and settle in England. It is not without significance that he, rather than, say, a prominent figure in the Irish literary renaissance such as A.E., should be Stephen's main antagonist.

Stephen's 'answer', given, as so often in *Ulysses*, in interior monologue, recalls his former friend Cranly's plan to recruit 'eleven true Wicklowmen to free their sireland' (U 236) and includes proverbial images of subjected Ireland culled from nationalist lore and Yeats's plays: 'Gaptoothed Kathleen, her four beautiful green fields, the stranger in her house' (U 236). Writing *Paradise Lost*, writing *Hamlet*, seems in some way to be related to the struggle to liberate Ireland, although in this, as in all things, we should make allowance for the Joycean singularity: *Ulysses* is not Joyce's contribution to the liberation of Ireland; rather, the centuries-old struggle for freedom is Ireland's contribution to his *Ulysses*. As a straight-faced Stephen will explain to an uncomprehending Bloom in Episode 16: 'You suspect [...] that I may be important because I belong to the *faubourg Saint Patrice* called Ireland for short. [...] But I suspect [...] that Ireland is important because it belongs to me' (U 748).

As if he'd been overhearing Stephen's thoughts, Eglinton 'censures' what he sees as the presumption of the new generation: 'Our young Irish bards, [...] have yet to create a figure which the world will set beside Saxon Shakespeare's Hamlet' (U 236). He thinks he's delivering a verdict but is, unwittingly, uttering a challenge: Stephen will take him at his word and deliver – in ten years' time – Leopold Bloom. Later on, in a paragraph that jumbles together in Stephen's mind the echoes of a many-sided conversation, one of the participants – in all probability Eglinton, as these thoughts appear in his essay 'Irish Books' – states: 'Our national epic has yet to be written […] Moore is the man for it. A knight of the rueful countenance here in Dublin' (U 246). This 'national epic' will, of course, be *Ulysses*, for which Stephen is already making mental notes: 'See this. Remember. […] Listen' (U 246). Might Stephen and Bloom, the acerbic intellectual and well-rounded *homme moyen sensuel*, be equated with Don Quixote and Sancho Panza, with protagonism ultimately being awarded to the squire, which, in Part II of *Don Quixote*, he is always on the verge of attaining and which Kafka grants him retrospectively in 'The Truth About Sancho Panza'? Given that Joyce practised multiple systems of reference, that Stephen may at times be Telemachus, Icarus and Hamlet, or Molly Bloom, Calypso and Penelope, it isn't altogether unthinkable. But, if we can list this as a 'correspondence', it's only fleeting: Joyce didn't set out to write *Paradise Lost*, or *Hamlet*, or *Don Quixote* for that matter (that task would be left to his contemporary Pierre Menard, who began work on his literal version of *Don Quixote* in 1918, the same year Joyce wrote the chapter we're discussing): he set out to write the *Odyssey*. If there is a ghostly father in this novel, it isn't Shakespeare but Homer; Homer, who's mentioned twice in this chapter and never again in all of *Ulysses*; Homer, whose traces, such as the chapter titles included in the *Little Review* instalments, would be erased from the published book and who is therefore 'a ghost through absence', for the ideal precursor should, like the ideal author – as Stephen, and Flaubert before him, envision them in *A Portrait of the Artist* – be everywhere and nowhere. But if Homer is the ghostly father, who is Shakespeare? 'A great brother poet?' (U 235). Hardly likely: master–servant relationships don't encourage fraternity. And if Stephen is neither son nor brother, then what is he? Nephew? Is Shakespeare being cast in the role of Uncle Claudius, the usurper? And if so, what has been usurped exactly?

When Eglinton brings Milton into the fray, Stephen, in his mind, counters the great Protestant poet's sublimity with Dante's eloquence at its most vulgar:

> Orchestral Satan, weeping many a rood.
> Tears such as angels weep.
> Ed egli avea del cul fatto trombetta. (U 236)

Nor is it only Dante's earthiness that comes to Stephen's aid, but his Italian. In literary agon, the closer the language, the shakier the alliance. As Stephen says of Shakespeare, 'A man's worst enemies shall be those of his own house and family' (U 265): rivals, in literature, are those who speak the same language. But Shakespeare and Milton are antagonists not only because their mastery of the English language challenges Joyce's, but because theirs is a preordained mastery: in the archetypical colonial double bind, the colonized are deprived of their language and forced into another which, they are warned, will never be entirely theirs. In a colonial setting, it isn't even necessary for the precursor to arrive earlier. They can come later, at their entire ease, and *usurp* the role of precursor.

Homer, in this sense, is not an enemy or rival, because Joyce's relationship with him, or *Ulysses*'s relationship with the *Odyssey*, is not verbal. According to Ellmann's biography, the young Joyce once remarked to Padraic Colum that the Greek epics lay outside the tradition of European culture: Europe's epic was the *Divine Comedy*. Joyce, we know, and Stephen Dedalus after him, had no Greek. Of course, this can be seen as another mark of cultural dispossession: as Brian Friel reminds us in his *Translations*, the Irish hedge schools, where education was imparted in Gaelic, were strong in the classical languages; but, after their eradication, direct translation between Greek and Gaelic was lost, and Greek became the privilege of the Trinity- or Oxford-educated Irish – usually the Anglo-Irish, like Wilde. The equally Oxford-educated Buck Mulligan rubs this in in Episode 1: 'Ah, Dedalus, the Greeks. I must teach you. You must read them in the original' (U 3). Homer, therefore, is hardly ever quoted in *Ulysses* (he is in that chapter – by Mulligan): the relationship between *Ulysses* and the *Odyssey* is not, strictly speaking, intertextual.

Across the channel, Virginia Woolf suffered the same dispossession, not for being Irish, but for being a woman, and she, and her character Septimus Warren Smith, in their bouts of madness, were both taunted by the sparrows – in Greek. Like Joyce, like Woolf, Borges had no Greek; like them, he sought to overcome this inferiority by turning it into a strength: 'My opportune ignorance of Greek', he argues in 'The Homeric Versions', 'has turned the *Odyssey* into an international library of works in prose and verse.' Borges didn't think much of *Ulysses*'s Homeric correspondences: the narrator of his 'The Approach to Al-Mu'tasim' deplores the fact that 'The repeated but irrelevant points of congruence between Joyce's *Ulysses* and Homer's *Odyssey* continue to attract (though I shall never understand why) the dazzled admiration of critics,'* while Borges's character, Pierre Menard, 'author of the *Quixote*', distinguishes his own project of rewriting a great classic from that of *Ulysses*, alluded to and dismissed as one of those 'parasitic books that place Christ on a boulevard, Hamlet on La Cannabière or Don Quixote on Wall Street'. Yet what he questioned was Joyce's method, not his aim: Borges also realized that his writing – and all of Argentinian literature with it – had to go back to Homer to invent a tradition of its own and wrote, in 'The Maker', an imaginary biography in which Homer himself becomes a forerunner of Borges's knife-wielding *orilleros*, and in the process fused the bard's blindness with his own. And in his story 'The Immortal' he imagines Homer living on into the early twentieth century, forgetting his Greek, forgetting he ever wrote the *Iliad*, forgetting he once was Homer, to take on the name of Joseph Cartaphilus and become by then an avatar of the wandering Jew – somewhat in the manner of Leopold Bloom. Taking over Homer, translating him into one's own culture and language without the benefit of Greek, was an endeavour both Joyce and Borges felt they *had* to make.

Italian, on the other hand, was fully mastered by Stephen and Joyce – or would be by the time they were ready to write *Ulysses* – and verbal echoes of Dante's poem are scattered throughout their novel: Dante is enlisted into the battle on a verbal level. But if Milton's Protestant severity can be countered with Dante's Catholic profanity (in his University

* All translations of Borges by Andrew Hurley.

College days 'Joyce exalted Dante at the expense of Milton, whom he fiercely rejected', we read in Ellmann's *James Joyce*), Shakespeare embraces all styles and is perfectly capable of playing Dante to his Milton. When asked by Frank Budgen which book he would take to a desert island if he could take only one, Joyce answered: 'I should hesitate between Dante and Shakespeare, but not for long. The Englishman is richer and would get my vote.' This answer puts Joyce's own dilemma in a nutshell: Shakespeare would be the author of his choice, but he is still 'the Englishman' – 'so familiar and so foreign', as Stephen says of their language in Chapter 5 of *A Portrait*. So the question abides: what is to be done about Shakespeare?

I choose to look for an answer in Borges's 'Theme of the Traitor and the Hero'. The story is set in 1824: a group of Irish patriots is about to stage an uprising against British rule when one of them, James Alexander Nolan, discovers that the traitor who had marred all previous attempts was none other than their leader and hero, Fergus Kilpatrick. Realizing the revelation might cripple their cause, they decide to stage a public assassination and lay the blame on the colonial rulers; Kilpatrick eagerly concurs. Urged on by time, Nolan is forced to plagiarize the works of 'the English enemy William Shakespeare', inserting scenes from *Macbeth* and *Julius Caesar* into the script for Kilpatrick's staged execution. When the bullet enters his heart, he is 'able to articulate, between two sudden effusions of blood, a few foreseen words'. We are not told if these words are Shakespeare's, but it's beautiful to think they were. This story may or may not have been prompted by Borges's reading of Joyce (we have no evidence either way), but the ideas it embodies – those of 'life imitating art' and 'fiction becoming history' – were undoubtedly inspired by Oscar Wilde, whose *The Decay of Lying* is alluded to in the story: 'The idea that history might have copied history is mind-boggling enough; that history should copy literature is inconceivable.' Perhaps it's no coincidence that two of the greatest champions of what has come to be known as 'anti-mimesis' – Wilde, an Irishman who dared hold the mirror up to the English, a 'jester at the court of his master', who eventually got the whip, and Borges – wrote from subjected or peripheral cultures: it's Caliban, after all, who sees – or doesn't see – his face in the mirror, as Wilde wrote in the preface to *The Picture of Dorian Gray* and Mulligan echoes in Episode 1 of *Ulysses*, prompting Stephen's definition of Irish art as 'the cracked looking-glass of a servant'; Caliban who, like Swift's Yahoos, is thought to have been partly based on images of the 'wild Irish' in English culture; Caliban who was chosen by Latin American writers, such as Aimé Césaire in *Une Tempête*, and Roberto Fernández Retamar in his *Calibán*, as a symbol of the archetypical colonial subject, whether Indian, negro or *criollo*, and who managed to condense the formula of linguistic dispossession and repossession into fourteen words: 'You taught me language, and my profit on't / Is, I know how to curse.'

The mirror reappears in Episode 15, when Stephen and Bloom gaze together into it after Lynch has quoted Hamlet's 'the mirror up to nature':

(*The face of William Shakespeare, beardless, appears there, rigid in facial paralysis, crowned by the reflection of the reindeer antlered hatrack in the hall.*)

SHAKESPEARE (*In dignified ventriloquy.*) 'Tis the loud laugh bespeaks the vacant mind. (*To Bloom.*) Thou thoughtest as how thou wastest invisible. Gaze. (*He crows with a black capon's laugh.*) Iagogo! How my Oldfellow chokit his Thursdaymomun. Iagogogo! (U 671)

Harold Bloom's interpretation of this puzzling moment, and language, reads thus:

Shakespeare the precursor mocks his follower, Stephen-Bloom-Joyce, in effect saying: 'You stare in the mirror, trying to see yourself as me, but you behold what you are: only a beardless version, lacking my onetime potency, and rigid in facial paralysis, devoid of my ease of countenance.'

This seems to put the blame on Stephen and Bloom, and ultimately on Joyce himself, their impotent creator, but it's also possible to find fault in the mirror itself: it is cracked, deformed, creative, as colonial or neocolonial mimesis – or anti-mimesis – must perforce be, and perhaps this loss is its gain; the language Shakespeare speaks in these last two sentences is already the language of *Finnegans Wake*.

But if Shakespeare's poetry cannot be engulfed, Shakespeare the man is up for grabs: if not a parody of the works, Stephen offers a travesty of the life, a fictional biography surrounded by a constellation of biographical near misses: the *reductio ad absurdum* of the 'authorship question' into a single word that anticipates the rumblings of *Finnegans Wake*, 'rutlandbaconsouthamptonshakespeare' (U 267), an Irish Shakespeare, a Jewish Shakespeare. Shakespeare has always been the ideal subject of such biographical ventures; as Eglinton says: 'of all great men he is the most enigmatic. We know nothing but that he lived and suffered. Not even so much. [...] A shadow hangs over all the rest' (U 248). Inevitably, what all Shakespeare biographers end up doing is patching up a 'character' with bits and pieces from the works: instead of attempting to interpret the works in terms of the life – the standard procedure of biographical criticism – they fashion a life to fit the works. Both Wilde and Joyce began their own enterprises with pet theories which they believed were grounded in the world of facts: for Wilde, the sonnets were written for a boy actor who changed Shakespeare's dramatic art; for Joyce, Shakespeare's cuckolding by two of his brothers plunged him into 'the hell of time of *King Lear*, *Othello*, *Hamlet*, *Troilus and Cressida*' (U 250), from which he emerged when a granddaughter was placed in his arms. But eventually both of them had to abandon all hope of serving them as straight biography, and wrote their musings down as fictions instead (Freud, on the other hand, enmeshed in mimetic superstitions by the demands of his method, would eventually despair of the task and embrace the Looney hypothesis).

Placing betrayal at the core of Shakespeare's fictional biography serves many ends: it connects with Helen's betrayal of Menelaus, which brought the Greeks to Troy, with Dervorgilla's betrayal of O'Rourke, Prince of Breffni, which brought the English to Ireland, with Bloom's cuckolding by

Molly, King and Prince Hamlet's by Gertrude, and Stephen's by mother Ireland, as we read in the 'Oxen of the Sun' chapter: 'Bring a stranger within thy tower it will go hard but thou wilt have the secondbest bed. [...] Remember, Erin, thy generations and thy days of old, how thou settedst little by me and by my word and broughtest in a stranger to my gates to commit fornication in my sight...' (513–14).

Father and son strive to cuckold one another: the father has already prevailed (otherwise the son would not be in a position to dream of it); the son's gambit is to symbolically erase this evil necessity and become a father to himself. By freeing fatherhood from biology, Stephen also frees it from history and geography: an Irish writer can father Shakespeare. This notion would be echoed by two writers from the New World: 'Whoever has approved this idea of order, of the form of European, of English literature, will not find it preposterous that the past should be altered by the present as much as the present is directed by the past,' writes T. S. Eliot in 'Tradition and the Individual Talent'; 'Every writer *creates* his precursors', suggests Borges in 'Kafka and His Precursors'.

Borges's 'Pierre Menard' deals with his chosen precursor in a most peculiar way. As said before, Menard's plans to rewrite *Don Quixote* were partly inspired by his discomfort with Joyce's endeavour: he didn't want to write another 'parasitic' book like *Ulysses*; 'his admirable ambition was to produce a number of pages which coincided – word for word and line for line – with those of Miguel de Cervantes'. This aspiration establishes him as the martyr and the hero of all Bloom's ephebes, for he is in effect saying 'I don't give a damn if my precursor wrote the book I meant to write before me, I'm going to write it anyway.' Menard at first considers the possibility of becoming Cervantes: 'Initially, Menard's method was to be relatively simple: Learn Spanish, return to Catholicism, fight against the Moor or Turk, [...] *be* Miguel de Cervantes.' But he eventually discards it as an easy way out: 'Being, somehow, Cervantes and arriving thereby at the Quixote – that looked to Menard less challenging (and therefore less interesting) than continuing to be Pierre Menard and coming to the Quixote *through the experiences of Pierre Menard*.' His dilemma is echoed in Professor Hermann Soergel's, the protagonist and narrator of 'Shakespeare's Memory', who has inherited the magical entity of that name and at first daydreams thus: 'I would possess Shakespeare, and possess him as no one had ever possessed anyone before – not in love, or friendship, or even hatred.' But eventually he must acknowledge that 'Shakespeare's memory was able to reveal to me only the circumstances of *the man* Shakespeare. [...] what matters is the literature the poet produced with that frail material.' The gift, as so often happens in Borges's stories such as 'Funes, His Memory' and 'The Immortal', eventually becomes a curse: 'in time, the great torrent of Shakespeare threatened to flood my own modest stream'. In remembering Shakespeare, Professor Soergel forgets himself.

'Poldy can challenge Shakespeare, or attempt to, the act being impossible to perform because the larger entity, in all literary agons, swallows up the smaller,' asserts Harold Bloom in *The Western Canon*. Yet Joyce does not, Charybdis-like, attempt to swallow Shakespeare whole, but takes quite a few Scylla-like nips (avoid the whirlpool of Charybdis, Circe had counselled Odysseus, and hug the cliff of Scylla, but do not attempt to fight her, for she is – like Shakespeare and the British empire, we might add – a nightmare that cannot die). '*Ulysses* tries to absorb Shakespeare on his own ground: *Hamlet*. Dublin is a large context but not large enough to swallow up Shakespeare,' Professor Bloom adds later on. I find it interesting that he should write 'Dublin' instead of 'Joyce'. Was he on the verge of admitting that, in the literary agon, the writer is not only fighting for himself but for his culture as well? Yet if *Ulysses* cannot 'swallow' the Shakespeare canon, maybe Irish literature can swallow English literature, which is what Joyce attempts in the 'Oxen of the Sun' chapter, where great precursors or literary fathers become an unnecessary evil, the paternity metaphor giving way to the maternity metaphor, agon being replaced by a slow gestation in the course of which the language of the enemy can become the mother tongue. Episode 14 offers a pastiche of English prose from early Anglo-Saxon literature to Dickens and Carlyle, and, eventually, the new language of the twentieth century, which anticipates that of *Finnegans Wake*. From the point of view of the individual writer, the chapter is a demonstration of James Joyce's virtuosity: *I* can write like any writer in the language. From the point of view of the cultural struggle, it presents English literature as a long march that culminates in Irish literature, inverting material domination on the symbolic level: the smaller entity swallows the larger. It's true that, in the 'Eumaeus' chapter, Bloom tells Stephen, 'It's all very fine to boast of mutual superiority but what about mutual equality?' (U 745). But it's also true that a subjected culture can only achieve equality by practising – not merely proclaiming – superiority.

It's always puzzled me that Shakespeare wasn't included in this list. The obvious answer might be that it's a list of prose writers, not of poets or dramatists. But I have often wondered, what if Joyce chose to limit himself to writers of prose in order to have a 'technical' reason – or excuse – for excluding Shakespeare, to shirk the task of imitating or parodying Shakespeare? Of course, Shakespeare's plots and situations can be parodied, and have been (how many parodies of *Romeo and Juliet* to date?), but not his style. Whoever attempts to parody Shakespeare's language or style will sooner or later discover it's Shakespeare who's parodying them. If anybody could have, it would have been Joyce: the fact that he chose not to should give us pause. In 'Scylla and Charybdis', Shakespeare is not imitated but intermittently quoted in italics or incorporated in the text in a technique we might term literary grafting: Joyce will take a snippet or scion of Shakespeare, graft it into his text and wait to see if it grows: Hamlet's words to the boy player, 'By'r lady, your ladyship is nearer to heaven than when I saw you last, by the altitude of a chopine' flower in *Ulysses* into 'He creaked to and fro, tiptoing up nearer heaven by the altitude of a chopine' (U 247); Richard II's words 'We must supplant those rough rugheaded kerns' and the dauphin's in *Henry V*, 'you rode, like a kern of Ireland, [...] in your straight strossers' clothe, with enriched alliteration, Eglinton's father 'a rugged rough rugheaded kern, in strossers with a buttoned codpiece' (U 265). I don't see these as allusions; allusions are meant to be identified, so that the identification will affect the way we read the text; rather, what these provide is a Shakespearean challenge for Joyce's text to rise to, and what we obtain when it does is Joyce's text Shakespearianized, empowered by the Englishman's words. To accommodate them, the narrator had to change: in Episodes 1 to 8, it was merely a camera eye and recording device: allusions, quotations and puns were confined to dialogue and interior monologue, the narrator not having mind enough for them. In Episode 9, it achieves a personality so that it may indulge in wordplay and become allusive, and ironical about its own allusiveness: 'He came a step a sinkapace forward on neatsleather creaking and a step backward a sinkapace on the solemn floor. [...] Twicreakingly analysis he corantoed off' (U 235); 'It is clear that there were two beds, a best and a secondbest, Mr Secondbest Best said finely.' [...] 'Antiquity mentions famous beds, Second Eglinton puckered, bedsmiling'(U 261).

Having had his say, Stephen steps out into the street, remembering how once, upon the very same spot, he 'watched the birds for augury' (U 279). The birds are absent, but an alternative vision is offered him:

> No birds. Frail from the housetops two plumes of smoke
>   ascended, pluming, and in a flaw of softness softly were
>   blown. Cease to strive. Peace of the druid priests of
>   *Cymbeline*, hierophantic: from wide earth an altar.
> Laud we the gods
> And let our crooked smokes climb to their nostrils
> From our bless'd altars. (U 280)

The image of the two plumes of smoke becoming one is usually understood as an anticipation of Stephen's 'fusion' with

Bloom; in Shakespeare's play it's preceded by a prophecy King Cymbeline finds on his bosom after waking from a dream:

> When from a stately cedar shall be lopped branches, which, being dead many years, shall after revive, be jointed to the old stock, and freshly grow, then shall Posthumus end his miseries, Britain be fortunate and flourish in peace and plenty.

The 'stately cedar', as interpreted by the Roman soothsayer Philarmonus, is King Cymbeline himself; the two 'lopped branches' are his two recovered sons, whom he thought dead. The grafting metaphor offers another image of reconciliation and growth that might, if applied to *Ulysses*, involve Stephen and Bloom, and perhaps, if my reading of the textual device is correct, English Shakespeare and Irish Joyce, inverting once again, in truly Joycean fashion, domination and precedence, the father being grafted onto the son. The prophecy also involves the appeasement of an imaginary cuckold, Posthumus (all of Shakespeare's great cuckolds – Claudio, Ford, Othello, Leontes – turn out to have been mistaken in the end). Celtic Britain invaded by the Romans figures Celtic Ireland invaded by the English, the parallels between the Roman and British empires having previously been elaborated in the 'Aeolus' chapter. The 'peace of the druid priests' (U 280), when applied to Ireland, is a dream of wish-fulfilment: Cymbeline freely decides to make peace with the Romans after defeating them in battle; it is peace on his own terms. The whole scene breathes 'the spirit of reconciliation' (U 249): Britons and Romans offer sacrifices on both their altars, to the gods of each, and the two ascending smokes merge and climb to the nostrils of their separate gods as one, just as, in Joyce's text, the combined words of the Englishman and the Irishman jointly climb to our ears and eyes.

Joyce's manuscript for 'Scylla and Charybdis' reads 'End of first part of *Ulysses*, New Year's Eve, 1918.' The armistice had been signed on 11 November. In Ireland, peace was still a few years away: it would come in 1923, roughly a year after *Ulysses* was published and independence achieved.

Wandering Rocks

The 'Retrospective Arrangement' of
Dublin in 'Wandering Rocks'

SHINJINI CHATTOPADHYAY

Shinjini Chattopadhyay holds an MA and an MPhil from Jadavpur University and a doctorate from Notre Dame. Her articles on Joyce have appeared or are forthcoming in *European Joyce Studies*, *Joyce Studies in Italy* and *James Joyce Quarterly*.

For a good part of the last two decades I had to commute daily from the northern part of Kolkata, India, to the city's southern edge. I traversed the same route every day – College Street Market, Sealdah Station, CIT Road, Park Circus, Ballygunge, Gariahat, Golpark, Jodhpur Park, and finally Jadavpur. Someone familiar with the city will know that each of these locations represent unique neighbourhoods of Kolkata. Whereas College Street and Sealdah Station constitute an old part of the city, often associated with congestion and overcrowding, Ballygunge and Jodhpur Park represent gentrified areas where upscale shopping enclaves are located. Each stop on my trajectory had its own unique history which inspired me to exaggerate it, rather naively, as an Odyssean itinerary. My itinerary from College Street to Jadavpur represents a snapshot of the transhistoricism and cosmopolitanism of Kolkata. Kolkata, as a post-colonial city, bears visible traces of British colonialism in its architecture and urban planning. The Victoria Memorial Hall, Howrah Bridge and the Monument act as explicit reminders of the city's colonial past. The city is also a confluence of Indians hailing from diverse cultural backgrounds. People from almost all states of India and a few neighbouring countries find their homes in Kolkata. For instance, whereas the Bara Bazar neighbourhood is the hub of the Marwari community, Chinatown is famous for its Chinese cuisine prepared with care by long-term Chinese settlers in the city. The diverse religious affiliations of the citizens are also evident in the urban fabric of Kolkata as Hindu temples, churches, mosques and synagogues peacefully coexist in the city. Growing up in such a multicultural and transhistorical city, I immediately found a parallel of post-colonial Kolkata in Joyce's colonial Dublin in *Ulysses*. Joyce's depiction of several layers of culture and history of Dublin illuminated for me the sedimentation of Kolkata.

Joyce's Dublin and the Kolkata I grew up in have various dissimilarities. They are set apart by a century. One is a city of the Global North and the other is located in the Global South. Yet I find irrefutable parallels between the two. Joyce's Dublin is constantly struggling to subvert the colonial domination of England and at the same time it is trying not to succumb to parochial nationalism. It is constantly trying to find a balance between coloniality and modernity. In post-colonial Kolkata, although British rule has ended, the city still regards its colonial history (or at least parts of it) as a nightmare from which it is trying to awake. But at the same time, the city also wishes to embrace the legacies of modernity and thereby continue certain colonial traditions as it tries to become a global location for modern living. It also attempts to preserve its unique regional identity, celebrate the diversity of the rest of the nation, and not submit to majoritarian nationalist impulses. The anti-colonialism, anti-nationalism and cosmopolitanism of Joyce's Dublin and my Kolkata make the two cities potential doubles of one another. Reading *Ulysses* helps me rediscover the transnationalism and transhistoricism of Kolkata. Although *Ulysses* is set in 1904 Dublin, the coloniality/modernity compound of Joyce's city echoes the post-colonial modernity of Kolkata. As I recollect my trajectory from College Street to Jadavpur, I think of the various streets and alleyways I could see from my bus, but never ventured into. Each corner of Kolkata, like Joyce's Dublin, is replete with numerous stories. In this regard, I believe, Kolkata resembles the 'Wandering Rocks' episode of *Ulysses* which provides glimpses of untold stories in Joyce's novel and is also one of my favourite episodes.

'Wandering Rocks' is one of the only two episodes in *Ulysses* which does not focus on either protagonist, Leopold Bloom or Stephen Dedalus. According to the Homeric parallel, 'Wandering Rocks' is the road not taken. In *The Odyssey*, Circe suggests to Odysseus two possible routes back to Ithaca – one is through Scylla and Charybdis, and the other is through the wandering rocks. Rocks are adrift in the ocean making it impossible for ships to navigate without risking a capsize. In *The Odyssey*, Odysseus chooses Scylla and Charybdis and the wandering rocks do not feature in his itinerary. But James Joyce inserts an episode on the wandering rocks in the Homeric trajectory of *Ulysses*. Since the wandering rocks present an alternative route never chosen by Odysseus in the Homeric text, 'Wandering Rocks' performs a similar function in the narrative of Joyce's novel. The episode creates a compilation of most of the characters that populate the universe of *Ulysses* and indicates all the alternative narrative strands that the novel could have pursued but does not in order to sustain its focus on Bloom and Stephen – just like Odysseus chooses not to go through the wandering rocks. The episode offers fragmented glimpses of the movements of individual characters across Dublin as they conduct their everyday activities. The nineteen subsections of the episode present interconnected itineraries of characters which draw attention to local details of Dublin and portray the city not just as the setting but as the main character of the episode.

'Wandering Rocks' carefully depicts the metropolitan laby-
rinths of 1904 Dublin and offers a vast repository of local
details. The plethora of street names, landmarks and monuments emphasize the mimetic specificity of the episode. Joyce's
intellectual compadre, artist Frank Budgen, has famously noted
that Joyce composed the episode 'with a map of Dublin before
him' and 'calculated to a minute the time necessary for his
characters to cover a given distance of the city'. While Budgen's
observation emphasizes Joyce's careful efforts to maintain
vraisemblance in depicting Dublin, it must also be noted that
Joyce constructed the 1904 Dublin in this episode, as in the
rest of *Ulysses*, with a temporal distance of at least a decade,
which the time-stamp, 1914–1921, in the epigraph of the novel
makes evident. The retrospective glance in the episode infuses
the mimetic specificity of Dublin with transhistoricism and
transnationalism. 'Wandering Rocks' situates the granular details
of 1904 Dublin within a network of transnational exchanges. The
episode depicts Dublin as a centre of metropolitan modernity and
at the same time acknowledges it as a colonial outpost which is
occasionally considered to be on the margins of modernity. It
depicts Dublin as a historical palimpsest that is in the process
of transcending its feudal past and transitioning to a future of
industrial modernity. In the episode, Dublin emerges as a location
that hosts the multifariousness of Irish identities that are being
shaped by the sometimes-contradictory forces of anti-colonial
resistance, nostalgia for a bygone past and commitment to a
cosmopolitan modernity.

The multi-layered past of Dublin becomes evident when
Ned Lambert, a seed merchant, presents a glimpse of the

complicated history of the city to Revd Hugh C. Love, a
clergyman who is recording the history of the Fitzgeralds, an
Anglo-Irish family with longstanding heritage going all the
way back to the twelfth century. Lambert stands in St Mary's
Abbey and announces that, '[t]his is the most historic spot
in all Dublin [...] The old bank of Ireland was over the way
till the time of the union and the original jews' temple was
here too before they built their synagogue over in Adelaide
road' (U 295). In a few sentences Lambert shows how a single
Dublin landmark can contain transhistorical traces from the
city's medieval past to its colonial present. He is correct in
pointing out that St Mary's Abbey is one of the most historic
landmarks of the city. The tenth-century abbey was the
oldest religious establishment in Dublin. Similar to the city,
the abbey also underwent several stages of transformation.
In the twelfth century it became a Cistercian abbey and in
1537 it was dissolved. It was later damaged by fire and the
surviving parts of the abbey were incorporated in the premises
of Messrs. Alexander & Co., seed merchants, as Gifford and
Seidman argue. Thus, the abbey began as a medieval religious
institution and ultimately became part of a modern commercial
establishment. Lambert also points out the abbey's connection
with the 'original jews' temple'. In 1835 a synagogue was built
in the chapter house of the abbey which in 1892 moved, as
Lambert rightly notes, to Adelaide Road in south-eastern
Dublin. The overlapping of the abbey and the synagogue
suggests that the history of Catholicism and Judaism in Dublin
is more intertwined than Mr Deasy would have it in 'Nestor'
(he claims to Stephen that Ireland is the only country that

has never persecuted the Jews because she has never let them in) (U 44–5). The abbey, with its palimpsestic past, indicates how a medieval religious institution can be absorbed within a modern commercial establishment and also signifies the multiplicity inherent within the religious heritage of Ireland by accommodating both Catholic and Jewish congregations.

St Mary's Abbey, in addition to signifying the heterogeneous religious heritage of Ireland, also stands witness to the historically tumultuous relations between Ireland and England. Lambert refers to the 1534–5 Kildare rebellion and accurately states that the council chamber of St Mary's Abbey was where Thomas FitzGerald, the tenth Earl of Kildare (otherwise known as Silken Thomas), had 'proclaimed himself a rebel' and renounced his allegiance to Henry VIII, King of England (U 295). He affirms that Ireland's relation with England continues to remain tempestuous when he draws attention next to the Bank of Ireland. He notes that the Bank of Ireland used to be located near St Mary's Abbey until the Acts of Union 1800. When he mentions a connection between the Bank of Ireland and the Acts of Union 1800, he again reminds the reader of the turbulent colonial relations between Ireland and England. The Acts of Union 1800 united the Kingdom of Great Britain and the Kingdom of Ireland to create the United Kingdom of Great Britain and Ireland (which was, of course, later repealed when the Republic of Ireland was formed). When the Irish parliament was dissolved by the Acts of Union, the House of Parliament was sold to the Bank of Ireland (1802) and it moved to a new location. The Bank of Ireland thus embodies the history of the dissolution of the Irish parliament.

When Lambert draws attention to the former location of the Bank of Ireland, he indicates an absent landmark. The landmark, by virtue of its absence, becomes emblematic of Ireland's subjugated sovereignty to England.

Ned Lambert's deep sense of history is, however, not shared by every other individual going about Dublin. It is especially contrasted by a group of British tourists and Haines, the British student. British tourists touring Dublin in cars look from 'Trinity to the blind columned porch of the bank of Ireland' (U 292). Their decision to tour Dublin in cars instead of walking around the city suggests that they are engaging with the city only superficially. They are merely sightseeing from a speeding car and not devoting the time to look closely at the monuments and landmarks that walking would have allowed them to do. They perceive Dublin as an exotic colonial other that they can only appreciate from a distance. Haines is similar to the tourists because he also has surface-level knowledge about Irish culture (in 'Telemachus' he assumes people in Dublin speak Irish and tries to speak Irish to the milkwoman) (U 16). In 'Wandering Rocks' he demands 'real' Irish cream (U 321). The emphasis on 'real' signifies that he has idealized concepts about the supposed authenticity of Irish culture and this notion of authenticity is founded upon a contrast with British culture that he implicitly regards as superior to the colonial Irish culture.

It is, of course, the viceregal cavalcade that makes most explicit the colonizer/colonized hierarchy. William Humble Ward, 2nd Earl of Dudley, accompanied by his entourage, goes to inaugurate the Mirus Bazaar in Pembroke township in his capacity as the Lord Lieutenant of Ireland. His cavalcade begins at the viceregal lodge in Phoenix Park and creates a grand spectacle when it traverses various streets of Dublin. The trajectories of most characters who appear in 'Wandering Rocks' intersect with the itinerary of the cavalcade and the characters generate varied responses to it. Miss Kennedy and Miss Douce of the Ormond Hotel (whom the readers will meet more extensively in 'Sirens') admire the cavalcade and Revd. Hugh C. Love makes 'obeisance unperceived' (U 325). However, their admiration is not replicated by every onlooker. For instance, Tom Rochford raises his cap to Lady Dudley only after he notices her eyes 'on him' (U 326). His display of respect does not come out of spontaneous admiration; instead, it is influenced by the fear of facing repercussions for accidentally appearing subversive and not acting as a submissive colonial subject. In contrast, Gerty MacDowell is less interested in the colonial power play and more invested in what Lady Dudley is wearing, at which she fails to get a good look because her view is obstructed by a tram and a furniture van (U 326). Unlike Gerty, Dilly Dedalus is not interested in Lady Dudley's couture or even the cavalcade and she is engaged in the French primer which she has recently purchased. But she also fails to get a clear view of the cavalcade because her sight is strained from reading the primer and she only manages to see 'wheelspokes spinning in the glare' (U 326). The most irreverent reaction is perhaps produced by the River Poddle which 'hung out in fealty a tongue of liquid sewage' (U 325).

The section describes at length how various onlookers view the cavalcade, but it does not reveal how the Lord Lieutenant views the crowd and the streets of Dublin until the very end of the episode. The omission of the Lord Lieutenant's point of view reminds the reader of the silencing of Haines's Irish in 'Telemachus'. The British aristocrat, similar to Haines, whose knowledge about Irish culture is superficial, is also detached from Irish traditions. His carriage traverses the historic streets of Dublin, but he pays little attention to the local details of the city or its people. The Lord Lieutenant, in contrast to Ned Lambert, who shows deep knowledge about the longstanding history of Ireland, is only interested in particular vignettes of Irish history which celebrate England's colonial domination. He overlooks most Dublin landmarks, and happens to acknowledge only a particular house that Queen Victoria is arguably said to have admired on her visit to Dublin in 1849 (U 328). His version of Dublin's history thus dismisses iconic landmarks and monuments in Ireland's past because it is generated from the position of the colonizer. The viceregal cavalcade across the city thus shows the disconnect between the imperial centre and the colonial outpost. It reveals the disempowerment and dispossession of the colonized and how they are marginalized by imperial hegemony.

'Wandering Rocks' does not represent colonial control over Ireland in isolation; it encloses it within the dichotomy of church and state. Joyce scholars have pointed out that whereas the viceregal cavalcade represents the aegis of imperialism, Father Conmee, at the beginning of the episode, represents the church. The character of Father Conmee is modelled after the real-life rector of Clongowes Wood College when Joyce was a pupil at the institution. In 'Wandering Rocks'

Father Conmee is seen travelling from Gardiner Street to the O'Brien Institute for Destitute Children, Artane, to make arrangements to place in the institute Patrick Dignam, the son of the deceased Paddy Dignam, whose funeral is portrayed in 'Hades'. Although Father Conmee is seen here serving the community by trying to do a good turn to the Dignam family, he represents a counterpart to the Lord Lieutenant to some extent. Whereas the Lord Lieutenant follows a selective history of Ireland, Father Conmee commemorates an idyllic history – both modes of history result in a partial detachment from reality. When Father Conmee walks on Malahide Road, instead of thinking about the Dignam family, he lets his mind wander off to the medieval sagas about the family of the Lords Talbot of Malahide. He thinks particularly about the betrothal of the son of Lord Galtrim and the daughter of Lord Plunkett, where the groom was called to war from the altar and was killed and thus the bride became 'maid, wife and widow in one day' (U 286). He nostalgically reminisces that '[t]hose were old worldish days, loyal times in joyous townlands' (U 286). He imagines a bygone idyllic past where everything was happy and peaceful. He conveniently disremembers moments of conflict, such as the chaotic periods of the Famine and the land disputes, and even dismisses the contemporary situation of brewing tension between England and Ireland feared to give way to an armed rebellion. This helps him to artificially construct an image of uninterrupted prosperity in Ireland. His use of 'townlands' confirms his hankering for the past because the word is emblematic of ancient land-holdings in Ireland. Urban modernity interrupts his chain of thoughts only fleetingly. When he walks along North Circular Road, he momentarily wonders why there is no tramline in such an important thoroughfare (U 283). But he does not ponder upon how trams represent technological modernity. Instead, while travelling on the tram he expects his fellow passengers to replicate his blissful reminiscences of the idyllic past. He disapproves of the 'solemnity of the occupants of the car', expressing a preference for 'cheerful decorum' (U 284). His inability to empathize with the 'solemnity' of his fellow passengers at a time when a large part of Dublin's population is ravaged by poverty shows his disconnection from the community. It suggests his disregard for the colonial condition of Ireland and his ignorance about the impoverishment of his fellow Dubliners which renders them unable to sustain a 'cheerful decorum'. Father Conmee's detachment from reality is made the most obvious when he boards a tram at Newcomen Bridge because he 'dislikes to traverse on foot the dingy way past Mud Island' (U 284). Father Conmee, by taking the tram, actively escapes from the squalor of Dublin. His engagement with Dublin suggests that although he traverses the streets of the colonial city, he often escapes to an imaginative and idyllic past and removes himself from the realities of imperialism and destitution.

The manner in which the church and the state often dismiss reality is made conspicuous especially in the figure of the one-legged sailor. The one-legged sailor fails to receive the benefaction of both the church and the state. Father Conmee notices that the sailor 'swinging himself onward by *lazy* jerks of his crutches, growled *some notes*' (U 280, italics mine).

It is interesting to note that instead of sympathizing with the condition of the sailor, Father Conmee notices a hint of indolence in his movement. He also refuses to hear the exact words the sailor utters and reduces them to indistinct noise. The readers find out in a later section that the sailor is saying 'For England [...] home and beauty' (U 289). He offers the sailor only blessings and does not give him any actual alms, citing the excuse that he has just the right amount of money to pay for his impending tram journey (U 280). He thinks, but 'not for long', of soldiers and sailors brought to such states of privation by war and ultimately manages to blame the sailor for bringing this misfortune upon himself by neglecting his duties to God (U 280). Father Conmee thus hypocritically disengages from the sailor just as he detaches himself from the realities of Dublin. However, he is not alone in his rejection of the sailor. The sailor is largely dismissed by his community and he is bitterly aware of the neglect dealt to him by society. He glances 'sourly' at the windows which remain unresponsive to his pleas (U 289). Even when he receives alms from people, he 'grumbles thanks' instead of showing enthusiastic gratitude (U 289). His lack of enthusiasm is caused by the fact that such acts of benevolence are infrequent, most people remain unmoved by his requests. When he comes to Eccles Street he receives a coin from Molly Bloom. Molly tosses the coin from her window and only her arm is visible while the rest of her body remains out of sight (U 289). The fragmentation of Molly's body suggests that she performs this act of charity only to allay her sense of guilt for her upcoming assignation with Blazes Boylan. She does not donate the coin out of sincere concern for the sailor, which is made conspicuous by the fact that she does not even take a proper look at whom she is donating to. The coin symbolically misses the mark and falls on the path (U 289). Molly missing the target underlines her lack of empathy with the predicament of the sailor and reveals the selfish intent behind her act of charity. The church and the community are joined by the state in their collective disregard for the sailor. The sailor growls a refrain from the song 'The Death of Nelson' which implores citizens to perform their duty for England. The sailor's physical disfiguration is proof that he has served England, but the state does not take responsibility for its subject in return. Moreover, the colonial status of Ireland signifies that the imperial state is especially negligent of its colonial subjects. The sailor, rejected by the church, the community, and the state, roams the neighbourhoods of Dublin and finds his ultimate refuge in the city streets.

The sailor is joined by other Dubliners who seek refuge in the city streets to varying extents. For instance, Simon Dedalus ignores his responsibilities towards his children and embraces the security of the streets. He gets an unpleasant surprise when he runs into his daughter, Dilly, in front of Dillon's auction rooms (U 304). Dilly demands money from Mr Dedalus to pay for domestic necessities. He vainly tries to deflect her request by commanding her to '[s]tand up straight' (U 304). Dilly eventually manages to get a shilling and two more pennies from Mr Dedalus in instalments which he begrudgingly parts with. When Dilly asks Mr Dedalus to seek money, he cites the excuses that 'no-one in Dublin would lend me fourpence' (U 305) and that he has 'looked all along the gutter in O'Connell street' and will try a different one next (U 306). He blames the city for not generating wealth and causing the penury of his family. He does not acknowledge his own inaction in redressing the destitution of his household. He avoids heeding Dilly's persistent plea for money and makes an opportune escape 'amid the din' of the viceregal cavalcade (U 306). He evades his domestic duties and seeks security in the streets of the very city which he blames for his impoverishment.

Mr Dedalus's accusations of paralysis against Dublin is partially disproved by another walker, Tom Kernan. Mr Kernan successfully books an order of tea for his company, Pulbrook Robertson, and he walks 'boldly' along James's Street, satisfied with his triumph (U 307). As he takes a walk, he replays in his memory his interaction with Mr Crimmins and recollects how he smoothly finalized the transaction (U 307). But he is not entirely immersed in his recapitulations and does manage to notice the history-laden streets of Dublin. Various Dublin streets remind him of different Irish patriots. When he approaches Thomas Street, he is reminded that '[d] own there Emmet was hanged' (U 308). He thinks of Irish nationalist patriot Robert Emmet, who was tried and executed for high treason for leading a rebellion against the British rule in 1803. When he turns into Island Street he thinks of two other Irish patriots related to the location, Jonah Barrington and Edward FitzGerald (U 309). Barrington had opposed the Acts of Union 1800 and FitzGerald was a key figure in the Rebellion of 1798. When Mr Kernan thinks of these Irish patriots, it shows that he is well acquainted with the history of Irish nationalist struggle. But he thinks of these times in a 'retrospective arrangement' (U 309) and contemplates what a chaotic time the past was. However, he considers the present insulated from the turbulence of the Irish nationalist struggle. The Easter Rising a little more than a decade later will, of course, prove him wrong. But for the time being, Mr Kernan, instead of admiring the feats of the Irish patriots, turns his attention to the viceregal cavalcade. He regrets not getting a glimpse of the Lord Lieutenant (U 310). His esteem for the cavalcade indicates that despite being well aware of the history of Irish nationalism, Mr Kernan does not oppose British rule in Ireland. He supports the colonial governance because it suppresses nationalist rebellions and brings some amount of stability which helps with his commercial endeavours. Since the colonial rule helps his capitalist ventures to flourish, Mr Kernan forsakes nationalist allegiances and supports the colonial rule.

Whereas Mr Kernan is satisfied to remain within the bounds of colonial Ireland, some of the young Dubliners aspire to transcend the national boundary. Stephen, in particular, looks towards continental modernity and embodies the quintessential modernist flâneur. Charles Baudelaire theorizes the flâneur as an urban figure who walks among the crowd and observes the city. The flâneur does not have a destination; their only purpose is to spectate various city scenes. Baudelaire writes that, '[f]or the perfect flâneur, for the passionate spectator, it is an immense joy to set up house in the heart of the multitude, amid the ebb and flow of movement, in the midst of the fugitive and the infinite'. Stephen is an ideal flâneur because he also finds his home in the streets of Dublin. He cannot return to his father's house and he has been usurped from Martello Tower by Buck Mulligan in 'Telemachus'. He therefore seeks refuge in the city streets and observes scenes of metropolitan modernity. Baudelaire explains that the flâneur observes minute and everyday details of the city, '[h]e delights in fine carriages and proud horses, the dazzling smartness of the grooms, the expertness of the footmen, the sinuous gait of the women, the beauty of the children, happy to be alive and nicely dressed – in a word, he delights in universal life'. Stephen also occupies himself with perceiving the everyday phenomena of the city and translates them into an artistic aesthetic. He aimlessly wanders the streets and spectates a jewellery store, a watchmaker's store and a book cart. He stands before the window of a lapidary and gem cutter and watches the craft in action. He infuses the mundane observation with lyricism: 'the lapidary's fingers prove a timedulled chain [...] Dust slept on dull coils of bronze and silver.' Similar to his stream of consciousness in 'Proteus', he again makes the burden of his university education explicit and continues intermixing his own thoughts with other works of literature. His observations bear echoes of Milton's *Paradise Lost*, John 1:5 and Yeats's *The Celtic Twilight*. He struggles to achieve originality. He continues observing city scenes and like a flâneur acknowledges the modernity of the city, '[t]he whirr of flapping leathern bands and hum of dynamos from the powerhouse urged Stephen to be on' (U 311).

A precondition of flânerie is that although the flâneur earnestly observes the city scenes, they themselves remain invisible to the urban crowd. In the case of Stephen this condition is breached. His trance as a flâneur is broken when his sister, Dilly, runs into him near the book cart. The encounter forces Stephen out of his anonymity. He is compelled to engage with the subjects of his observation instead of remaining a distant observer like the flâneur. He finds himself obligated to respond to Dilly's futile efforts at learning French. He warns himself '[s]how no surprise' (U 312). However, he does little to assist his sister and wallows in remorse in his inability to save her. He perceives Dublin as a city with no opportunities and hopes to go beyond it. But he cannot help but aestheticize even his expression of remorse. He alludes to a medieval text and articulates his remorse as 'agenbite of inwit' (U 19) ('remorse of conscience'). Thus, although Dilly momentarily forces Stephen to encounter reality, he soon slips back into his flâneur-self and resumes transforming perceived reality into fragmented lyricism.

'Wandering Rocks' largely follows the itineraries of male characters – Father Conmee, Simon Dedalus, Stephen, Tom Kernan, and others. Whereas most male characters have uninhibited mobility in the streets of Dublin, many of the female characters in the episode are found indoors. Molly Bloom is famously confined in her home for the whole duration of the novel and in 'Wandering Rocks' only her disembodied arm makes a fleeting appearance to give alms to the sailor. In contrast to Molly's brief appearance, the episode focuses at length on a few other female characters. These women, although not circumscribed exclusively within domestic spaces, are still located indoors. For example, Miss Dunne, Blazes Boylan's secretary, is seen in a state of stasis in her office, where she reads a sensational novel by Wilkie Collins and daydreams about getting a 'concertina skirt like Susy Nagle's' (U 294). Although Miss Dunne is in a state of immobility, she still occupies a safe space. But the young shopgirl who arranges Boylan's fruit basket at Thornton's fruits and flowers shop is in a more vulnerable position (U 291). The shopgirl bears traces of Bloom's daughter Milly, who is away for work in Mullingar. The shopgirl, like Milly, suggests that young women transcend the boundary of the household and are ready to join the workforce. But in the shop the girl finds herself subject to the predatory male gaze of Boylan. Boylan looks 'into the cut of her blouse' and lustily calls the girl 'a young pullet' in his mind (U 292). The girl is aware of Boylan's attention and her discomfort is reflected in the 'blushing peaches' (U 292). She keeps an eye on Boylan's advances with sideways glances and continues arranging the fruit basket (U 292). The shopgirl's position suggests that young women like her are forced to operate in unsafe work environments where their safety can be breached any time by characters like Boylan.

The women we see on the streets in 'Wandering Rocks' are also in a relatively disempowered position compared to the male characters. For example, the account of Bessie Sheehy's peregrinations in Dublin find space in the narrative only when she runs into Father Conmee in Mountjoy Square (U 280–1). Father Conmee, instead of acknowledging her as an autonomous individual, attributes her identity to her husband, Mr David Sheehy MP. Bessie Sheehy remains silent in the narrative and her exchange with Father Conmee is articulated only through the latter's stream of consciousness. Similar to Bessie Sheehy, another female character who is briefly seen on Dublin streets and also remains silent in the episode is the young woman Father Conmee spots near Malahide Road (U 287). The woman emerges from the gap of a hedge after an assignation with a young man (who will be identified later in 'Oxen of the Sun'). The woman exercising her sexual freedom is looked down upon by Father Conmee and he makes his disapproval apparent by blessing her 'gravely' (U 288). He speaks warmly to Bessie Sheehy, who appears to conform to traditional gender rules and looks unfavourably upon the young woman for her alleged promiscuity. Thus, as the shopgirl finds herself a target of the predatory gaze of Boylan, the young woman finds herself subjected to the critical gaze of the clergyman. Other female characters in 'Wandering Rocks' who have the privilege of voicing their own words also often find their freedom curbed. Dilly Dedalus enjoys uninterrupted mobility in the city. But her trajectories yield few positive results. Her itineraries lead either towards obtaining money from a reluctant father or seeking guidance from a brother wallowing in self-remorse. Similarly, Mrs Breen, with whom Leopold Bloom has a conversation in 'Lestrygonians', also has little control over designing her own trajectories. Although she has the privilege of mobility, she finds her itineraries largely determined by her husband, Denis Breen. In 'Wandering Rocks' she is seen being 'led' by her husband over O'Connell Bridge (U 309). Social expectations and gender traditions thus obstruct women's mobility in 1904 Dublin.

While the restricted mobility of women in the streets suggest that Dublin's urban modernity is yet to become more conducive to women, the prominent presence of electric trams signifies that the city is making considerable progress in technological modernity. Various characters such as Father Conmee and Master Dignum come across the tram system. The tram system connects various parts of the city and facilitates mobility among various neighbourhoods. The intricate tram network indicates that Dublin is leaving behind its rural past and approaching a mechanized future.

The itineraries of various characters in 'Wandering Rocks' show that individuals engage with Dublin in different manners. Some characters view the city as a transhistorical palimpsest, some ignore its turbulent past and imagine an ideologized history, some view its streets and monuments as markers of colonialism, some situate it in a transnational context, and some embrace its technological modernity. The episode captures how a medieval city transforms into a modern metropolis and negotiates with its coloniality. The episode not only depicts how different characters respond to Dublin's colonial position, but also foreshadows upcoming anti-colonial struggles. The General Post Office remains an unsaid presence in the episode which functions as an implicit reminder of the 1916 Easter Rising. Various streets and locations mentioned in the episode, such as Mountjoy Square, Eccles Street, Nelson Street, Ormond Hotel, Nassau Street and O'Connell Bridge, are situated within walking distance of the General Post Office. Therefore, when these locations appear on the itineraries of various characters, they bear an implicit reference to the General Post Office. During the Easter Rising, the General Post Office was used as headquarters by the leaders of the uprising. It was destroyed by fire in the course of the rising and later restored by the Irish Free State government in 1929. The General Post Office thus symbolizes Ireland's historical anti-colonial struggle. Its implicit presence enhances the transhistoricism of the episode. Its history of being destroyed and renovated stands as a metonym for Dublin as a city that relentlessly renews itself from its own ashes and exemplifies transnational and transhistorical urbanism.

Sirens

Sgt Joyce's Lonely Hearts Club Band

JOSEPH O'CONNOR

Joseph O'Connor's internationally acclaimed novels include *Star of the Sea*, *Redemption Falls*, *Ghost Light* and *Shadowplay*. His fiction has been published in more than forty languages and his awards include the Prix Zepter for European Novel of the Year. He is Frank McCourt Professor of Creative Writing at the University of Limerick.

As a child growing up in the Dublin of the 1970s, I was enthralled by the city's theatres and their lives.

'Playhouses', they were called by my Francis Street grandparents. Across the street from number 15, the tenement house where they had lived as newlyweds, the tenement house in which my father was born in 1938, stood the Tivoli, frequented by generations of Liberties people. A stageplay of my own was presented there in 1995, by which time the Tivoli was perhaps a little past its best. In its latter days it became a venue for amateur wrestling. If my aunts' and uncles' stories of Tivoli-based courtships are correct, I think a certain amount of that always went on there.

In a bout that was only ever going to turn out one way, the building recently met the wrecking ball and lost. Soon a hotel will rise from the rubble. Sometimes I picture the ghosts its future guests will glimpse in the en-suite mirror, faded Macbeths, shimmering Hamlets, luminous old Ophelias. Zozimus the blind balladeer, who haunted the Liberties all his long life, or the spectre of James Clarence Mangan, another local. When the minibar is emitting that strange, seductive hum in the night, it may be Thomas Moore.

John Field, friend of Chopin and inventor of the nocturne, was born in the Liberties' Golden Lane. Turlough O'Carolan, blind harpist, compositional genius, was said to have traded airs with Italian violinist Franceso Geminiani in Dublin, perhaps at St Patrick's, a theatre of sorts, its stars having included Dean Swift. One Dublin theatre, Smock Alley, had at one time *been* a church and the Quaker Meeting House in Temple Bar would become a cinema. Prayer house and playhouse were sometimes soul kindreds, shrines of spirit and music.

The Abbey had been founded by Yeats, Synge and Lady Gregory, the Gate by Hilton Edwards and the great Michael MacLiammoir, who might even in my childhood still be noticed in the throughfares of Dublin, dandyish in morning dress and mascara.

Charlie Chaplin and Laurel and Hardy had played the Olympia in the antediluvian era when it was Dan Lowry's Music Hall. Further back, when dinosaurs roamed Phoenix Park, Handel's oratorio *Messiah* had received its world premiere in a Dublin theatre, the Great Music Hall on Fishamble Street, itself not five minutes from the Liberties. The lead soprano, an Englishwoman, Susannah Cibber (her brother Thomas Arne wrote 'Rule Britannia'), had been involved in a much-publicised adultery case back in London, a lurid tale involving informants, hasty retreats and spyholes drilled through walls. Perhaps with an eye to the box office, Handel knew what he was doing in casting her. As she came to the climax of 'I know that my Redeemer liveth' on opening night in Dublin, a clergyman in the audience, overwhelmed by the transformative intensity of her performance, stood up and cried out, through the halo of his tears, 'Madam, for this be all thy sins forgiven!' Molly Bloom would not be the first unfaithful soprano to grace the boards of Dublin. Mrs Cibber got there centuries earlier.

Bram Stoker met his idol Henry Irving in a Dublin theatre and left Ireland to be his secretary in London. *Dracula* would not have been written had that meeting not happened. O'Casey and Shaw had served theatrical apprenticeships in Dublin, so had Willie Pearse and Joseph Mary Plunkett. At a theatre called the Antient Concert Rooms on Brunswick Street, now renamed Pearse Street, James Joyce had performed as a tenor. Disappointed to come second in a singing competition, he tossed his silver medal into the Liffey on the way home.

It was important that you knew all this, my parents seemed to feel. The city was a backwater but its playhouses were portals.

We lived near Dún Laoghaire, the seafront conurbation once known as 'Kingstown', not far from where *Ulysses* opens. The Martello Tower and the Forty Foot were part of our daily world. I saw Howth, across the bay, every morning of my teens, from the train on my way to school. Unbelievably, the Gas Company Showrooms in Dún Laoghaire, a large shop that sold cookers and cannister-fuelled campfires, had its own theatre in the back of the store. (Later the premises became a branch of Eason's bookshop. It is now a Chinese restaurant.) On the seafront sat the Pavilion, like a beached Art Deco liner, crumbling into its one-time finery. At the end of a laneway in Seapoint was the tiny Lambert Puppet Theatre, whose repertoire included Wilde's 'The Selfish Giant'.

In the city centre, even the national bus depot had a theatre, the Eblana, a former newsreel cinema once intended to entertain the waiting passengers. Perhaps the news was too bad for anyone to want to see it. Anyhow, the bus people donated the space to Thespis. A mews-alley behind Baggot Street was home to the Focus, where modern American and European works were staged. If the priest who taught me English for the Inter Cert wanted to stop us misbehaving, he'd say, 'Lads. I'm warning you. Quit playacting.'

But the greatest of Dublin's theatres, to me, was the Gaiety, on South King Street just off St Stephen's Green. A busy, working playhouse built by two brothers in the late nineteenth century, it offered everything from grand opera to folk gigs, farce to Shakespearean tragedy, Lloyd Webber to Sean O'Riada. Once a year, at Christmas, it was where many Dublin children were brought to see pantomime. That was a night you longed for.

You headed up to that high balcony of dark, velvet plush, or into that parterre of alabaster pillars and creamy stucco nymphs, settled back with your bag of toffees, though it was impossible to settle, let the sound from the orchestra pit wash over you.

Every time you heard it, it was new, strange and gorgeous. You didn't know then that it would *always* be new and strange and gorgeous, would forever strum the heartstrings and stir recognitions.

Playhouse.

Is there any more exciting sound than an orchestra tuning up?

The *spit* of a snare drum, the shimmering, brushed cymbal, a plunking, spangling banjo brought into the ensemble for a comedy number. A trumpet's blowsy bawl, a naughty phrase of boogie-woogie piano, the seethe of impatient violins, a chime-tree, a gong. An exhilaration of harp arpeggios, billowing like wavelets, and a foghorn of responding bassoons. An orchestra tuning up means unimagined wonders are about to happen. It says you can leave reason at the door.

It's the sound that opens the Beatles' masterpiece known to millions by the truncation 'Sergeant Pepper', and it's the sound Joyce has in mind as his 'Sirens' sequence commences, not with an overture but a gathering, a shuffling-together. His characters are choristers-in-wait, and they're watching from the wings as the houselights thrillingly start a slow fade.

Themes are introduced, tossed around, repeated, inverted, curtailed, transposed, italicized, struck through, before the conductorial command 'Enough, Begin!' is uttered from some podium beyond the page and Joyce's own Day in the Life resumes its glorious unroll.

Somebody spoke and I went into a dream.

There are cities (Rome, Oxford, London) that come to us as a colour scheme. *Ulysses* is a concept album, a soundtrack. 'Sirens' intensifies the music, charges every phrase with acoustic. Like David Bowie's *Berlin* trilogy or the 'ambiences' of later Brian Eno, like Laurie Anderson's 'O Superman', Yoko Ono's 'Fly', Laurel Halo's 'Quarantine' or Mira Calix's 'Exchange and Return', this is storytelling as sonic wash. *Ulysses* knows words are sounds before they are anything else. The man who began his *Bildungsroman* with a moocow walking down the road understood that the power of the nursery rhyme is pre-verbal.

Music, the most universally loved and evocative of all art forms – perhaps the only art form that really *is* universally loved – is also by far the most abstract. Music is made of noise and the absence of noise. It doesn't sound *like* anything but itself. As Bloom muses in 'Sirens', it's a matter of mathematics. But it's also something more. 'Why minor sad?' (U 361).

Joyce's soundscape can be difficult to enter on first attempt, but that's because there are things in life that are difficult to articulate. A difficult style is often nothing more than the first awkwardness in getting something unusual, weird or strange said. This was the view taken by J. M. Synge: 'Style comes from the shock of new material'. Later, that style will come to seem natural and smooth. Old forms can seem unable to contain material that is radically new, especially in a time of cultural transition. Joyce, for instance, was aware that the Irish extracted new sounds from English. Much as African Americans took up viola and piano to make jazz, Joyce played tricks with the syntax and cadence of English; and in both cases the older instruments and languages were hard put to contain the subversive new energies speaking so weirdly through them. Eno, that great maker of soundscapes – the contemporary artist whom Joyce most resembles – understood this, noting that that which marks new sounds as 'ugly, uncomfortable and nasty' eventually becomes their signature. He points out that artists like Frank Zappa and Bryan Ferry mix and match sounds from the past to create 'fiction and energy' and in this way can be compared to playwrights who invent characters and write lives around them. In 'Sirens', Joyce does just that. Had a recording studio been available to him, he would have been Brian Wilson. Since it wasn't, he made one out of language.

Where does he place it? In a city of self-medicators. Half the populace never drink, are high on the Pledge; the other half have a buzz on all the time. Homes are often unhappy, poor or smoky. The pub is the public house.

Miss Douce and Miss Kennedy, 'Bronze by gold', two barmaids, are on duty in the Ormond Hotel. They trade licks of slightly eroticized conversation and girls-together laughter. ('He's killed looking back.' [...] 'Oh, Miss Douce! Miss Kennedy protested. You are a horrid thing!') (U 335). It's coming on for four o'clock. Customers enter and leave. Some sing. Others tickle the ivories.

Amid the crooners is half-wrecked Simon Dedalus, his 'dancing days over' (U 350), as he puts it. The useless, loquacious, handsy father of Stephen – 'Pappy was a rat', Stanislaus Joyce summarized bleakly – foosters and flirts, terminally out of his depth, fantasizing that wisps of his pipe baccy are 'her maidenhair, her mermaid's' (U 336) (thus unwittingly redefining the phrase 'shag tobacco'). Among the listeners is downbeat Leopold 'Poldy' Bloom, saucy novel in his pocket and a song contest going on in his heart.

A Jack-the-Lad, Blazes Boylan, ambles in for a vivifying snifter, en route to his booty-call with Marion, Bloom's wife. In an image designed to erotically dement a certain type of Irishman since it yokes together his two most favourite leisure activities, the sight of a barmaid's fingers sensually fiddling with a beerpull engorges masculine ardencies. Never has the slang term 'hand shandy' suggested itself more.

Secretly, while all the above delights are unfurling, Bloom is engaging in the Edwardian equivalent of online sexting, penning hanky-spanky letters to a woman he hasn't met. At least, he thinks his correspondent is a woman – I think she may be a man, in which case *Ulysses* is yet again decades ahead of its time and Bloom is the first character in the history of European literature to be catfished. There's a whole lot of shaking going on.

In other words, the symphony of 'Sirens' bubbles with sexuality, befitting a chapter that takes as instigation the myth of the sprites so irresistibly beguiling that their song lured mariners to doom. It's a theme explored by songwriters from Wagner to Stephen Patrick Morrissey of The Smiths in one of his cheerier numbers, 'Shakespeare's Sister'. But if music be the food of love, Joyce says, let's play. He crams his sentences with instruments.

Harp, horn ('have you the horn?' U 669), tympanum, pipe, fife, cello, double bass, trombone, dulcimer are only some of the assembled cast, as is the most beautifully evoked piano ever given to literature. 'He pressed (the same who pressed indulgently her hand), soft pedalling, a triple of keys to see the thicknesses of felt advancing, to hear the muffled hammerfall in action' (U 339). Joyce's bandstand is bulging and bugling with possibilities. The flam and paradiddle of his plosives ('Pat paid for popcorked bottle', U 340). The power chords of his nouns. Windmilling the language like Pete Townshend a guitar. ('A sail! a veil, a wave upon the waves', U 329.)

Wonderfully, Joyce himself is present in the chapter. The 'tap tap' (U 368, 369) heard throughout the early parts of the sequence is his baton, before becoming, in time, a walking stick. Like a painter adding himself into the corner of a crowd scene, like a songwriter doing backing vocals but not obtruding upon the stars, he becomes part of what is being created, enters its very texture. Portrait of the artist as a bandleader.

Then, there is the magnificent orchestration of his verbs. Shoes creak. Bells ting. Chords crash. Trays of china chatter. Coins ring. Giggles peal. Joyce chucks around puns like glitter-dust at Glastonbury. Laughter is 'trilling'. Tenors 'get women by the score' (U 353). Although 'Sirens' is wonderfully, resoundingly clever, this is no mere cleverality but an act of imaginative audacity. The jingle of a cab-horse's harness over cobbles might be bedsprings. Indeed, horse-music is whinnied and clopped so frequently throughout the chapter that the reader is reminded of one irreplaceable treasure of Dublin slang, 'ride' as both verb and noun. In other parts of Ireland, the word has one syllable. In the capital, it has one and a half or the full two. (Since the international mega-success of Sally Rooney's novels, 'ride' may have ridden abroad like a seahorse.) Odysseus blocked his men's ears with wax so they wouldn't hear the Sirens, as Miss Kennedy sticks her fingertips in her own ears to banish a creepy man she doesn't want to know about. Much depends on what you want to hear.

Is 'Sirens' understandable? Maybe that's the wrong question. Too often, we look to great literature for mottoes. ('Shakespeare,' Bloom huffs. 'Wisdom while you wait.') 'Sirens' is not asking to be understood but listened to, experienced. Joyce is Jimi Hendrix demolishing 'The Star-Spangled Banner', Miles Davis floating *Sketches of Spain*. He's Janis Joplin exploding Soul into another immensity, Etta James doing 'I'd Rather Go Blind'. He's bebop before bebop and Beat before Kerouac. Give him a top, he'll go over it. In a way, that's the point.

He'd love to turn you on.

In 'Sirens', Joyce rises above the role of listener (highly though he rates it), becoming an instrument recording the quotidian racket that a later quartet of his townsmen would call 'Rattle and Hum'. But his inarticulate speech of the heart is George Eliot's roar from beyond the silence, too. This is part of the brilliance of 'Sirens', that the reader constructs it, indeed *re*constructs it every time it is encountered. Press play, drop the needle, click on 'Sirens' once more, and the song remains the same but is different. Joyce gives us the sheet music but it's we who bring it to life. To quote Eno a last time, we must 'stop thinking about artworks as objects and start thinking about them as triggers for experiences. What makes a work of art good for you is not something that's already inside it but something that happens inside you.'

The Joyce of 'Sirens' is fascinated by what happens inside you, in every sense. Looking back to Blake and Whitman, forward to Ginsburg's 'Howl' and Patti Smith, the body (containing 'organs') is itself a sort of cathedral, a holy instrument incapable of profanity. Blood surging in the auditory canals fills a seashell with the susurration of the ocean; piss trickling into a chamber pot might be poetry. A burp, a groan, a gasp, a sigh, a half-snatched-back sentence, a mumble, a hiccup, a blurt, a yawwwn, all are worthy of membership of the choir. Crumlin's finest troubadour, Philip Lynott of Thin Lizzy, when introducing his group live on stage, or thanking the roadies, would twinkle suggestively in his Dubbalin accent to the audience 'Make a lorra noise'. 'Sirens' does.

Laughter and sexual bliss are brilliantly transposed, mirrors of joyous helplessness, the body going jazz. 'Douce gave vent to a splendid yell, a full yell of full woman, delight, joy [...] I wished I hadn't laughed so much. I feel all wet [...] And then laughed more [...] All flushed (O!), panting (O!), all breathless [...] Ah, panting, sighing. Sighing, ah' (U 354–5). The reader is left in little doubt that the O! doesn't stand for Oedipus.

It anticipates the prolonged ecstatic sonata that is Molly's orgasmic soliloquy but, in a moment all the more beautiful and touching because he doesn't know it's happening, Bloom chimes with it, in a different way. 'Sea, wind, leaves, thunder, waters,' he ponders, 'cows lowing, the cattle market [...] There's music everywhere' (U 364). His wife, close to sleep, will dreamily enrapture and sanctify the physical world, too:

I love flowers Id love to have the whole place swimming in roses God of heaven theres nothing like nature the wild mountains then the sea and the waves rushing then the beautiful country with the fields of oats and wheat and all kinds of things and all the fine cattle going about that would do your heart good to see rivers and lakes and flowers all sorts of shapes and smells and colours springing up even out of the ditches primroses and violets nature it is as for them saying theres no God I wouldnt give a snap of my two fingers for all their learning. (U 931)

Joyce's psalmody allows the couple to be closer than they think; perhaps, for a moment, closer than they are. Sinners both, but singing from the same hymn sheet.

Joyce remarks in one of his letters that 'Sirens' took him five months to write. I slightly hate myself for knowing that the chapter contains 12,218 words (I just had to look). (Having read the book.) That's a rate of around eighty words per day. Imagine the patience, the sheer perfectionism, the craft, all it took to get it down to what it is. Joyce has so much to teach all writers. Write with fire but edit with ice. Wait, rewrite. *Work* for the word. Don't ransack your thesaurus, instead *listen*. As the lyric of the old African-American spiritual has it, 'Ninety-nine and a half won't do'. And 'Sirens' teaches us that prose must aspire to the performative; it's not enough to tell a story, the words need to zing. In another letter, Joyce says he was unable to listen to music for a long time afterwards. He sacrificed much to give us the glorious sound of the Sirens.

Interestingly, in Dublin everyday speech, the word 'sound' has particular nuances. First of all, it is a connotation of agreement, affirmation or acknowledgement, a way of saying you have heard and taken on board the point. Ask a Dublin waitress for a pint and a sandwich and she might respond 'sound'. Tell the taximan you want the airport via North Eccles Street, you're in a bit of a hurry, he'll say 'sound' as he flicks on the meter. In that sense it is a version of Joyce's beloved 'Yes', an assertion of empathy and solidarity. It also means a sort of seaworthiness, a readiness for the trip. When the doctor puts away her stethoscope and pronounces you 'sound', there is nothing much the matter, you're shipshape.

Then, to be described as a 'sound' man or woman by Dubliners (a 'sounder', I notice younger Dublin people saying of late) is to be granted the deep but unshowy respect of your peers, to be admitted to the highest order they acknowledge. A sounder is reliable, reasonable, dependable, tolerantly generous, slow to judgement. Soundness could never be claimed for the self; that would be bad taste, like calling yourself heroic. You cannot be a sounder and a bounder simultaneously (though at least one former Taoiseach made the attempt). In any sort of trouble where you need plain sense to be talked to you, cleave to the counsel of a sounder. Every president of Ireland from

Mary Robinson forth has been sound. Synge was sound. Yeats wasn't. No sound man could ever be a self-publicist or any sort of nuisance. His soundness is a gold standard by which others are measured, true as the forgotten tuning fork that vibrates throughout the margins of 'Sirens'. In a city where a tall story has always been overvalued, soundness is regarded as rare; the sound are to be serenaded. Every Dubliner ever born would feel honoured to be described as sound, but one Dub is sounder than most. For his many faults and foibles, his kinks and coy secrecies, Leopold Bloom may be the soundest man in all of literature.

But the mixtape that is *Ulysses* has its murkier tones. There is also the Dark Side of the Bloom. 'Sirens' does not suggest that pain can be sung away, far from it. Rather that is a way of fleetingly putting down the burden of being us, of escaping the prison of the self. The paradox, of course, is that when truly great music is experienced, we return to the self with a more enhanced sense of what being us involves. Dylan said you don't need a weatherman to know which way the wind blows. But oddly enough, you do.

A song of broken love, 'The Lass of Aughrim', turns 'The Dead' into a ghost story so huge and powerful that we never saw it coming, an Argo looming from Galway with snow-dampened sails. In the same way, 'The Croppy Boy' is the moment around which everything in 'Sirens' coheres. Not a traditional ballad but a work by songwriter Carroll Malone, it was published in *The Nation* in 1845, on the eve of the catastrophic Great Famine. A work about disguise, it is itself in disguise, but clad in the clothes of authenticity. The lyric presents itself as a first-person tale of betrayal (a yeoman captain is dressed as the priest to whom the boy makes confession) arising from the United Irishmen rebellion of 1798. The narrator has been executed, is addressing us from beyond the grave; thus 'The Croppy Boy', like 'The Dead', is a ghost story, as is *Ulysses* itself. Rudy Bloom and Paddy Dignam are among the phantoms of the Ormond, hanging around with the sold-out Croppy among half-finished glasses and unemptied ashtrays, too late in the afternoon, too early in the evening, for anyone to be hitting the sauce. 'Sirens' is a drinking song, but Joyce never lies to his characters. Closing time is always closer than they think.

In another version of the Croppy lyric, made famous by the Clancy Brothers (as a young teenager I saw them play a thunderous homecoming gig, in the Gaiety), the narrator as he ascends the gallows is 'denied' by his father and sent to immortality unparented. So, the perennial Joycean recitative of paternal unreliability is there, masquerading as sung lament. It sidles up to us hand in hand with the story of Robert Emmet, himself the protagonist of several rebel ballads. His famous speech from the dock was interrupted by the hanging judge, Lord Norbury, who counselled him to consider his father's reputation and not to preach sedition in court. Interestingly, Emmet refers to his dead father as a 'shade' in the classic text of the address, a word meaning either a ghost or, in Irish slang, a policeman. In 'Sirens', the mangled speech is counterpointed with Bloom's rasberrying response to it. The humour of *Ulysses* can often be Pythonesque ('I fart in your general direction' taunts a character to the Holy Grail Knights). But it is always deployed for a reason. The jokes often ask, 'Am I funny? Why? What is being laughed at? By whom?' Textual scholarship has long established that Emmet's speech from the dock, a speech so famous that people all over the world learnt it by heart – thus a party-piece, not unlike 'M'appari' in 'Sirens' – was reconstructed from the mutually contradictory notes of a number of scribes, was in other words an artefact, perhaps partially an artwork. More than sixty variant texts of the speech exist. We might think of them as what they probably are, cover versions, remixes. Far from mocking the revolutionaries' courage, 'Sirens' mocks credulity. Be careful what you sing for. You might get it. For Joyce, Emmet has become as empty a symbol as the viceregal carriage, largely because of inherited rhetoric, not rebellion.

Ulysses was first published over several years in serial form (a notable example of the singles predating the album), but in the summer of 1920, around the time he was working on 'Circe', the first commercial blues recordings were made. Delicious to imagine that he might have heard one. Unlikely, I know. And yet, Paris was Europe's high capital of jazz. Joyce the guitarist had an ear for the new. And the colour appearing most frequently in 'Sirens' is blue (sometimes in the form of 'blew' or 'bloo'), the only colour that, pluralized, is also a musical genre.

Blue was also, at Joyce's insistence, the colour of *Ulysses*'s cover. And it's part of his hero's surname, no coincidence. If a headline were required to summarize the 'Sirens' chapter in nine words, it might read 'Stuck Inside of Ormond with the Blazes Blues Again'.

As with Irish and English traditional balladry, the blues is a sort of collective inheritance, a patchwork originally composed by storytelling geniuses whose names we will never know. Verses, images, couplets are reused. Streamlets flow in and out of each other, tributaries are formed. Among the stock characters is the cuckolder, the sexually skilled opportunist trysting with an unfulfilled married woman. He appears in the Howlin' Wolf number 'Backdoor Man', so called because he vanishes into the night as hubby comes home. Sometimes, as is the case in Muddy Waters's 'Long Distance Call', the dalliance is a matter of gossip, euphemism or surveillance. On other occasions, the infidelity is a matter of nudge-heavy humour because the husband, unlike the audience, doesn't realize he's being cheated. In that way, it's a pantomime for grown-ups. If anyone thinks 'Little Red Rooster' is about avian husbandry, my advice would be, never go farming. The remarkable capacity of the blues to know two things at once stirs echoes in the Sirens' song.

Blazes Boylan, backdoor man, wears blue, like Joyce's book. But at one level he's easier to read. In strictish four-four, he advances up the quays; there's never any question where he's heading or what will happen when he gets there. You suspect he's going to be damn good at it – what Brendan Behan termed 'a sex mechanic' – and that Molly will enjoy many an O and a Yes in the coming hour, but you don't particularly feel Blazes is going to enjoy it all that much himself. Maybe that's why he had to stop in for the gin? (A 'stiffener' is one Dublin slang term for a quick drink.) The magnificently swaying bum of a carthorse anticipates other rhythms and satisfactions, a metronome Bloom doesn't want to give ear to. Anticipating a line from Bessie Smith's double-entendre-packed 'Sugar in my Bowl', he thinks 'I feel so sad' (U 329, 330), because what else is to be said or done at this moment? He doesn't want to leave Molly; she probably doesn't want to leave Bloom. Here, Joyce the operatic balladeer is also Joyce the bluesman, drifting slipstreams of sex, archipelagos of coupledom, facing into a crossroads he is not equipped to face, with only his devils for wisdom.

At the outset of this essay, I risked the reader's patience by recollecting a number of lost Dublin theatres and music halls. The best and most comprehensive book on that subject is by the late journalist Philip Ryan. His son and namesake became known by the stage name Philip Chevron, lead singer and guitarist with Dublin group The Radiators, later The Radiators from Space. A punk band like no other, they crammed their lyrics with Joycean references, borrowing also from German cabaret and Brecht. Their important record *Ghostown*, in my view the finest Irish rock album of all time, could not have been brought into existence without *Ulysses*. Linguistically ambitious, stylistically bold, it is as though Stephen Dedalus stole a Fender Strat from some foul rag-and-bone shop in an alleyway behind the Ormond and taught himself the three-chord trick. Kitty Ricketts, the pillar and the kips all appear, with the crusty elegance and pitiless squalor of a crumbling city that, in my childhood, had still not gone. Chevron's musical odyssey would lead him into another genre-smashing post-punk Irish outfit, The Pogues, with whom he played until shortly before his too-early death, doing much to infuse

247

that band with vital creative spark and save it, perhaps, from self-parody. The spirit of 'Sirens' is still alive and dangerous, sometimes encountered where you'd least expect it.

Where might we look now, in contemporary Irish music, for wordsmith dexterity and earthy capaciousness of the sort Joyce bequeathed us? Perhaps to the burgeoning rap and R&B scene led by Denise Chaila, the Rusangano Family and Godknows from Limerick, who blend multicultural modes and stoked staccato lyrics with a certain stamp of Munster no-bullshit iconoclasm, to spectacular and danceable effect. A writer fascinated by concealments, Joyce would have dug the mask-wearing Rubberbandits for their rapid-fire brio and playfulness. You feel he'd relish Conor O'Brien's sinuous and unearthly melodies, the lyrical insights and restless intelligence of Sorcha Richardson and the piano-based off-kilter intimacies of Patrick O'Laoghaire, who performs as 'I Have a Tribe'. He'd adore the brilliant Camille O'Sullivan, French-Dublin chanteuse, who burns every playhouse down with her torch songs. The 'spoken word' scene of performers like Stephen James Smith, Erin Fornoff and David Balfe would thrill him, too, for this is chant as well as poetry, needing an audience of live listeners to close its circuits and loose its sparks. Saint Sister, the fabulous duo of Belfast's Morgan Macintyre and Gemma O'Doherty from Derry, on Irish harps, ethereal (even Siren-like) harmonies and electro-pop synthesizers, might have him penning paeans of bliss. But I think his favourite living Irish poet would be his fellow Dubliner, Paula Meehan, and anyone who has ever heard her read will know why. She inhabits her extraordinary poems like a Sean-Nos singer inhabiting a song, eyes closed, swaying gently, lofting words to the air, both present and absent, absence *becoming* presence, doing something at once ancient and urgently of the now, with joy and a songster's respect. He has descendants who don't know about him and others who do. Some people drive the train. Joyce laid the tracks. 'Sirens' is a high revelation.

In other ways, he would find twenty-first-century Ireland strange. It would strike him as odd that you can't smoke in a pub but you can buy a condom and a croissant in a petrol station. You wonder how he'd approach the task of orchestrating a scene set in a Dublin hotel bar nowadays, what he'd be listening to from his nook in the corner.

On the Liffey's northside quays, you can see the boarded-up Ormond. As I write, it's been closed for months and looks derelict. In June 1985, a student at University College Dublin, I went there to hear a gig by the peerless Sonny Condell, who played strange, beautiful songs based on passages from *Ulysses* and didn't say much about why. You got it or you didn't. No problem either way. The door to the night and the rain was open. Sonny wasn't asking anyone to stick around.

But for those who did – I'm so glad I was one of them – the world was about to change. The house lights went down. On a stage made of language, 'gin-hot words' began singing. They've never truly stopped because their theatre never closes. It's there between the covers of a sea-blue book whose ghosts translate their shadows into music.

That's what 'Sirens' says. A song is full of shadows. Hurts you happened into and heartaches left to come. But those who come to music will find meaning and substance when the grace called healing has begun. Joyce never pretends that our lives are other than they are – he is too great an artist for evasions. But what sights along the way, and more vitally, what sounds.

'O rocks' (U 194), says Molly.

'Sirens' does.

Cyclops

A Sneer and a Smile

DEREK HAND

Derek Hand is Dean of Arts and Humanities at Dublin City University. He has written major works on John Banville and John McGahern, as well as *The Cambridge History of the Irish Novel*.

What'll It Be?

Leopold Bloom poses a riddle early on in the day that a 'Good puzzle would be cross Dublin without passing a pub.' Nothing is impossible, of course, but it would be difficult. Everyone knows that *Ulysses* is the modern epic of the everyday. However, that many of the characters wander through Dublin, not just passing by pubs but loitering a while within, suggests the heroic deeds of the past have dissipated somewhat in the contemporary world. To talk of the heroic epic mediated through a bunch of down-at-heel flâneurs might seem incongruous. But both versions of the novel are equally valid. The 'Cyclops' episode, set in Barney Kiernan's public house on Little Britain Street, like all the other episodes in *Ulysses*, encapsulates the themes and concerns of the whole. In this episode, though, that notion of doubleness that underpins the novel's world – every person, idea, emotion having both an opposite and a parallel – is much more pronounced. Here, despite the focus on a one-eyed perspective with the Citizen espousing a very narrow and exclusionary version of Irishness, the reality emerges that nothing is ultimately either/or, as potential multiplicities abound. And so, famously, the 'Cyclops' episode nods to its Homeric predecessor by reimagining the epic with Leopold Bloom in verbal combat with the one-eyed bombastic Citizen (loosely based on GAA founder Michael Cusack) in Barney Kiernan's public house on Little Britain Street – Bloom waving his cigar becoming the comically diminutive version of the burning stake that Odysseus plunged into the eye of the Cyclops. The central action of the episode, the argument between the Jewish Bloom and the nationalist Citizen about Irish identity and belonging, is significant in terms of Ireland's cultural and political development then and now. With most of the characters gathered together in the pub being well on their way to being a little worse for wear, and one – Bob Doran on one of his periodic benders – paralytic with drink already taken, the grandeur of that heroic moment, and the significance of the dispute, is burst with each pint drunk. As a snapshot of 1904 Dublin, it doesn't look that promising: a world of success, of action, of articulating a real progressive sense of what an independent Ireland might be, seems to be somewhere else in both time (the past) and space (anywhere else but here). And yet, it is 5 p.m., and these men, or some of them at least, are having a drink after work, looking for entertainment and a bit of an escape from the humdrum. The presence of alcohol means that things are never as they seem, that perceptions and actions are a little off-kilter, more pronounced and exaggerated.

A significant clue is in the name: 'public house'. A pub is a place of gathering and conversation. While there are always drinkers who drink alone, the real business is to meet up with whoever might cross the door. Everyone is equal, but those with money and means are more equal than the others. There are various types of establishment for drinking on display in *Ulysses*: Davy Byrne's moral pub seems good for a spot of lunch, the Ormond Hotel's bar allows for a song or two to be sung, even if it is the afternoon, and Burke's is the perfect terminal spot for a late-night carousing session. Each place possesses its own mood and clientele. Being close to the courts on Green Street, one can guess that in Barney Kiernan's, the day's hot topics are important. Information, or rather news (as in what is relevant), is the fundamental currency of the pub, and this pub in particular. There is no bad or good news, just news, so politics, history and sport are all important and worthy of discussion. And there are regulations, of course: it is, after all, a 'licensed premises', but it is the rules of engagement, the codes that allow *both* discussion *and* the drink to flow, that are critical. Many of the men (and it is very much a men's only space) have been spotted elsewhere in *Ulysses* during the day. The likes of Joe Hynes, J. J. O'Molloy, Martin Cunningham, and Crofton or Crawford or 'whatever you call him' slip in for a drink. And, of course, Leopold Bloom also comes inside. Barney Kiernan's is a place where people come and go on their way to somewhere else, though the Homeric link indicates that the pub is a site of entrapment that needs to be escaped. People have roles to play, with specific information to offer and peculiar bugbears to espouse. So beneath a mask of conviviality, of the conventions of manners, lurk many Irish neuroses just waiting to bubble to the surface.

What Are You Looking At?

The one-eyed nationalist – the Citizen – embodies all that is narrow and backward in the Irish politics of 1904. He has all the answers to the country's contemporary ills, which are firmly set at the foot of Britain's imperial impositions on Ireland. When it comes to the national question a pervading and oppressive sense of outrage permeates the individuals gathered in the pub, and most explicitly the Citizen. The problem is that this outrage is debilitating, both for the individual and the country, precisely because that outrage becomes the singular response. It is understandable, though, because the odds, if not the very rules of the game, are stacked against Ireland in the colonial relationship. The parameters of the debate are already written in this scenario, with the imperial centre setting the agenda. Its consequences can be seen in every aspect of Irish life and culture. For example, his idea of a great Irish past is mocked by the presence of mere fragments of the Irish language in the Citizen's speech: 'A chara'; 'Slán leat'. And he knows it, as he tells the group of men about the state of the Irish language in Ireland with city councillors labelled 'the shoneens that can't speak their own language'. So he both articulates the problem while simultaneously embodying it. That Barney Kiernan's pub is located close to the seat of law in Ireland is also significant. The rule of law is decided elsewhere, is indeed a very real expression of the power of the imperial master and a means of creating the colonial space and ruling it. Still, all the characters in the pub display deference to the law, seeing it as the vehicle to right wrongs, even as it oppresses. Denis Breen, walking the streets of Dublin threatening to take a libel action for the card sent to him with the cryptic 'U.p: up' (U 386), is called a 'bloody lunatic' (U 415), but perhaps they all are in their shared enthralment to the very system that subjugates them.

The Citizen rightly focuses on the colonial economic system that places Irish manufacturing and the Irish economy on a lower rung than that of the imperial centre:

What do the yellowjohns of Anglia owe us for our ruined trade and our ruined hearths? [...] We had our trade with Spain and the French and with the Flemings before those mongrels were pupped, Spanish ale in Galway, the winebark on the winedark waterway. (U 423–5)

It becomes a list of lament and woe, calling out all that is wrong and has been taken away. The consequences of this economic reorientation towards the imperial centre and the imbalance it causes are many. That sense of past glories set against present-day humiliation seeps into all aspects of Irish life and culture with power, be it economic, political or cultural, always situated anywhere else but here. And it does not take much for the sense of hurt to explode into view. The conversation becomes more heated as the Citizen and the other men in the pub warm to their topic and move on to corporal punishment: the material means by which power is wielded. But, again, the Citizen is correct in his analysis of how force and violence are at the heart of the system, the essential means by which imperial control, indeed all political control, is exerted.

Bloom has entered the pub at this stage and his contribution to the discussion only confirms his outsider status, which has been a feature of all of his interactions throughout the day. Now, though, his Jewish background comes to the fore both for the unnamed narrator of the episode and for the Citizen, whose simplistic perception of Ireland's identity and his xenophobia is affronted by his presence. Bloom points out that 'force' and state violence are the same everywhere and that if Ireland were free, it would be deployed in the same fashion as it is elsewhere:

> But, says Bloom, isn't discipline the same everywhere. I mean wouldn't it be the same here if you put force against force? (U 427)

Such nuanced critique falls on one blind eye and two deaf ears. At its heart, though, such thinking exposes the dead-end of the sentimental nationalism of the Citizen and his narrow-gauge conception of Irish identity. His perception is the product of the prevailing overarching system, the imperial system. So his Irishness is not so much about difference but about opposition. Simply put, to be Irish is to be not English. And that's it. It might be recalled that the pub is located on Little Britain Street, emphasizing Ireland's lowly status in this strictly hierarchical relationship and, indeed, how that 'Ireland' is merely a projection of Englishness. He goes on to talk about putting force against force, about tapping into the emigrated Irish far-flung to all parts of the globe, and bringing England's misrule to an end:

> And they will come again and with a vengeance, no cravens, the sons of Granuaile, the champions of Kathleen ni Houlihan. (U 428)

Heady sentiments indeed. The reader gets the sense that this has all been said many times before. There is a call and response quality to the exchanges, with some bystanders happily acting as a chorus to the Citizen's operatic histrionics. The result of all this force ought to be a new Ireland. Instead, in truth, the future gestured towards is merely a notion of some great Irish past. Earlier, concerning Ireland's economy, it was declared that

> — And our eyes are on Europe, says the citizen. We had
> our trade with Spain and the French [...]
> — And will again, says Joe. (U 425)

Stephen Dedalus mused earlier in the day about the nature of the Irish historical narrative as a 'nightmare from which I am trying to awake'. Here, too, Ireland's story of failure is accepted and dominates the conversation. From the deforestation of the land and the loss of control of Irish ports, to the dominance of English culture in the newspapers, all aspects of Irish life are touched by the colonial malaise. The issue is that this cataloguing of all the wrongs done to Ireland is far too easy for these barroom know-it-alls. Much more difficult would be to begin to resist this prevailing narrative, actually move beyond words, and trying to tell a different story. But the 'And will again' implies that the future will only be an unimaginative restoration of what was before, rather than the radical embrace of the as yet unknown and unsaid.

Bloom's debating style certainly riles the Citizen. The narrator comments that Bloom's recourse to fact and detail is a maddeningly known characteristic of him:

> I declare to my antimacassar if you took up a straw from the bloody floor and if you said to Bloom: Look at, Bloom. Do you see that straw? That's a straw. Declare to my aunt he'd talk about it for an hour so he would and talk steady. (U 410)

Minutiae, though, get in the way of the Citizen's narrative of woe and want, prompting him to question Bloom's nationality, echoing Shakespeare's Captain Macmorris in *Henry V*:

What is your nation if I may ask? says the citizen. (U 430)

Bloom's reply is simple: 'Ireland [...] I was born here. Ireland.' All acknowledge the undisguised anti-Semitism here in the pub, even Bloom.

> — And I belong to a race too, says Bloom, that is hated
>   and persecuted. Also now. This very moment. This
>   very instant. (U 431–2)

Bloom directly confronts the anti-Semitic slur in the immediate moment of the 'here and now' of Barney Kiernan's pub at approximately 5.40 p.m. on Thursday 16 June. This is a direct challenge to the thrust of the Citizen's narrative. And he goes on to really provoke the Citizen's worldview when he declares:

> — But it's no use, says he. Force, hatred, history, all that.
>   That's not life for men and women, insult and hatred.
>   And everybody knows that it's the very opposite of
>   that that is really life.
> — What? says Alf.
> — Love, says Bloom. I mean the opposite of hatred.
>   (U 432)

In the hyper-male world of 1904 Dublin, this statement is simply unacceptable. Having just called out the anti-Semitic sentiments of the Citizen, Bloom now exposes the system of masculinity to scrutiny. Culture and history collide at this moment so that we see how limited colonial construction of Irishness is linked to the masculine realm, which is also seriously proscribed and limited. All hierarchical systems operate in a similar fashion: there are winners and losers, there are those who dominate and those who are conquered, and here Bloom connects the imperial mindset with the actions of these Dublin barflies. And, of course, the one-eyed Citizen and the others are too blind to see that their belittling of Bloom in their questioning of his masculinity and making fun of his cuckolded state are merely mirroring how the English infantilize and abuse the Irish. It is the pivotal moment in the episode and tempers begin to rise after it. In a way, what Bloom does is make history personal and immediate. Rather than talk in terms of the anonymous nation, he brings in the actualities of the individual and the realities of life as is lived by women and men. In the colonial world, where the colonizers control the historical narrative, this is a manoeuvre signalling the potentials of a revolutionary rupture. He gives voice to other possible realities and an alternative future.

Bloom's declaration is the beginnings of a critique of the Citizen's narrow nationalism, seeing similarities rather than differences and intimating that if a new Ireland is just an inverted mirror image of the colonial regime, then Ireland will remain unfree. In this novel of modern heroics, none of Bloom's actions are presented as grand. Still, that he acts at all is what is important. In comparison to the sentimental group of men who are happy to sneer and smile with equal measure at a verbal level, Bloom actually does things in the real world. As has been noted already the location of Barney Kiernan's pub – close to the law courts – signifies the centrality of the law in this colonial world. But Bloom knows there's a difference between law and justice in Ireland. The reason he is in Barney Kiernan's is to see if he can meet with Martin Cunningham and sort something out for the widow of poor little Paddy Dignam, whose death insurance might be in default. The law might say one thing, but Bloom wants to find a workaround that will make things right. Just after his outburst about love, he quickly makes an exit to find Cunningham. It is an excuse, because Bloom is aware of what he has said and how it might not fit with the general tone and thrust of the increasingly drunk clientele of the pub. In his absence it's said that he gave the idea of 'Sinn Féin' to Arthur Griffith. It may or may not be true, but its irony is seemingly lost on the gathering: Bloom doesn't mourn Ireland's history, nor sing or cry over it. Instead, he gets things done. And that's problematic, and demands not just a verbal rebuke but a physical one as well.

In the great nineteenth-century novels, the medieval world of physical derring-do and adventure became verbalized jousting, so that when George Knightley in Jane Austen's *Emma* proclaims that his rival Frank Churchill's handwriting style is like a 'woman's', we don't think that he'll follow through on it and add injury to insult and give him a box in the head. In Barney Kiernan's pub, though, while the aspersions on Bloom's masculinity are all too similar, there *is* the added threat of actual violence when the Citizen chases him out of the pub and throws a biscuit tin at the retreating Bloom. It is comic, to be sure, but highlights how disruptive the articulation of Bloom's vision has been.

You Had To Be There!

The presence of alcohol has a distorting effect on the action in the episode. While these particular moments of interaction between Bloom and the Citizen are clear, they occur in a milieu of people coming and going, as snippets of conversations are half overheard. While the argument about nationality and Irish identity revolves around a one-dimensional sense of belonging, the pub itself is a location where a multitude of things are happening simultaneously. The dynamics of the pub, with the stress on the spoken word, means that anything can happen at the level of language. Drink heightens the emotions at work within the group so that the men in the pub move rapidly from happy to sad, serious to comical. Every point and idea and proposition is thus elevated or humbled, celebrated or devalued in the moment. There is an element of the fantastic at work here. For Alf Bergan, Paddy Dignam is still alive:

— Paddy Dignam dead! says Alf.
— Ay, says Joe.
— Sure I'm after seeing him not five minutes ago, says Alf, as plain as a pikestaff.
— Who's dead? says Bob Doran.
— You saw his ghost then, says Joe, God between us and harm. (U 388)

Anything is possible at this in-between hour. Nobody is precisely sure of who anyone else actually is. Of Bloom it is asked:

> — Is he a jew or a gentile or a holy Roman or a swaddler
> or what the hell is he? says Ned. Or who is he? No
> offence, Crofton. (U 438)

Crofton is a Protestant Orangeman, we are told, but the narrator is never quite certain of his name: Crofter, Crofton or Crawford. Perhaps he is all three? Famously, there are no new jokes in Joyce's *Ulysses*, and here we witness the comforts of the well-known gag at work. With the talk of nationality and the idea of home and belonging being put to Bloom, he answers, 'A nation is the same people living in the same place' (U 430). This prompts Ned Lambert to declare:

> — By God, then, […] if that's so I'm a nation for I'm
> living in the same place for the past five years. (U 430)

The injection of humour here is perhaps an attempt to diffuse the situation, but it only serves to isolate Bloom even more. The humour of the men creates a sense of shared community, with each happy to play their part and say their line:

> — Stand and deliver, says he.
> — That's all right, citizen, says Joe. Friends here.
> — Pass, friends, says he. (U 381)

The men are still boys, playing their childish games of make-believe, and for a moment existing in a state of timelessness.

Time's Up: Have You No Homes To Go To?

But all good things must come to an end, and the world of throwaway remarks and debate and argument must be brought back into the real world. Bloom's hasty exit from Barney Kiernan's public house sees him warming to his theme of celebrating his Jewish difference and further antagonizing the Citizen:

> — Mendelssohn was a jew and Karl Marx and
> Mercadante and Spinoza. And the Saviour was a
> jew and his father was a jew. Your God. (U 444–5)

Chased by the raggle-taggle group of men and led by an irate Citizen, Bloom ascends into heaven:

> When, lo, there came about them all a great brightness and
> they beheld the chariot wherein He stood ascend to heaven.
> (U 449)

Even though it is an ascension that occurs only at the level of language, it affords, nonetheless, a triumphant conclusion to the episode: Bloom has escaped the sphere of the one-eyed Cyclops, his defence of an alternative Ireland, more inclusive and humane, clear both to the men gathered in the pub and to the reader. Indeed, it might have served as a fitting way to bring the entire novel itself to a close. After all, where left is there to go after the hero has transcended the all-too-fallen world of Dublin in 1904?

James Joyce's brilliance is to indicate that there are no pat endings, no neat conclusions where all the loose ends are tied up and 'The good end happily, and the bad unhappily,' So despite the possibility that the fantastic is the dominant in the episode, where everything might be turned on its head, reality is never too far away. Therefore when Bloom's ascension is undercut in the description of the angle of his elevation being 'fortyfive degrees over Donohoe's in Little Green Street like a shot off a shovel' (U 449), the reader is brought back to earth with a bang.

One More For The Road?

It is, as stated, an episode in which anything can happen, in which all polarities are reversed, even momentarily. The narrator of the chapter – an unnamed little Dubliner who works as a debt collector – offers the only straightforwardly first-person narrative in the novel. Thus the reader sees Bloom as others see him. His difference to the other men is made apparent, but the Nameless One does have a grudging respect for him all the same. He acknowledges his ability to stand up for himself and his steadfastness in sticking to his point. The narrator, to be fair, is quite democratic in his prejudices, because he doesn't have a good word to say about anyone. Indeed, there is a sense in which it is the Citizen – as a Dublin 'character' – who is being made fun of here, as well as Bloom. All these men know which buttons to press in order to rile him up and get a rise out of him. His performance has been seen before and, to be sure, it'll be seen again.

It might be remembered that this is a story told, perhaps later that day, or at some other time after the fact and the reader, like the putative listener, can take it as seriously as they want, or not, as the case may be. It is a story told for entertainment, highlighting the foolishness of men and, perhaps inadvertently, intimations of everyday heroics. As he has throughout the novel, Bloom, once again, is shown to embrace the realities of his own life: he doesn't acquiesce to the mob's demands and become just like them, which would be the trouble-free option. Who wouldn't want to be someone else? Even for a day or an hour? The pub and drink offer that fleeting possibility of such diversion. But Bloom remains abstemious during his time in Barney Kiernan's, choosing the more challenging and authentic option of being just himself, with his flaws and the inevitable tribulations and trials he must endure. As the poet W. B. Yeats said: 'heart mysteries there'. Mysteries for Bloom and mysteries for us.

Nausicaa

JHUMPA LAHIRI

Jhumpa Lahiri is a plurinational writer who has written many works, focusing on themes of cultural transition, loneliness and the gains and losses of translation. Recently, she edited a major collection of Italian stories and wrote the novel *Whereabouts* in Italian, which she subsequently translated into English.

For as the eyes of bats are to the blaze of day,
so is the reason in our soul to the things which
are by nature most evident of all.

Aristotle, *Metaphysics* Book 2

1

Like Gerty and Bloom, I am distracted by the bat in 'Nausicaa', Episode 13, fluttering in the gathering summer twilight over sea and strand.

Gerty sees it first, just after Father Conroy gives the benediction and the evening bells chime. At that very instant, she sees 'a bat [that] flew forth from the ivied belfry through the dusk, hither, thither, with a tiny lost cry' (U 473).

The squeaking bat flies back and forth. Coming and going, neither silent nor still.

Once the nocturnal animal appears, Gerty's mood shifts to an interior realm, to dreams 'no-one else knew of' (U 473), to a confession album in which she writes her deepest thoughts in violet ink. She thinks of the private language of poetry, 'so sad in its transient loveliness' (U 474). Only seventeen, she is acutely aware of the passage of time, of years 'slipping by' (U 474). She is also aware of a mysterious man staring at her in the darkness, who had already been 'drinking in her every contour' (U 471) a few pages back. Now the 'magic lure in his eyes' (U 474) makes her think of love and the concomitant desire – corresponding, perhaps, to the movements of the bat circling the air – to 'be wild, untrammeled, free' (U 475).

Her reflections are interrupted by the start of a public spectacle: another element that appears in the sky. Roman candles begin to burst, and as they do, Gerty begins to experience a tingling, not due to the fireworks but inspired by the 'eyes that were fastened upon her', and a 'whitehot passion [...] silent as the grave [that] made her his' (U 475–6). When they lock eyes, she notices that 'his hands [...] were working' (U 476). Such is her response to being the object of a mysterious man's masturbation that 'she seemed to hear the panting of his heart, his hoarse breathing' (U 476). Her thoughts shift again, from love to the 'dead secret' (U 476) of sex. Now she can 'almost feel him draw her face to his and the first quick hot touch of his handsome lips' (U 476).

Just before Gerty notices that the man has begun looking up her legs, towards her underpants, the bat reappears. She senses more than sees it; she refers to it not as animal, but rather as an abstract, odd, unidentifiable entity: 'Something queer was flying about through the air, a soft thing, to and fro, dark' (U 477). As the man surreptitiously glimpses her 'wonderous revealment', she lets him look. She trembles 'in every limb' (U 477), unashamed that he 'kept on looking, looking' (U 477), and she desires to cry out to him: 'She would have fain cried out to him chokingly [...] the cry of a young girl's love, a little strangled cry, wrung from her, that cry that has rung through the ages' (U 477). Gerty's suppressed cries of pleasure are both specific and archaic, both rooted to the moment and existing out of time. Her 'little strangled cry' echoes, analogously, the three words grouped together to describe the bat's 'tiny lost cry' earlier on, and concludes with alliterating adjectives alluding to the bat's presence: 'O soft, sweet, soft' (U 477).*

I'll pause here to stitch together a few key themes that begin to unfold once Gerty notices the bat flying hither and thither: darkness, dreams, destiny, desire, direction, death. I'll also link this thematic unfolding not only to the unfolding of consciousness that transpires in these pages, but to the spirit of the very first line of Episode 13 of *Ulysses*, in which the summer evening folds 'the world in its mysterious embrace' (U 449).

(Fold: to indicate a sense of enclosure and protection. Folding: as in bending, altering and succumbing. Folded: to describe the wings of bats as they sleep.)

Following this erotic exchange, both public and private, the mysterious man is identified as Leopold Bloom. As we leave Gerty's point of view and enter Bloom's, it is the bat that serves as a narrative pivot, binding her consciousness to his: 'That was their secret, only theirs, alone in the hiding twilight and there was none to know or tell save the little bat that flew so softly through the evening to and fro and little bats don't tell' (U 478). Bloom echoes Gerty's description of the bat (and her own cries) as 'soft' with the adverb softly.

The bat is witness to what has just transpired: a sexual connection based on sight as opposed to touch, a connection that is as 'innocent' as it is sordid. The bat, complicit, is the only repository of Gerty and Bloom's shared knowledge – a

---

* In Evelyn Waugh's *Brideshead Revisited*, when Charles Ryder, riding in a car one summer at twilight between the wars, lights a cigarette and puts it into Julia's lips, he recalls: 'I caught a thin bat's squeak of sexuality, inaudible to any but me.'

secret that no one (except the reader) is privy to. The bat intuits and plays the role of someone to whom secrets are confessed. But is what just happened – the climax-centrepiece of the episode – really a secret? Why is it that little bats that don't tell? Are they little bats, or are they the 'exasperating little brats', as Cissy Caffrey's twins are previously called: children who may or may not have also witnessed what has just taken place as Bloom puts his hands down his pants and the Roman candles are bursting?

2

What might this bat signify? Let's turn, like Gerty, to the dictionary (where she finds out, in Walker's pronouncing dictionary, 'about the halcyon days and what they meant') (U 462).

The English 'bat' has multiple meanings. It is twice a noun in addition to a verb. It is the word for a stout wooden stick or a cudgel, perhaps used for sport, and, one can safely say, an object with a phallic shape. The ball the children are kicking on the beach calls for a bat of this variety. Remember, too, that Gerty keeps her iron, with which she presses her underwear, on something called a 'brickbat' (U 456), which is a piece of brick that can be used as a club-like weapon, and is also synonymous with a criticism or barbed remark.

The verb 'bat' can mean to hit or to strike. 'Bat around (or about)' means, a bit like Bloom throughout *Ulysses*, to wander aimlessly, to drift. This bat is of Celtic and old French origin (a *batte* is a pounding element). The other bat, the winged one, dating from 1575, according to the *Oxford English Dictionary*, is the alteration of the Middle English *bakke* and refers to the flying nocturnal mammals of the order Chiroptera. The *OED* also mentions *blatta*, in medieval Latin, for a beetle-like insect that avoids the light and turns active after dark.

Another way 'bat' functions as a verb is to wink or to flutter, as in batting one's eyes or lashes (whereas Gerty's hopes are 'fluttering' U 455). Thus not batting an eye (or eyelash) means to show no affection. The etymology of this bat stems from the Middle English *baten* and Old French *batre* ('to beat') and means 'to flap wings wildly or frantically'. If one stops to consider this web of meanings, one appreciates how these meanings, though distinct, are also intertwined and in communication with one another, especially when it comes to the fluttering associated with the winged beast, and to the instinctive fluttering associated with the human eye.

Bats, to whom human beings are unquestionably related, link us through their various connotations and associations to a series of additional creatures, including bugs and rodents, both grounded and airborne.

3

With multiple meanings in mind, let's consider the bat, either different or the same, that appears in the second part of 'Nausicaa' – when we are firmly ensconced in Bloom's section – rousing him from a dense sequence of memories:

Ba. What is that flying about? Swallow? Bat probably. Thinks I'm a tree, so blind. Have birds no smell? Metempsychosis. They believed you could be changed into a tree from grief. Weeping Willow. Ba. There he goes. Funny little beggar. Wonder where he lives. Belfry up there. Very likely. Hanging by his heels in the odour of sanctity. Bell scared him out, I suppose. (U 492)

Why, I'll ask off the bat, is the Bat missing its t? Not once but twice, then twice more in this passage? Why has the formation of the word been truncated, suspended? And is it beggar or bugger?

Bloom believes, initially, that the bat is a bird before changing his mind. And that change causes Bloom himself to assume the bat's perspective and 'change' into a tree. The reference to metempsychosis ('Met him pike hoses' as Molly puts it elsewhere in the novel, changing a single word into four) underscores not only the act and fact of change, but associates bats explicitly with souls.

Like Gerty, Bloom ascribes the Bat to the belfry. But where is the bat coming from, really? From *A Portrait of the Artist as a Young Man*, certainly: in chapter 5, we find three references. In the first two instances, they become adjectives, by means of simile, to describe the soul. The first is Stephen Dedalus's 'own, batlike soul waking to the consciousness of itself in darkness and secrecy and loneliness'. An identical phrase, with the exact same arrangement of words, appears later in the same episode, but describes a woman: 'she was a figure of the womanhood of her country, a batlike soul waking to the consciousness of itself in darkness and secrecy and loneliness, tarrying awhile, loveless and sinless, with her mild lover and leaving him to whisper of whispered transgression in the latticed ear of a priest.' Pinging through the episode, 'batlike soul' is itself a case of textual hither and thither. Finally, we have a passage in which a collective batlike consciousness is evoked: 'And under the deepened dusk he felt the thoughts and desires of the race to which he belonged flitting like bats, across the dark country lanes, under trees by the edges of streams and near the pool mottled bogs.'

In each of the instances in *A Portrait*, as in 'Nausicaa', bats are linked with desire, with secrets, with sleeping and waking, with transgression and movement and the dark. Moreover, 'batlike' refers twice to the soul, and therefore to Homer, who writes at the start of Book 24 of the *Odyssey*:

> Then Hermes called the spirits of the suitors / out of the house. He held the golden wand / with which he cast a spell to close men's eyes / or to open those of the sleepers when he wants. / He led the spirits and they followed, squeaking / like bats in secret crannies of a cave, / who cling together, and when one becomes / detached and falls down from the rock, the rest / flutter and squeak—just so the spirits squeaked, / and hurried after Hermes, lord of healing.

Hermes is leading the souls of Penelope's dead suitors down to Hades. In Homer, as in Joyce, we find references to eyes, to sleep, to secrets, to movements, to sounds. The souls are *turned into* bats in Homer. That is to say, they free themselves from physical existence – from the body – in bat form. Is 'batlike soul' in *A Portrait* Joyce's translation and borrowing of this bat-based transmigration of the souls in *Odyssey* 24? Can the whole of *Ulysses* be read not only as a borrowing and migration but transmigration of the soul of Homer's epic poem, transformed into the form of Joyce's novel?

A few other intertextual points of origin to consider: when Bloom speaks of weeping willows, his texts unfolds backward to Dante, and to Statius and Ovid and Virgil before that:

Inferno 13 (interesting coincidence): Virgil asks Dante to break off a branch in a dense forest full of repulsive, 'wide-winged' harpies who shriek strange laments (more later on repulsive winged women). 'I snapped the tiny branch of a great thornbush, / and its trunk cried: "Why are you tearing me?" // And when its blood turned dark around the wound / it started saying more [...] / Men were we once, now we are changed to scrub' (Musa, lines 32–7).

Thebaid 9: in the forests of Arcadia, we also find an oak tree 'dying on the ground, torn with many a wound, its leaves fallen and its branches dripping blood' (lines 595–7).

Metamorphoses Book 2: when Phaethon's weeping sisters are turned into trees, their mother 'tries to wrest their bodies from the trunk / and breaks the tender branches with her hands, / but blood flows dropping from the joints, as if from a wound'.*

Aeneid 3: when Aeneas, on a beach, also breaks off a branch that begins to pour blood: 'Soon as I tear the first stalk / from

---

* Translation by Yelena Baraz and Jhumpa Lahiri.

its roots and rip it up from the earth [...] / dark blood oozes out and fouls the soil with filth' (lines 33–5). Later, he hears it clearly speaking, 'a wrenching groan rising up from the deep mound / a cry heaving into the air' (lines 46–7).

Bloom, in desiring Gerty, does not touch her. Though he possesses her, he does not cause her to break or bleed.

4

The bat is called a 'Ba' a third time: 'Ba. Again. Wonder why they come out at night like mice. They're a mixed breed. Birds are like hopping mice. What frightens them, light or noise?' (U 492). Bats are now compared to mice, now to men: 'a little man in a cloak [...] with tiny hands. Weeny bones. Almost see them shimmering, kind of a bluey white' (U 493).

The conflation of bat and mouse rings a bell. A fragment from Varo's *Mennipean Satires* suggests something similar about the bat's essentially hybrid essence: 'Factus sum vespertilio; neque in murices plane neque in volucribus sum' (I have been made a bat; I am neither clearly mouse not bird). *Factus sum*: this suggests a state of transformation. But from what previous state?

Bats, in Bloom's imagination, are a mixed species even though they are wholly mammals. They are of course distinct because they are the only mammals that fly. To review, Bloom's bat is compared to a bird, a mouse, a priest-like man with a cloak, and a man with hands (appendages that distinguish humans from other animals, and are also the part of the body that allows Bloom to reach sexual climax with Gerty).

The bat's double nature is underscored by its double environment: both boundless air and inner, enclosed space. Their habits, as Bloom notes, are also double and contradictory: they are both bothersome and fearful, they either sleep or flutter madly about. Bats, being winged hot-blooded mammals, are both foreign (as Bloom is described throughout the episode) and familiar.

(Throughout history, across cultures, bats are always portents. Their significance fluctuates. Either good omens or bad omens, depending on how you look at them.)

Before proceeding, I feel compelled to linger on the bat's oscillating and contradictory nature, and therefore to circle back to Primo Levi's story 'Quaestio de Centauris' in which the main character, the centaur Trachi, is a mixture of horse and man. The story opens with an alternative creation myth, authored by centaurs, honouring all things hybrid, including bats, which are the children of 'an owl and a mouse'. And yet female centaurs are described, by the male centaur himself, as 'squalid monsters'. Later, Trachi, acutely sensitive to acts of procreation and birth across species, allows the first-person narrator of the story to glimpse a bat that 'had just brought into the world six little blind monsters, and was feeding them minuscule portions of her milk'. The lactating bat is, needless to say, female. Levi, like Pliny the Elder before him, draws attention to the fact that they are emphatically female, and the only winged beasts who nurse their young.* Her children, of unspecified gender, are both monstrous and sightless. (I'll build more on mothers, monsters, lactation and menstruation later.)

Interestingly, Levi uses the word *pipstrelli* in the first instance and *mostriciattoli* in the second, a word which, with its pejorative suffix, means, simply but colourfully, 'little monsters'.† They are diminutive versions of the monstrous female centaurs in the story. *Mostriciattoli*, small generic creatures of unknown taxonomy, are distinctive for being hideous and/or deformed. Alternatively, *mostriciattoli*, in Italian, is another way of saying little brats.

(A personal coda to my consideration of hybridity in 'Nausicaa': it has been through reading Joyce that I have learnt that writing is a cross between consciousness and observation.)

5

There is a fourth time, in the metempsychosis passage, that the three-letter word 'bat' is missing its t:

---

* Pliny the Elder: 'The only viviparous creature that flies is the bat, which actually has membranes like wings; it is also the only flyer that nourishes its young with milk, bringing them to its teats. It bears twins, and flits about with its children in its arms, carrying them with it.' (*Natural History*, Book 10, LXXXI, line 168 ff. Much of Book 10 is dedicated to birds; bats are the last winged creatures he discusses, before moving on to snakes, humans, *et al.*)

† Monsters, from the Latin *moneo*, meaning to warn or presage, was 'originally a religious term used of a supernatural phenomenon which conveys a portent or an omen.' (Fordyce) These omens could be favourable or unfavourable. Virgil uses the word in connection with the bleeding tree in *Aenied* 3: 'horrendum et dictu video mirabile mostrum'. In English: 'I see a terrifying portent, amazing to tell.'

Ba. Who knows what they're always flying for? Insects? That bee last week got into the room playing with his shadow on the ceiling. Might be the one bit me, come back to see. Birds too. Never find out. Or what they say. Like our small talk. And says she and says he. Nerve they have to fly over the ocean and back. Lots must be killed in storms, telegraph wires. Dreadful life sailors have too. (U 493)

Here a bee (another three-letter creature which both shares and is the first letter of our flying mammal) is a being intertwined with the bat's predatory nature. They – be they bees or bats – reveal little. They are cryptic. They are incommunicative, but tend to eavesdrop. They are brave to fly over the sea, but also risk their lives in doing so. In the next sentence, the bats morph into humans again: those, specifically, who live on (and off) the sea, bound to nature, to water, to a fluid element, to infinite patterns of to and fro.

6

Evening deepens in 'Nausicaa', and after meditating on metempsychosis and superstitions, the bat re-emerges. 'Twittering the bat flew here, flew there. Far out over the sands the coming surf crept, grey' (U 494). Words and phrases evoked in the following lines include slumber, night breeze and 'a red eye unsleeping, deep and slowly breathing, slumberous but awake' (U 494–5).

While Gerty's bat flew softly to and fro, Bloom's now moves in more emphatic, anaphorous way ('flew here, flew there'). The bat is now associated with the agitated active adjective 'twittering', which is placed (in a lovely example of hyperbaton) at the start of the sentence. Twittering reminds us again of the bat's chirping, bird-like nature; twittering shares its first two letters with twilight, a key word in this episode. Twittering is a kind of squeaking, which we've encountered in Homer. Squeaking rhymes with speaking. Sex can provoke the squeaking of a bed.

The deepening darkness provokes, in Bloom, an intermediate, transitional state of drowsiness: a mood of suspension between sleep and awareness that underscores all the other states of suspension in this episode: the suspension needed for flight, also the suspension between day and night, between eyes that are open and closed.

Is the red eye the bat's, or Bloom's? And aren't red eyes meant to be the devil's?

The English word 'bat' may conjure thoughts of encroaching darkness, but the Latin term, *vespertilio*, containing vesper/twilight, insists on it, literally folding evening into the word itself, as does the ancient Greek *nykteris*, which contains the word for night, 'nyx'. In Greek and Latin, the word and whereabouts of the creature are marvellously one.

All of 'Nausicaa', from the very first sentence, is an ode to evening: to the coming of darkness and to life and consciousness that awakens, Dracula-like, according to rhythms and habits presumably contradictory to those of humans.

Vespertilio is the term Dante uses when he describes three-headed Lucifer in the final canto of the *Inferno*. From each of his heads descends a pair of bat wings:

Sotto ciascuna uscivan due grand'ali, / quanto si convenia a tanto uccello: / vele di mar non vid' io mai cotali. / Non avean penne, ma di vispistrello / era lor modo; e quelle svolazzava, / sì che tre venti si movean da ello... (Canto 34, lines 46–51)

Charles Singleton translates as follows:

From under each there came forth two mighty wings, of size befitting such a bird—sails at sea I never saw so broad. They had no feathers, but were like a bat's. And he was flapping them, so that three winds went forth with him...

(In using *vispistrello*, Dante transitions, like dusk, from the Latin *vespertilio* to *pipistrello*, the Italian word for bat.)

7

But we must return to Ovid's *Metamorphoses* to learn the origin of the word *vespertilio* itself. In Book 4, which may also be a crucial point of origin for Joyce's bat, we encounter the two female daughters of King Minyas, who are punished for scorning Bacchus's feast day. They are transformed when 'the day had completed its course, and the time was approaching / which couldn't be firmly established as either darkness or light / but a kind of disputed no man's land between night and day...' (lines 399–401). The transformation occurs at the exact same time of transition 'Nausicaa' spans and describes. The metamorphosis is immediately preceded by a spectacular show of fire and lights that remind us of the exploding Roman candles: 'the building suddenly seemed to be shaken and flames to leap / from the oil-rich lamps; the room was aglow with flickers of fiery / red and filled with specters of howling beasts' (lines 402–4). To escape the conflagration, the sisters must search for darkness, where, Ovid writes, their 'limbs shrivelled up and a membrane / stretched across them to trap their arms in gossamer bat wings' (lines 407–8). Once transformed into bats, their speech is also altered: 'their minuscule bodies would only / allow them to sigh for their lot in the thinnest and shrillest of squeaks' (lines 412–13). The episode concludes by linking their name to the moment when daylight shifts to dark: 'Their haunts are covered spaces, not trees; as they loathe the daylight, / they fly in the night and take their Latin name from the evening' (lines 414–15).

Key points in Ovid: that bats are originally female, that their wings are punishment for profanity, that they emit squeaks, and that they are lovers of darkness.

Darkness declines two ways in 'Nausicaa': it is both the darkness of evening and blindness. There is as much attention paid to compromised eyesight as there is to acts of seeing in 'Nausicaa', and their coexistence provides ongoing tension throughout the episode.

Evening is evoked, at one point, in threes: 'The shepherd's hour: the hour of folding: hour of tryst' (U 494). 'Nausicaa' is full of trios, full of auspiciously repeating threes. The episode opens with three girls on a beach and ends with three chimes of a cuckoo clock.*

---

* More threes: 'Three cheers for Israel. Three cheers for the sister-in-law he hawked about, three fangs in her mouth' (U 496). Also: 'Pray for us. And pray for us. And pray for us' (U 492).

8

Bloom's reflections on the dark intensify along with the shade of the sky. 'A star I see. Venus? I can't tell yet? Two. When *three* it's night.* Were those nightclubs there all the time? Looks like a phantom ship. No. Wait. Trees are they? An optical illusion. Mirage. Land of the setting sun this. Homerule sun setting in the southeast. My native land, goodnight' (U 490–1).

(There's Homer again, embedded into the word 'homerule', referring to Ireland's campaign for self-government.)

Bloom observes celestial bodies that are fixed, also those that shift, that drift, that appear and reappear. And yet in spite of movements, of hither and thither, of nocturnal visions, the fact of time inexorably passing in only one direction prevails. Evening evokes elegy, the setting sun, with daylight behind us and the temporary oblivion of sleep to come. Memory might suggest and awaken, but it can never restore or replace. Bloom summarizes the brutal truth: 'Never again. My youth. Only once it comes' (U 491).

In 'Nausicaa', seeing is wanting, seeing is feeling, seeing is controlling, seeing is complying, seeing is deceit.

(I think back to Ovid, and to hundred-eyed Argos who could not keep a single one open in the end, and of poor Io who was turned into a cow.)

I pluck out at random the following citations related to vision in 'Nausicaa': 'blue eyes [...] glistening with hot tears' (U 451); 'Eyes dancing in admonition' (U 451); 'That squinty

---

* Italics mine.

one' (U 479); 'Peeping Tom' (U 480); Gerty who can 'see without looking' (U 468); Edy Boardman with shortsighted eyes who squints at Gerty 'with her specs, like an old maid' (U 469). Bloom, it seems, can see quite well in darkness as far as a girl's underwear is concerned. Towards the end of the episode, when Bloom finds a piece of paper on the strand: 'he brought it near his eyes and peered. Letter? No. Can't read' (U 497). Prophetic words pertaining to the novel's author, afflicted by severe vision problems for much of his adult life and nearly blind when he died.

'Blind as a bat': a phrase attributed to Aristotle that provides the epigraph to this essay. Aristotle speaks of human blindness, not due to the literal inability to see, but to understand or recognize bad or obvious things. Attributed, as science has proven, falsely to bats. In fact, bats are not technically blind. They were believed to have poor eyesight due to their manner of flying hither and thither, without any clear or apparent direction. Thus 'blind as a bat' is the result of a (mistaken but also observant) human point of view.

('North Richmond Street, being blind': the words that begin the short story 'Araby' have been lodged in my mind for many decades now. I have never lost sight of them.)

9

The bat, in its meandering freedom, in its skittish fluctuations as perceived by human eyes, embodies the very technique of stream of consciousness, the very mechanism of Joyce's singular literary language – organic and winged and hot-blooded.

The adjective 'batlike' characterizes the 'easy flow of indirect speech' in 'Nausicaa' (van Caspel), moving from one consciousness to the other, alternating, embedded in a novel that consists of a male narrator that becomes, at different points, also a woman. Batlike are Joyce's voices and vision and various points of view.

(Fluttering, flitting, flirting, flapping, fluctuating, flight, flux.)

Wings belong to the devil, to bats, to devilish bats. Also to Daedalus, Joyce's totem of freedom who, with his man-made wings, represents flight and freedom but also attendant, tragic dangers.

And yet there is also a profound element of stillness in 'Nausicaa'. We might read the entire extended physical description of Gerty at the start of the episode as ekphrasis: a rhetorical device that stills the flow of narrative down. Stillness is born from Bloom's fatigue, sitting on the beach at dusk. For much of the episode, Bloom, sitting still, is watchful as opposed to moving about. 'Better not stick here all night like a limpet' (U 496), he says to himself.

10

Bats may seem to blunder about, but in fact they navigate by echolocation: a sophisticated sensory system that functions thanks to high-pitched sounds whose very echoes are interpreted in order to navigate and prey. Theirs is a form of secret communication humans have no access to. We only detect the physical manifestations of echolocation in observing the way they move. In 'Nausicaa', Gerty and

Bloom also engage is secret communication: 'Still it was a kind of language between us' (U 485), Bloom says.

(Bats are born interpreters and translators of an idiom that defies human perception. Bats, like translators, have double natures. Both bats and translators, in composition and in comportment, are creatures betwixt and between.)

Echolalia, meanwhile (a term found just before echolocation in my dictionary), is the spontaneous and involuntary repetition of words and phrases, and refers specifically to that phase of a child's development in which language is learnt through repetition. Echolalia is how language moves from one generation to another. We see evidence of this phenomenon at the start of the episode, when Cissy asks her baby to say 'I want a drink of water' and he repeats 'A jink a jink a jawbo' (U 450). Echolalia is part of the intense maternal activity in this episode, which includes mothers passing language down to their children. Further ahead, Cissy tries to teach her son to call his father by name: 'Say papa, baby. Say pa pa pa pa pa pa pa' (U 464). What is interesting here is that the mother, in teaching her infant to speak, speaks as the infant would. Role reversal, in other words; she becomes the child. He replies first with 'Haja ja ja haja' and then 'Habaa baaahabaaa baaa' (U 464). The p's become b's and resemble Bloom's aforementioned series of 'Ba's'; the father becomes a truncated, then an elongated version of the word 'bat', and also conjures the sound of sheep, which we often count to get to sleep.

11

'Bats in the belfry': an idiom dating back to the late nineteenth century that means eccentric, crazed, intensely confused or even possessed by the devil. Bats in the belfry describes erratic thought patterns, not in bats, but in humans. The mind, batlike, Bloomlike, flitting from one thought to the next. Bats in the belfry locates these creatures in a consecrated space and ties them to that part of the church in which bells are enclosed, and from which sound is produced, transmitted and set free. When Bloom wonders where the bat lives, and says 'Belfry up there', is he ruminating on the figure of speech in addition to the bat's presumed physical lair?

'Like a bat out of hell': an idiom for extreme velocity, inspired by the speed at which they fly, and presupposing their origins are 1) underworldly, 2) infernal. This idiom associates bats incontrovertibly with the devil, but emerges only during the First World War, when aviators likened fighter planes to the only mammal that survives in the sky. The expression appears for the first time in 1921, in a novel by Dos Passos, one year after *Ulysses* was first published and one year before it was published in its entirety.

But why, if bats are indeed associated with the devil, are they flying so quickly away from him?

Gerty is a 'hot little devil' (U 479). Molly is a devil, too, when she has her period. 'Devils they are when that's coming on them. Dark devilish appearance' (U 481). A woman's fertility turns her temporarily satanic. Later on, Gerty is a 'little limping devil' (U 482).

Both Paul van Caspel and Hugh Kenner believe that the bat, by which Bloom both is and is not unsettled, is no other than his rival Blazes Boylan, the man who has slept with his wife. Van Caspel writes: 'He had noticed the animal before [...] and the shape his thoughts take (note the pronouns!) shows that he conceives of it as a male being.' He is referring to Bloom's penultimate awareness of the bat: 'Bat again. No harm in him' (U 498). But how can our bat be merely male, in an episode steeped in complex questions of maternity and female sexuality? An episode in which, says Fritz Senn, 'we enter, for the first time, a predominately female world'? An episode in which Gerty, a virgin, is also compared to 'a second mother in the house' (U 461)? An episode that describes women with 'children's hands always round them', with 'sour milk in the swaddles and tainted curds. Oughtn't to have given that child an empty teat to suck' (U 486). No, our bat, an intermediary, darts decisively between male and female gazes, between Gerty's repressed sexuality and Bloom's shameless erotic satisfaction.

The three witches in *Macbeth* (we never see them fly, though it's been believed for centuries that witches do) throw the wool of bat into their cauldron to concoct their hell-broth. That play also revolves around the language of night, of seeing – 'Is this a dagger which I see before me?' – and of sleep. Lady Macbeth summons thick night so that her knife 'see not the wound it makes, / Nor heaven peep through the blanket of the dark'. Earlier in that same speech, she asks to be unsexed: 'Come to my woman's breasts / And take my milk for gall...'

Is the bat in 'Nausicaa', in an episode that comments extensively if ironically on female beauty and also on the ageing female body, to be interpreted as a squalid monster, or as a nourishing mother? A soft something that accompanies our deepest desires? Or a bothersome pest?

('Old bat', it's said, to mean an irritating older person, and in particular, an old, annoying woman.)

Are the three friends on the shore on the same spectrum with other ill-omened winged women such as harpies and sirens?* With Virgil's bestial, shape-shifting Allecto, a fury summoned by Juno, Ulysses's consort, to raise mayhem and cause war?†

(Stephen Dedalus worships a bird-girl in *A Portrait* as evening falls. But she is an altogether different form of hybrid female, representing a pure beauty that leads to epiphany. When Stephen sees the bird-girl, there are no bothersome bats in the background. In spite of her avian aspect, her wings are never mentioned.)

The three vengeful Furies, or Erinyes (first mentioned by Euripides to be a trio, to be black-visaged and to be winged), live in the underworld, in the darkness of Tartarus, and are sent to punish men for their wrongdoings, and especially disobedience. They have snakes entwined in their hair and fly on bat-like wings.

('Batter my heart, three-person'd God': note the bat nestled inside 'batter' in Donne's Holy Sonnet XIV. Is Joyce building the case for a form of devilish trinity, with the bat substituting for the dove as Holy Spirit?)

---

* In *Aeneid* 3, harpies are described as monsters, also hybrids: 'the faces of girls, but birds! A loathsome ooze / discharges from their bellies, talons for hands, / their jaws deathly white with a hunger never sated' who produce 'ruffling, clattering wingbeats' (lines 263–5; 274).

† For a colourful description of the Furies see *The Aeneid*, lines 324ff of Book 7, which, incidentally, opens with divine portents and oracles regarding marriage to the foreign hero of the poem. Allecto, at line 476, 'takes flight on her black wings'.

The Furies in Aeschylus are daughters of the night. In Ted Hughes's translation of the *Eumenides*, they are described as gender fluid as well as sinister: 'I would call them women but they are not women [...] Black, like the rags of soot that hang in a chimney, / Like bats, yet wingless'. They say: 'Night is our mother, we live in her womb.'

Sophocles's Furies, meanwhile, in *Oedipus at Colonus*, are 'Daughters of darkness and mysterious earth' (line 40). H. J. Rose reminds us that 'any underworld power is apt to be connected with fertility, because it is out of the ground that crops grow'.

The bat, unlike Daedalus, is designed to thrive in the air. The bat, flying only at night, does not run the risk of plunging into the sea due to the sun's power and heat. The bat, of whatever gender, is by definition linked to three crucial female elements: night, fertility and the shape-shifting moon.

12

The final bat, at nearly the very end of the episode, may or may not be the same bat as before. The article is indefinite. 'A bat flew. Here. There. Here. Far in the grey a bell chimed' (U 499).

Here/There/Here (three words again) mimic the sound of the bell, in the belfry, from which the bat presumably emerges.

These words, indicating direction, indicating either present or future or past, are syntactically separate now. The unfolding of 'Nausicaa' proceeds from bat to bell to the three chimes of a cuckoo clock that lives on the mantelpiece in the priest's house. I read the cuckoo as another form of bat in the belfry: a winged creature, popping out of its enclosure, as three priests tuck into fried mutton chops with catsup, chatting, feeding their bodies as opposed to the spirit.

Throughout 'Nausicaa', Bloom is tunnelling into memory, plunging backward into time. He is also out of sync. Suspended, as I've argued. Without time.

A few pages earlier in the episode, at half past four, just before sun sets, Bloom realizes that his watch has stopped (Gerty noticed him winding it earlier, or so she thought). From then on he must intuit the passage of time by sight, through the quality of the light, as an animal or an ancient sailor would. Earlier: 'Very strange about my watch. Wristwatches are always going wrong. Wonder is there any magnetic influence between the person because that was about the time he' (U 487). The sentence is truncated, its sense suspended. Later: 'Must be near nine' (U 498). Perhaps the presence of bats help him to mark the hours. In this sense, bats are metonymy for time.

Speaking of suspension, as the episode draws to a close, Bloom attempts to write a message in the sand, to Gerty, with a bat-like stick. But the message, too, is truncated. He writes: 'I. [...] AM. A' (U 498). Then says to himself, 'No room, let it go' (U 498). In the message, he refuses to identify himself. He leaves the sentence, and himself, in suspense (just as the last sentence of the episode), before the three final chimes of the clock, lacks its predicate and leaps into the void: 'the foreign gentleman that was sitting on the rocks looking was' (U 499).

I'll pause very briefly to consider the philosophical question of time's movement. Linear or circular? I gather time is able to move back and forth only in the mind, and that it oscillates especially effectively in literature.

In writing about the directionality of time, Hans Meyerhoff observes that death, or the lack of time, is in fact unfolding time's final destination, at least as far as the individual consciousness is concerned. Meyerhoff (who has written extensively about time in Joyce) reminds us that time is bound up with metamorphosis: 'from Heraclitus to Bergson, time is identical with "becoming"'. He writes: '... the significance of a timeless dimension in experience, the self, the work of art, or beyond experience can be fully appreciated only when it is placed within the context of the melancholy, gloomy reflections ensuing from the direction of time towards death and nothingness'.

'Nausicaa' moves towards another awareness of time in the abstract: the cuckoo* that chimes, that emerges bat-like from its enclosure. This, too, is a memory. The trajectory of the episode, as it concludes, is rooted – also suspended – in the past, and ends on a note of nothingness.

(Incidentally: in the middle of writing this essay, a watch that I had not removed from my wrist for two years, a timepiece that I wore day and night, disappeared mysteriously.)

13

A final deviation regarding destiny: this rereading of 'Nausicaa' took place as a massive brood of cicadas began singing in the trees of the central New Jersey town in which I live. In spring they had emerged from their seventeen-year-old sleep underground, and having moulted and shed their exoskeletons,

---

* Echo perhaps of 'cocu', French for 'cuckold'?

they transformed into red-eyed, winged creatures, ready to mate. Their screeching serenade, as majestic as it was monstrous, accompanied my thinking and writing about Joyce. Day after day they fluttered around the house and along the streets in a blundering way, living and dying everywhere one turned. They sat on bushes and branches with wings folded, and copulated on sidewalks, wings overlapping, for all to see. They were neither nocturnal, nor mammals, and far smaller than bats, and yet I could not help but ponder certain correspondences.

Nausciaacicada. Nausicada.

Before the flying insects completed their febrile life cycle I flew to Italy, where Joyce began *Ulysses* and I concluded these comments. My roaming reflections emerged from my original copy of the novel, purchased nearly a quarter-century ago when I was in college, in 1987.* Annotated and revisited over the years, it conjures up the past. Who knows why as I read it this time – I believe for the third time – I was so struck by the bat?

Hither, thither, me, the reader.

Princeton-Rome 2021

---

* When I was an undergraduate student, which was when I discovered Joyce, there was a class at Columbia University that was another trinity of which Joyce formed a part, called 'Eliot Joyce Pound': EJP for short. A class, boiled down to three letters, I would have liked to have taken had my schedule allowed.

Oxen of the Sun

Prescience and Parody

RHONA MAHONY

Rhona Mahony served as Master of the National Maternity Hospital at Holles Street. She is an obstetrician, an Honorary Fellow of the American College of Obstetricians and Gynaecologists, an Eisenhower Fellow and sits on the board of the Little Museum of Dublin.

One hundred years after the publication of *Ulysses* there is still a maternity hospital on Holles Street. Parts of the building have changed little since 16 June 1904, the date on which 'Oxen of the Sun' describes Mina Purefoy's three-day labour. In the twenty-first century the hospital heaves under the responsibility of 9,000 births per year. Joyce could not have known that the management of prolonged labour would become one of the major endeavours of the National Maternity Hospital, nor could he have fully imagined the ways – existential, social and medical – that the questions raised in 'Oxen of the Sun' would remain relevant to future generations.

Despite the extraordinary showcasing of his literary and linguistic abilities, nowhere more evident than in this episode, Joyce struggled hugely with the publication of *Ulysses*, as he had with *Dubliners* before that. He had been writing *Ulysses* for seven years before he was adopted by Sylvia Beach in Paris and inculcated into the unique community of her bookshop Shakespeare & Company, where he was much admired as a leader of emerging literary modernism. The publication of a version of the 'Nausicaa' episode of *Ulysses* in *The Little Review* had previously led to a legal case in the US which hampered further publication. Most publishers demanded that he substantially change the text but Joyce refused. Beach ultimately decided to publish *Ulysses* as a limited and private edition available only by subscription directly from the publishers. This publication was a nightmare for the printers, as Joyce required constant revision, but Beach insisted it should be published as Joyce wished. Curiously, just as Mina Purefoy gave birth to a son while the men delivered a drunken exposition of literary styles, it was a female publisher who gave 'birth' to Joyce's book and indeed continued to provide him for some years with the means that he consistently lived beyond. This struggle with the gestation of the novel reflects one of the central themes of this chapter – the tension between artistic creation and procreation. Joyce eventually produces a book and Mina Purefoy a son.

On the third day of Mina Purefoy's painful and protracted labour, Leopold Bloom wanders aimlessly around Dublin, knowing that his wife Molly will make love to another man in their home that day. Late in the evening, Bloom is drawn to the maternity hospital to check on Mina. Here he meets Stephen, some medical students and a group of men getting drunk in the waiting room. As they sit drinking, the midwives quietly care for the women who labour. The language of this chapter is an extravagant ensemble of developmental literary genres reflecting the embryology of language, while the central action focuses on the conversation of men as they drink and discuss birth, contraception and sex. From the empathy of Bloom to the overt misogyny of the men's discussions, it is the largely unseen women who quietly achieve while the men do little. Their drunk and bawdy conversation is both ridiculous and an affront to the work of the hospital and the risk endured by women giving birth. The nurses are professional and hard working and Mina endures the traumatic birth of her ninth child while crediting her husband for this feat. Though a cast of ludicrous male characters dominate this episode, it is an absent son who haunts the pages – Rudy, the baby boy delivered by Molly Bloom eleven years before. Since their son died eleven days after his birth, Molly and Bloom have struggled and grown apart as they try to grieve him. Unable to go home and face Molly, Bloom waits for the arrival of another woman's son, surrounded by his memories of Rudy. Rudy and Bloom defy the comedy and complexity of 'Oxen of the Sun's literary exposition and bring us back to the universal themes of birth, grief and the impotence of human and artistic endeavour.

The structure of 'Oxen of the Sun' is drawn from the embryological stages of pregnancy and Joyce wrote it with the aid of a text of embryology. He explains the structure in the schema he drew up to help readers understand and navigate *Ulysses*. His notes were contained in nine notebooks – a nod to nine months of pregnancy. A series of parodies reflect the development of language and literary growth analogous to the embryonic development of a fetus. The chapter has forty paragraphs, consistent with forty weeks of pregnancy, and is divided into three sections reflecting the classical division of pregnancy into three trimesters. Bloom arrives at 10 p.m. at night, a possible play on the 10 cm of full dilatation signifying the second stage of labour. Mina Purefoy's name is a reference to Richard Dancer Purefoy, who was a Master of the Rotunda, and Mina delivers her ninth child – a child for every pregnant month.

Much of the action in 'Oxen of the Sun' is verbal, as the characters hold forth on topics of birth, sex and love. Parallels are created between the narrative of the characters and the literary or mythical figures drawn from the particular style of the narrator. Thus Bloom becomes Sir Leopold and the members of the cast are transformed into romance heroes, allegorical personages, Victorian moral crusaders and ancient knights, in parodies that trace the development of the English language. This is not quite a linear process, consistent with a fetal embryological model, instead employing looser categories of fiction to create a patchwork of literary styles. As the different styles jostle to create effect, Joyce darts from one parody to another, illustrating the limitation of any one style to portray a person or event completely. In presenting a particular aspect, other aspects are omitted and therefore successive literary styles struggle to convey sufficiently the depth and breadth of human experience. T. S. Eliot argued that Joyce had exposed the 'futility of all the English styles'. Joyce himself constantly revised his texts and in the very cleverness of the parody play there is a certain impotence that parallels the struggles of the ordinary men described. Bloom's humility and humanity transcend the complexity and artistry of the parodies. Conversely, the interior monologues and spoken words are wonderfully expressive, returning us time and time again to the underlying themes of grief and lost or wasted opportunity.

Since Rudy died, Bloom has been unable to reach orgasm during their lovemaking. This physical impotence has been mirrored in a growing separateness within their marriage. Bloom knows that while he is out walking about Dublin for a day, Molly is having sex with Blazes Boylan. No matter how often Bloom thinks of the happy times he shared with Molly, particularly before the death of Rudy, the shadow of Boylan is never far away. Joyce has created Boylan but gives him little approval, apportioning him only three words of interior monologue – like 'a young pullet' (U 292) as he eyes up the female assistant in Thornton's shop. In those three words Boylan is relegated to the role of cheap womanizer and his easy opportunism seems particularly offensive in the context of the loss Molly and Bloom share and the love that brought about the birth of their son Rudy.

In 'Hades', 'Sirens' and 'Oxen of the Sun', Bloom thinks of his dead son and imagines what he would have been like if he had lived. 'He would be eleven now if he had lived' (U 80). 'See him grow up. Hear his voice in the house [...] My son. Me in his eyes. Strange feeling it would be' (U 110). Unlike the visions of Bloom's mother, father and wife, the vision of Rudy does not speak to him and is incomplete, conveying a sense of irretrievable loss. In 'Oxen of the Sun', Bloom meets Stephen at the hospital and his memory of the four- or five-year-old Stephen dressed 'in linseywoolsey' (U 553) at the get-together at Matt Dillon's is combined with thoughts of Rudy and the corselet of lambswool that Molly knitted for his burial. In one of the most sentimental parodies, Stephen is presented as a potential son. Written in the romantic style of Malory, the parody laments, 'Now Sir Leopold that had of his body no manchild for an heir looked upon him his friend's son and was shut up in sorrow for his forepassed happiness [...] so grieved he also in no less measure for young Stephen for that he lived riotously with those wastrels and murdered his goods with whores' (U 510). In this romance, the somewhat profligate Stephen is portrayed as a good child led astray. Redemption will be provided for both Stephen and Bloom as Stephen gains a father and Bloom a son. Sadly, there can be no such happy ending. Later in the chapter, Bloom reflects on his youth as a schoolboy, as a door-to-door salesman and on his first sexual experience with a prostitute. His reminiscences lead him to once again remember Rudy: 'No son of thy loin is by thee. There is none now to be for Leopold' (U 541). Bloom's grief is mixed with his own sense of inadequacy manifest physically in sexual dysfunction and rooted in a sense of paternal failure. Bloom blames himself for Rudy's death in the heartbreaking sentiment in 'Hades': 'Our. Little. Beggar. Baby. Meant nothing. Mistake of nature. If it's healthy it's from the mother. If not the man. Better luck next time' (U 120).

Bloom's sense of impotence as a father is accentuated in the setting of a maternity hospital. It is also an obvious place to seek a son, and as the chapter progresses Bloom comes to care for Stephen, soothing him in the thunderstorm as one might a child. Additionally, Stephen and Bloom represent alter egos of Joyce, with Stephen representing the writer as a young man and Bloom a more mature Joyce. The three share a range of autobiographical details, which help to illuminate the human dimensions of the text. Joyce and Stephen had alcoholic fathers, plunging their families into poverty and alienating them from their sons, while Bloom's father, Rudolph, died by suicide. In each case there is a sense of paternal abandonment and complex failure in paternal relationships. The death of any child is beyond awful for any parent, but for Bloom, the tragedy must have been magnified by his own father's suicide. Joyce initially attended Clongowes but when the school fees could no longer be paid, he subsequently attended the Christian Brothers and Belvedere College. After some dissolute years in University College Dublin, Joyce travelled to Paris to study medicine but ultimately embarked on a writing career. His time in Paris was interrupted when he was called home to his mother, who was dying. Similarly, Stephen travels to Paris to further his career as an artist but is called home to nurse his dying mother, subsequently struggling with his evolving identity and unrealized artistic talent.

While studying at Belvedere, Joyce rejected Catholicism and Stephen similarly has no time for this religion. Stephen refuses to join the nationalist movement and feels alienated from his peers and yearns for companionship. Joyce was greatly affected by the death of his university friend Francis Sheehy Skeffington, murdered by a British officer during the Easter Rising of 1916. Skeffington was a pacifist and a champion of women's rights and is undoubtedly partly commemorated in the character of Bloom, whose empathy towards women is vividly displayed in 'Oxen of the Sun'. There is also repeated reference throughout *Ulysses* to Bloom's rejection of war: 'How can people aim guns at each other? Sometimes they go off. Poor kids' (U 495).

These biographical factors may also have inspired Joyce to reject the preoccupation of many of his contemporaries with the Irish mythic hero Cuchulainn. In place of the cult of glamourized combat and justified violence, Joyce aligns his narrative with the Greek legend of Odysseus, the very human Greek hero who did not much want to go to war. In Homer's *Odyssey*, Odysseus returns home following the end of the ten-year Trojan War. It is a hazardous journey and Tiresias and Circe have warned Odysseus to avoid the island of Thrinacia, which belongs to Helios and which is home to the oxen of the sun – sacred livestock of the sun god Helios. Any harm to these cattle is punishable by annihilation. Despite the warnings, Eurolychus, one of the crew on Odysseus's ship, begs to be able to land on Thrinacia to prepare supper. Odysseus eventually consents. They are subsequently held on the island for a month by an unfavourable storm created by Poseidon and their stores are depleted. Odysseus goes to pray for help and in his absence, Eurolychus convinces the crew to kill the cattle as a sacrifice to the gods and to provide food. They feast for six days, but on the seventh they set sail and are killed in a storm created by Zeus. Only Odysseus is spared because he alone has committed no sacrilege. He manages to reach Calypso's island of Ogygia, although he is held captive there for a further seven years.

So, the island of the sun god Helios becomes Holles Street in 'Oxen of the Sun', where the attitude towards gender roles and associated discourse can be explored. The women in labour should be sacred; the nurses attending them quietly allowed to discharge their life-giving duties. Instead, the women are on the margins of the text, heard but rarely seen, with the men the dominant focus. They are a motley crew who largely behave disgracefully, and their conversations are littered with misogyny and violations against sacred fertility. They sit drinking in the hospital waiting room and loudly discuss sex, contraception and pregnancy and make all kinds of deeply inappropriate comments, oblivious to their surroundings and the risk endured by women giving birth. The maternal death rate at the time was 350/100,000 and infant mortality was some 150/1,000. Today the maternal mortality rate at NMH is

3.6/100,000 and the perinatal mortality rate is 3–4/1,000. The then Master of the hospital, Sir Andrew Horne, 'the able and popular master', summed up the perils of childbirth somewhat uniquely: 'once a woman has let the cat in to the bag [...] she must let it out again to save her own' (U 550).

As the men continue to drink, they become rowdy and a nurse comes to the door of the waiting room and 'begged them [...] to leave their wassailing for there was one quick with child, a gentle dame, whose time hied fast' (U 506). Just as Odysseus's crew had received two warnings not to violate the oxen of the sun, this is the first of two warnings the men will receive and which they will ignore. The conversation goes on; Stephen enacts the Eucharist and goes on to argue that art rivals motherhood in its creative ability, which seems quite a stretch in the setting of the maternity hospital and given that Stephen's artistic career has not yet come to much. Stephen also argues that Mary was technically the child of her son: 'was but creature of her creature' (U 511). In the midst of Stephen's efforts, Punch Costello begins to sing a bawdy song and Nurse Quigley enters the room and delivers the second warning as she angrily chastises the men for their inappropriate behaviour. Rather than observe the warning, Costello curses her and the men go on to discuss bizarre sexual wedding ceremonies and Stephen launches into a lewd poem while Costello returns to his bawdy song.

Outside Alec Bannon has just arrived from Mullingar and he meets Buck Mulligan and they make their way to the hospital for a drink. Bannon is in pursuit of Milly Bloom and describes her as 'a skittish heifer, big of her age and beef to the heel' (U 519). This is followed by an unpleasant sexualised conversation centred on cows as they commit further sacrilege. The fact that Milly is Bloom's daughter adds layers of horror.

When they arrive at the hospital, Buck hands around mock business cards that advertise: '*Mr Malachi Mulligan. Fertiliser and incubator. Lambay Island*' (U 525). He plans to set up a fertilizing farm and to offer his dutiful yeoman services for the fecundation of any female. It is difficult to imagine much demand for these particular services. And on they go. Eventually, Bannon shares his new love interest without realizing that she is Bloom's daughter and the men go on to discuss condoms.

These conversations in the waiting room are ridiculous and while they can be comical in places, they are underpinned by a deep-rooted misogyny. In this place, the objectification and denigration of women is particularly misplaced and the underlying sexual immaturity of the men's conversation is deftly exposed. The labour of women giving birth contrasts starkly with the men's hopeless efforts to grapple with issues of reproduction. The men are all talk while the women give birth.

Both Stephen and Bloom offer a challenge to the contemporary notions of gender that underpin the waiting room conversations. When the men's bawdy conversation is interrupted by the thunder clap representing the storm created by Zeus to kill the men who had slaughtered the oxen of the sun, Stephen is petrified: 'Loud on the left Thor thundered: in anger awful the hammerhurler. Came now the storm that hist his heart' (U 515). After all the male bravado he is revealed as deeply insecure and terrified of his sinful past: 'the voice of god that was in a very grievous rage that he would presently lift his arm up and spill their souls for their abuses and for their spillings done' (U 518).

Bloom in turn has wandered around Dublin all day, but apart from placing an ad in the paper appears to have achieved little of note. For all his innovation in business there is an aching loneliness in his life. His reflections on his past life are infused with melancholy and years of sexual dysfunction have contributed to the breakdown of his marriage. The Blooms' marriage is contrasted with the Purefoys': Mrs Purefoy's husband is happy at home with his eight children and while the men might laugh at him, 'the old bucko [...] could still knock another child out of her' (U 534).

Yet alongside these worldly failures, Bloom's character is revealed as far more impressive than the other men in the waiting room, in ways that are at variance with traditional constructions of masculinity. The antithesis of a military hero, Bloom is humble and caring – his concern for others and particularly women conflicts with the machismo of the archetypal warrior. He is hugely empathetic and shows great kindness to those around him. As he enters Holles Street at the beginning of the chapter, Bloom apologizes to Nurse Callan for not greeting her when he last saw her in town and is saddened to learn that an acquaintance, Dr O'Hare, has died and they share a moment 'in wanhope, sorrowing with one another' (U 503). He remains sober when the men are getting drunk and remains attuned to the suffering of women in labour. Bloom is a gentle Odysseus – the one who doesn't commit sacrilege by demeaning women with gratuitous insults. He has no sword or white horse, he endures no glittering battle, but his basic decency and independent humanity set him apart.

When Nurse Callan enters the waiting room and calls the medical student Dixon out as he is needed on the delivery ward where Mina Purefoy has finally given birth to a boy, Costello calls her a monstrous fine bit of cowflesh and suggests that Dixon has practised his bedside manner with her. Bloom is nauseated by this 'missing link' and contends that 'those who create themselves wits at the cost of female delicacy' are beneath 'proper breeding' (U 553). We see Nurse Callan not as the other men in the waiting room do, but as Bloom does – a dignified character that exudes an air of authority. She had been Bloom's former landlord some years earlier when the Blooms had been struggling financially and had sublet a room in Nurse Callan's house on Holles Street.

Incidentally, it is perhaps no surprise that this kind of strong, independent nurse would feature in 'Oxen of the Sun'. At the time that *Ulysses* was being written, Irish nationalism was organizing, culminating in the Easter Rising of 1916. Cumann na mBan played a central role in preparing for the rising, and a number of female medical students played a prominent role in the events of Easter Week. Elizabeth O'Farrell carried the white flag of surrender around the rebel strongholds at great risk and later trained in Holles Street as a midwife. Although no women were executed in 1916, a number were imprisoned for their part in the rising and bravely endured both the fighting and the appalling conditions of incarceration. When the Free State was ultimately formed in 1922 – the year in which *Ulysses* was published – women were rewarded for their efforts by effective exclusion from public life. It would be six decades before the Irish Dáil would contain more than ten women.

Alongside the medical characters and symbolic use of pregnancy and birth, the episode in the 'House of Horne' (so called by Joyce because Sir Andrew Horne was Master of Holles Street from 1894 to 1925) also discussed substantive medical issues that would be relevant in Irish life for decades. Albeit in drunken conversation, the characters engage in their own lively debates on the nature of sex, birth and obstetric care. At one point, the 'right witty' scholars are discussing whether doctors should save the mother or the baby in a difficult childbirth. They generally agree that it's better to save the mother and 'the world was now right evil governed' as doctors prefer to save the baby. Stephen argues that Catholics prefer this as the infant goes to limbo and the mother to purgatory. He also contends that Catholics oppose contraception because they think people are simply a means of reproduction and they oppose abortion because the fetus acquires a soul in the second month. Bloom quips that the church prefers to let the mother die because they make money from both baptism and funerals.

This conversation was indeed prescient. The Irish Free State was a state in which Catholic teaching and state policy were deeply intertwined, particularly in the arena of women's health and reproductive rights. Arguably one of the most egregious laws passed in the Free State was the Criminal Law Amendment Act of 1935, which decreed that the procurement or sale of contraceptives was a criminal offence. It had a long tail and few will forget the spectre of the Irish state taking action against the Irish Family Planning Association for the illegal sale of condoms at the Virgin Megastore in Dublin in 1991. Interestingly, in 1904 and prior to 1935, contraception was available in Ireland, and the men discuss the procurement of a condom 'as snug a cloak of the French fashion as ever kept a lady from wetting' (U 530).

Decades after the drunken men in 'Oxen of the Sun' debated whether a baby or a mother should be saved, Ireland grappled with a related question in 1983. Fearing the introduction of abortion to Ireland, powerful lobbies put pressure on two successive governments to hold a referendum for a constitutional amendment that would effectively confer equal right to life to the mother and the fetus and thus make it virtually impossible to legislate for termination of pregnancy in Ireland.

This amendment created huge difficulty for women and clinicians caring for women in the context of maternal risk, women's physical autonomy and the compassionate management of fatal fetal anomaly. Ultimately, this amendment was removed following a 2018 referendum, paving the way for subsequent legislation permitting termination of pregnancy in restricted circumstances.

Central to 'Oxen of the Sun' is the protracted labour of Mina Purefoy, with Nurse Callan telling Bloom that she has 'seen many births of women but never was none so hard as was that woman's birth' (U 504). On hearing that she is having a long and very difficult labour, Bloom 'felt with wonder women's woe in the travail they have of motherhood' (U 504). Later, as he sits in the waiting room, he hears a woman cry out in one of the delivery rooms and hopes that Mina Purefoy will not be too much longer in labour and he reflects on the suffering women face in childbirth: '[w]oman's woe with wonder pondering' (U 507). Prolonged labour is a relatively common problem in childbirth, affecting first labours particularly, and is caused most commonly by inefficient uterine activity, abnormal fetal position such as occiput posterior (so-called 'stargazer') or obstructed labour associated with a baby that is too big to navigate the maternal pelvis. The first caesarean section was carried out in the NMH in 1901 for a prolonged and obstructed labour in a woman with a contracted pelvis related to rickets. She survived and was discharged home after a mere thirty days.

Four decades after the publication of *Ulysses*, the NMH was to become a world leader in the management of prolonged labour and elements of the treatment protocol developed in the early 1960s are practised all over the world today. The underlying philosophy is based on the prevention of prolonged labour in nulliparous women with singleton pregnancies and cephalic (baby is head first) presentations. Labour should last no more than twelve hours. The accurate diagnosis of labour is of critical importance and the protocol includes one-to-one midwifery care in labour and antenatal classes that educate women in relation to what happens to their bodies during labour. If nulliparous labour is slow, oxytocin is used to ensure an efficient uterine contraction. Like 'Oxen of the Sun', the AML manual is divided into three sections, with the first section examining key aspects of labour, the second section containing visual records and the third examining perinatal outcomes.

The language of the AML manual avoids technical and Latinate terms because they 'frequently serve as a cloak that obscures true meaning'. Valuable as that might be, it is open to other critiques. In one section the manual lays out the role of mothers: 'An expectant mother owes it to herself, her husband and her child [...] to be well briefed [...] The disruptive effect of one disorganized and frightened woman in a delivery unit extends far beyond her individual comfort and safety and there should be no hesitation in telling her so [...]' For all the misogyny in 'Oxen of the Sun', on hearing of Mina Purefoy's predicament from Nurse Callan, Bloom is moved to empathize rather than instruct in relation to women's suffering in labour. I think the manual's language might reasonably be described as a parody of a paternalistic style and it might be time for a revision.

It is worth noting in this context a fascinating exchange of outcome data from the NMH that became the subject of a somewhat erudite row contained in a series of papers in the *American Journal of Obstetrics and Gynaecology* during the 1980s. The discussion focussed on appropriate rates of caesarean section (CS) and prolonged labour. These papers explored the ability of AML protocols to prevent prolonged labour using oxytocin while maintaining low CS rates without compromising the baby's outcome. The papers went back and forth, including 'An Answer to the House of Horne' by Professor Ken Leveno and subsequently 'A Response from the House of Horne' from NMH. The final retort was contained in the 'House of Horne Revisited'. Despite the fact that the papers debated the management of prolonged labour, Mina Purefoy did not make the title.

There is no longer any waiting room for men at NMH – indeed there are hardly any male bathrooms in the cramped, outdated facilities, which retain some of the long wards that would have been commonplace in hospitals in 1904. Nowadays, it is unusual for a father not to be present at a birth, although the manual, which is still in print, suggests, 'The extent to which husbands should be influenced to remain with their wives during the entire course of labour and delivery remains an open question. Experience suggests that women have far more to gain from the presence of a female companion who is not only sympathetic but also well informed...' In my experience, most men are profoundly moved by being present at the birth of their children and it is wonderful as an obstetrician to see a couple welcome their baby into the world. The inability of some fathers to attend the birth of their children during the Covid-19 pandemic was a source of great distress.

Thankfully, women no longer labour for three consecutive days. At the time of the publication of *Ulysses*, caesarean sections were rare and fraught with morbidity and mortality, especially before the introduction of antibiotics, blood transfusion and safe anaesthesia. When the AML was introduced in the early 1960s, section rates at NMH were 5 per cent. They are now around 30 per cent, and while rising CS rates globally remain a cause of great concern, perinatal outcomes have improved dramatically, although this is largely due to advances in neonatal care. Nonetheless, in all the celebration of new life, grief is never far away, and people continue to mourn babies who have died. Elements of the physiology of pregnancy and birth remain elusive. Midwives continue to care for their patients with extraordinary skill and contrary to their portrayal in 'Oxen of the Sun', doctors and medical students do not sit drinking with friends as they await a birth. Nowadays, doctors are increasingly female, and it is not at all unusual to find an entirely female cast in the delivery room or operating theatre.

Sadly, misogyny continues to flourish, and especially in the cowardly anonymity and scarcely literate language of social media that might warrant additional parody if Joyce were writing now. The worst excesses of the waiting room conversations are amplified daily in current social media through hateful language that persistently denigrates women. The unacceptably high prevalence of gender-based violence today comes at huge cost to women and society and should serve as a daily reminder of how misogyny can harm and kill women. The tale of the destruction of the oxen of the sun remains a salutary one and Joyce's deft exposure of the deep-rooted misogyny that pervades the men's conversations in this chapter is sadly as relevant today as it was on 16 June 1904.

Wars continue to be fought around the globe and human relationships continue to thrive and fail. Joyce would surely be delighted with the rich legacy of his writing. *Ulysses* will continue to bring forth conversation, thought and literary endeavour for centuries to come and for many more years than an average human lifespan. In this way the tension between artistic creation and procreation is soothed. Words, whether spoken or written, will continue to help us explore the lives we live, but however brilliantly assembled, words will never tell the whole story. And among all the words, babies will continue to be born, and all kinds of different lives lived. Ultimately, with the safe arrival of Mina's son, 'Oxen of the Sun' concludes on a note of hope and redemption, just as the sun and rain follow the thunder that terrified the men. 'The air without is impregnated with raindew moisture, life essence celestial [...] God's air, the Allfather's air' (U 554).

Circe

Night–Rule in Nighttown

CAITRIONA LALLY

Caitriona Lally grew up in Dublin and graduated from Trinity College. She is author of *Eggshells* (a novel about a flâneuse wandering in post-crash Dublin) and of *Wunderland*. She is the winner of the 2018 Rooney Prize and the 2019 Lannan Fellowship for Fiction.

Contrary to parenting advice, I put my two toddlers in front of the television when they rise early, to delay fully engaged parenting. Some TV shows are wholesome, educational and utterly dull, but the ones I try to orchestrate an addiction to are either wild and funny or magical and beautiful. The kinds of shows you might imagine occurring to a trippy genius in a rush of hallucinatory inspiration. The 'Circe', or Nighttown, episode of *Ulysses* hits all four of my criteria: wild, funny, magical and beautiful.

Although I studied English at third level, I fled from *Ulysses* because it seemed to demand too much time and effort to make a decent go of it. Twenty years after graduating, I published my first novel, *Eggshells*, based on a female protagonist, Vivian, who believes she's a changeling and walks the streets of Dublin looking for a portal to the Otherworld. Interviewers and reviewers asked if I was influenced by *Ulysses*, a question I was uneasy with. I hadn't read *Ulysses* when I was writing *Eggshells*: if I had, the similarity of the setting would probably have caused me to lose courage, feary of looking like I was trying to emulate or in some way respond to Joyce. As many Dublin citizens can claim, Joyce had lived near me, Leopold Bloom's house on Eccles Street is within spitting distance of my house, and my protagonist walked similar routes to Bloom. But when I eventually read *Ulysses*, the 'Circe' episode stood out for me as a stand-alone slice of chaos, one I was thrilled to have an excuse to delve into again.

Some Representations of the Mythical Circe in Other Literature

1. *Homer's* The Odyssey

Homer's magical language shows Circe's soft power in luring sailors into her palace on the island of Aeaea with her 'spellbinding' voice, weaving an 'enchanting' web on her loom. She serves Odysseus's men a feast in which is concealed a potion and uses her wand, her hard power, to turn them into pigs. Hermes had given Odysseus moly, a plant-talisman that saves him from Circe's powers, and she is in awe of him for not succumbing to her spell: 'Never has any other man withstood my potion, never [...] You have a mind in you no magic can enchant' (Book X). After a year as Circe's lover on the island, Odysseus asks to go home. Circe tells him to first travel down to the Underworld to consult the ghost of Tiresias, the blind gender-bending Theban prophet, for advice on journeying safely home. Odysseus meets his dead mother in Hades, like the scene in *Ulysses*'s 'Circe' where Stephen Dedalus's mother comes back to life in a Miss Havisham-style bridal get-up.

2. *Ovid's* Metamorphoses

Ovid calls Circe 'the dread goddess' (Book XIV) who hides the transformative herbs inside the sailors' feast to sedate them before turning them into pigs. Her palace is 'thronged' with the victims she had turned into beasts.

3. *Shakespeare's* A Midsummer Night's Dream

The form of a dream-play is similar to the structure of the 'Circe' episode. The character Titania, daughter of a Titan, refers to either the huntress Diana who turned Actaeon into a stag or Circe who turned men into pigs. The fantasy elements that take place in the woods on midsummer night are transformative, with Bottom's head turned into an ass's head and Titania duped into loving the new bestial Bottom. Bloom's head in a pillory has ass's ears.

4. *Louise Glück's poem 'Circe's Power'*

> I never turned anyone into a pig.
> Some people are pigs; I make them
> Look like pigs.
> I'm sick of your world
> That lets the outside disguise the inside.

These lines began to change my thinking about Circe. I had viewed her as a witch, luring innocent men to her palace to be turned into beasts on a whim. The older literature I read hadn't examined Circe's motivations from *her* perspective, just the consequences for the men. Glück's poem made me question *why* Circe turned these visitors into pigs, how had they behaved *before* the spell. Like a Gaelic football match watched on television versus live in the stadium: on TV you might only see the dramatic act that causes a player to get a yellow or red card, in the stadium you witness the player's opponent chipping away at him for the duration of the match before he loses temper and lashes out in full view.

5. *Madeline Miller's novel* Circe

Miller takes this notion of culpability to a level where the reader wants the men not only turned into pigs but dismembered and roasted. In this version, the obvious threat to a solitary woman of a gang of warfaring sailors landing on her island is portrayed in a horrific rape scene. Miller's Circe manages to stop the entire crew from raping her by turning them into pigs, and pre-emptively turns all men forever after who enter her palace into pigs. It builds on Glück's notion of the innateness of the pig-like behaviour, the magic spell bringing out what is already there, compared to the male-scribed myth of innocent men randomly pigged by a witch.

The Circe of Miller and Glück made me look at Bella Cohen and her prostitutes afresh. A brothel scene written from the perspective of a man is going to give a certain point of view. Bella, the Circe equivalent in *Ulysses*, and the younger prostitutes are portrayed as sly, bawdy, greedy, but a novel from the inside of the brothel might show how the women's prior experiences have coloured their behaviour.

Piggishness

The piggish theme recurs throughout the episode, from the first description of Bloom: 'the bonham eyes and fatchuck cheekchops of Jollypoldy the rixdix doldy' (U 566). When Jacky Caffrey runs into him he is 'on weak hams', he buys pig's crubeen and sheep's trotter and then says, 'Eat it and get all pigsticky' (U 580). Mrs Yelverton Barry (one of Bloom's accusers) calls him 'Pig dog'

(U 594), and while he is in the pillory for sexual misdeeds, the Artane Orphans chant, 'You hig, you hog' (U 616) at him. The Sins of the Past list Bloom's perversions, calling him 'the gross boar' (U 649). Bloom himself says 'O, I have been a perfect pig' (U 660). In the brothel, Bloom changes to a pig-like woman, snuffling and rooting on the ground, threatened by Bella to kill and eat the Bloom-pig. This all links to Glück and Miller's Circe, whose spell unleashes the essence of what's innate in the men; Bella-Circe draws out an existing piggishness.

Worlds Apart

Nighttown in *Ulysses*, the island of Aeaea where the mythical sorceress Circe lives, and the wood a league outside the town in *A Midsummer Night's Dream* are islands or pseudo-islands where anything can happen. Characters leave their usual contexts and move into an adjacent fantasy space where they are tested and challenged and act without society's constraints. Reality has shifted and boundaries have dissolved. There is a sense of a last hurrah in the middle three acts of *A Midsummer Night's Dream*, a night of sexual shenanigans at a hen or stag party before order being brought by a wedding, a kind of what-goes-on-tour-stays-on-tour before the confines of marriage. Nighttown has a similar function: anything can happen in this gothically grotesque dreamscape. It is David Lynchian, extreme, nightmarish. The macabre and monstrous are the norm, there are apparitions and spectres, ghosts and ghouls. Meaning is reversed or given new applications: there is a satanic black mass; Bloom carries a wizened old potato as a talisman (moly); the prostitutes Biddy the Clap and Cunty Kate see knights duelling chivalrously for their honour instead of drunk soldiers gunning for a punch-up.

Nighttown is carnivalesque, as in Mikhail Bakhtin's definition, subverting norms through humour and chaos. The episode seems to fit into Bakhtin's four categories of the carnival sense of the world: familiar and free interaction between people, eccentric behaviour, uniting everything that is usually separate, and profanation.

Time

It's just before twelve o'clock midnight in the Monto, the witching hour when magic is at its strongest and anything can happen. On the stroke of midnight, Cinderella's beautiful dress turns back to rags, her carriage to a pumpkin. It's a time of transformation, of magical potential; Theseus in *A Midsummer Night's Dream* calls it 'fairy time'. It's a liminal time, the chronological equivalent of a thin place, crossing the threshold between two days. Oberon asks Puck, 'What night-rule now about this haunted grove?' There is night-rule in Nighttown, where anything can and does happen. In Freud's personality theory, the id is the unconscious energy that aims to satisfy basic needs, urges and desires, and Bloom's id is on show in 'Circe'. Freud called the id 'a chaos, a cauldron full of seething excitations', stating that there's 'nothing in the id which corresponds to the idea of time'. This is apparent in the dreamy sense of timelessness in 'Circe', where there are overlapping chaoses, dreams and realities.

Stephen and Bloom spend one hour in Nighttown, around midnight; Odysseus spends one year in Aeaea with Circe; and the characters spend one night in the woods in *A Midsummer Night's Dream*.

Portals

The entrance to Nighttown feels like a portal transporting people between worlds; Bloom calls it entering 'hellsgates' (U 578), reinforcing the sense of it being elsewhere, other. In one of Bloom's hallucinations, the recently deceased Paddy Dignam returns to the Underworld through the portal of a coalhole. Bloom's grandfather, Virag, returns from the Underworld through the chimney flue that he 'chutes rapidly' (U 628) down like a macabre Santa Claus. He is 'sausaged into several overcoats' (U 628) as well as a brown mackintosh, a Fran Dempsey Fortycoats character from the 1980s children's TV show. King Edward VII appears in an archway, a liminal space between life and death; the real Edward had also reputedly used the tunnels as portals between the Monto brothels and the outside world. In the nightmarish pandemonium scene at the end of 'Circe', a portal to hell opens: 'A chasm opens with a noiseless yawn' (U 695).

Portals have fascinated me since reading *The Lion, the Witch and the Wardrobe*, and I made many attempts as a child to find the door in the back of the wardrobe. I thought that if I could just catch it off guard, I might be able to find Narnia and, more importantly, that exquisite Turkish Delight the Ice Queen gave Edmund. My novel's character Vivian walks around Dublin looking for thin places, where the barrier between this world and the next are more permeable. She goes to Middle Third in North Dublin in an effort to find a gateway to Middle Earth, and tries to find a holy well in Nassau Street on May Day (a thin place at an especially thin time) but ends up circling sunwise three times around disused public toilets instead. The failure of the hunt was what interested me most.

Will-O'-The-Wisp and Hellish Links

The traffic lights at the entrance to Nighttown are 'red and green will-o'-the-wisps' (U 561), the ghostly light over bogs and marshes that mislead travellers and send them astray. In Irish mythology, the will-o'-the-wisp (named Jack or Will) is doomed to haunt the bogs with a light as punishment for a misdeed. It contains an ember from the fires of hell, to illuminate his way through the twilight world to which lost souls are forever condemned; it wouldn't take much of a stretch to compare the drunk men visiting Nighttown to these condemned lost souls. Jack places the ember in a carved turnip to serve as a lantern. Growing up in 1980s Ireland, before pumpkins became widely available, my mother carved unwieldy turnip-meat into a Jack o' lantern, which we brought trick-or-treating at Halloween. In *A Midsummer Night's Dream*, Puck, the mischievous trickster who causes all the mistaken love matches and orchestrates chaos, is likened to a will-o'-the-wisp. And in Milton's *Paradise Lost*, Satan is compared to a will-o'-the-wisp when he leads Eve to the Tree of Knowledge.

There are other hellish echoes in 'Circe', with reference to Lucifer, Satan, Beelzebub. The pandemonium scene near the end of the episode is sparked from the fire Bloom had seen across the Liffey at the start of the episode, in the same way that a mundane event from reality becomes warped into something huger and scarier in a nightmare. It's a genuine horror of a scene, with an eclipse, the city's dead rising up, a chasm opening and people jumping into the void, but it's also reminiscent of a child's bad dream, with dragon's teeth rain and witches on broomsticks.

Bloom's journey to the underworld of his imagination, meeting people from his past whom he's wronged, reminded me of Dante's *Inferno*, with Dante being guided through hell by Virgil to see how sinners are treated. Similarly, I thought of Dickens's *A Christmas Carol* and the film *It's a Wonderful Life*, in which Scrooge and George revisit their past lives. Bloom is a more isolated traveller, however; these other characters have guides.

The Monto, Past and Present

Nighttown is Dublin's Monto, the largest red light district in Europe in the late nineteenth and early twentieth centuries. The Monto was, according to the 1885 *Encyclopaedia Britannica*, 'the worst slum in Europe', a square mile enclosed by Talbot Street, Amiens Street, Gardiner Street and Gloucester Street. The brothels were known as the kips, the area the digs or hells' gates, and the madams as the kip-keepers. Circe's Bella Cohen is modelled on a real kip-keeper of the same name who ran a brothel at 82 Mecklenburgh Street (Joyce places her at 81). The real Bella Cohen provided services on the kinkier end of the spectrum, which is possibly why he landed on her for a madam.

I looked at the Monto on various Dublin maps, from Rocque's 1756 map to a recent Ordnance Survey map. Montgomery Street, after which the Monto was named, began as World's End Lane in the nineteenth century, a harbinger of its grim future. Old Rope Walk on Rocque's 1773 map is now Gardiner Street; The Strand morphed into Amiens Street; and North Cope Street and Moland Street became Talbot Street. Great Martin's Lane became Mecklenburgh Street in the eighteenth century before turning into Tyrone Street in the nineteenth century and Railway Street today. Mabbot Street became Corporation Street and is currently James Joyce Street. So:

Old Rope Walk – Gardiner Street
World's End Lane – Montgomery Street – Foley Street
Mabbot Street – Corporation Street – James Joyce Street
Great Martin's Lane – Mecklenburgh Street – Tyrone Street
   – Railway Street
Gloucester Street – Sean McDermott Street

The changing of street names and mixing up of house numbers adds to the shape-shifting feel of the area, a warren where you don't know where you stand (both figuratively and literally, if rumours of secret tunnels are to be believed). I know from researching my novel in Dublin's 2011 streets that even a decade later, some of my references to buildings or bus routes are dated. The extension of the Luas tramline north in 2017 changed the landscape, whereas Joyce's tramlines at the entrance to Nighttown (setting the Gothic tone with 'skeleton tracks') have since been demolished. Hunting for any remnants of street names from Joyce's time, I could only find Gloucester Square and Place, Mabbot Lane and Beaver Street, where Bloom stops to watch the fight. Mabbot Street's current existence is as a bus stop, bus stop 4380 on Gardiner Street.

I attempted a literary pilgrimage around the Monto, following the shadows of Stephen and Bloom from Connolly Station at Amiens Street and crossing onto Talbot Street. The overhead railway bridge takes the road at a slant, the same bridge the 'Circe' lads walked under. There's a hardware shop where Bloom went to Antonio Rabaiotti's and apartments at Olhousens, where he bought the animal feet. Le Bon Crubeen restaurant is presumably an homage to Bloom's pig's trotter, bought ten doors down. There's a new pub on the corner where Bloom stood to look south at the fire: this pub went from Cormack's in Joyce's time to Mother Kelly's to 74 Talbot Street today. On the corner of Talbot and James Joyce Street (Mabbot Street in Joyce's time), where O'Beirne's pub stood, is an office block housing Irish Water, so there's still a liquid link.

I headed down James Joyce Street and turned right onto Railway Street, the site of Bella Cohen's brothel. High old walls display uplifting phrases and hopeful murals and a girl on a swing, and there are white crosses on the walls of the former Magdalene Laundry that Bloom pretended to be visiting on a charity mission. I wondered whether taking a photo or writing some notes would be more obtrusive – there's something uncomfortably patronizing about intruding on a neighbourhood that has never experienced wealth to document it. Hastening my unease, a group who had seemed absorbed in an argument about money owed suddenly became united in asking what exactly I was taking a photo of. Not being able to explain even to myself what I was looking for, I moved quickly on to Buckingham Street, known in my family for trips into town in the car in the 1980s. We would park at the Macushla – a former ballroom turned into a bingo hall (now a credit union) – which became a byword in my family for being miles from your intended destination. There were lock-hard men – that benign form of extortion in which men in peaked caps 'helped' drivers to park their cars by shouting 'Lock hard!' before taking a donation to mind the car, although where this threat came from was never made clear. Rounding by Amiens Street to come back where I started, where Leopold Bloom and Stephen Dedalus started, I realized I had found nothing of Circean note so I took a sugary figary and had coffee and a cinnamon bun. Bloom would have approved.

Commemorative Plaques

In one of Bloom's fantasies, the Late Lord Mayor Harrington proclaims, 'That the house in which he was born be ornamented with a commemorative tablet and that the thoroughfare hitherto known as Cow Parlour off Cork Street be henceforth designated Boulevard Bloom' (U 601–2). Given that excess humility didn't seem to be an issue for Joyce, I wonder if he suspected a street would indeed be named after him (as well as a bridge and a couple of statues) and that commemorative plaques would adorn the many houses he lived in around Dublin. The Joyce family lived in around eighteen houses, moving to cheaper and cheaper houses as James's father's fortunes fell. I live around the corner from the house on 7 St Peter's Terrace (now Road), where Joyce's mother, May, died. The commemorative plaque is next door on 5 St Peter's Road: either it's a mistake or the number of the house has changed as well as the name of the road. If I lived there, I'd like to know which side of the wall May Joyce's ghost frequented.

1901 Census

I hunted in the North Dock area of Dublin's 1901 census for hints of the Monto's past. In line with my other thwarted seekings, I couldn't find Bella Cohen's 'disorderly house' but I found the house of Eliza Mack, another famous kip-keeper, at 85 Lower Tyrone Street. Mrs Mack is listed as Head of Family with five female lodgers in their twenties, and a servant in her thirties. The madam is the Lodging Housekeeper, while the younger women's occupations are given as housemaid, dressmaker, milliner, lacemaker and waitress. I found a clump of houses in the lower numbers of Lower Tyrone Street with a similar setup: several unmarried female lodgers in their twenties with a middle-aged female Lodging Housekeeper, mostly widowed, and a servant in her thirties. There's something quietly devastating about seeing the names of these young women who likely lived tough, tough lives; it makes the story very real.

Lists

I firmly believe that few situations in life cannot be improved on by making a list, and I'm not sure it's within my capabilities to write a novel without a list-obsessed character. I think list-loving Joyce would approve of this list of the lists in 'Circe', a kind of meta-list. There are lists of: Bloom's crimes and misdemeanours; items distributed by Bloom's bodyguard at the parade (within that list there's a list of the World's Twelve Worst Books); suicide methods of attractive women for Bloom; 'objects of little or no commercial value' (U 612) being thrown at Bloom (a reversal of items distributed by Bloom's bodyguard a few pages earlier: when good lists go bad); valuable items collected by a rich American for the diseased and pregnant Bloom; adjectives describing the grotesque Ben Dollard; Bloom's teenage fantasies; dance moves performed in the brothel; horses in a race; items Bloom is pelted with (again), Bloom's accusers, who are chasing him (including the almost Twitter hashtaggy compound word 'andsomemarried womanrubbedagainstwidebehindinClonskeatram' U 686); and birds of prey swooping in during the pandemonium scene.

Disclaimer: None of my lists are exhaustive. They have grown with each reading and could possibly grow with more readings but time has been exhausted.

Sex

Joyce had a fairly vigorous sex life with Nora Barnacle, as evidenced by his letters, and it might not be too wild a guess to suggest some of Bloom's fantasies in this episode had a basis in truth. The recurring pig theme from 'Circe' is reflected in Joyce's letter to Nora in which he tells her he fantasizes about flinging her down and 'fuck[ing] you up behind like a hog riding a sow'. He also begs her in a later letter to 'flog, flog, flog me viciously on my naked quivering flesh!' This plays out in the masochism scene in Bella's brothel. His fantasies about his wife farting, on him or at him I couldn't quite get from the prepositions of the letter, are realized in 'Circe' with Bloom being turned on by Bella farting on him.

List of sexual practices, fantasies, kinks and fetishes mentioned:

Eprochtophilia, coprophilia, voyeurism, fisting, transvest-itism, public masturbation, foot fetish (podophilia), sadomasochism in the form of debasement (being forced to clean pisspots thoroughly or drink the contents (urophilia)), hair-pulling, slapping and whipping (impact play), facesitting or queening, frotteurism, watching while his wife has sex with her lover (cuckolding or troilism), mpreg (the fantasy of male pregnancy, which led me into a fascinating Internet labyrinth). There are other paraphilias I struggled to find the official definition of, for example, being turned on by sitting where a woman recently sat. When I lived in Japan, my boss told me to lock my bicycle indoors because there had been several thefts of women's bike saddles by a local man who was turned on by the same thing as Bloom. (The fetish of sniffing women's bike seats is called snedging or snarfing.) Researching this essay has taught me more things than I could ever have wanted to know.

Bloomusalem

With its 40,000 rooms, Bloomusalem, 'a colossal edifice with crystal roof, built in the shape of a huge pork kidney' (U 606), is Bloom's hallucinatory, megalomaniacal messianic version of New Jerusalem. In the Bible, New Jerusalem is a cube the size of 12,000 stadia, somewhere between 1,400 and 1,500 square miles. Bloomusalem reminds me of the Crystal Palace in London's Hyde Park for the Great Exhibition of 1851, the Wizard of Oz's green glass palace in the Emerald City, and in terms of scale, Borges's infinite Library of Babel. Indeed, rereading 'Circe' many times felt like entering the Library of Babel with its labyrinthine, nonsensical segues; new pathways emerging on each reading, sending me sidelong into completely unrelated texts and seeing new connections to random things. In *Imaginary Cities*, Darran Anderson writes of New Jerusalem or Nevertown, 'Attempts to replicate the heavenly citadel on earth have predictably run aground at great human cost. Where the attempts were restricted to a lone figure they could be seen as admirable if misguided.' An epitaph for Bloom perhaps, Admirable if Misguided.

Compound Nouns

I love German compound nouns for their unwieldy ramming together of disparate words to make a longer one, with no hyphen. Joyce's compounds are similarly gloriously hyphen-free, they'd give German compound nouns a run for their money. My favourites from this chapter are the alliterative ones:

'plumpuddered' (U 659), 'silversilent summer air' (U 659), 'his mane moonfoaming' (U 675), 'clipclaps glovesilent hands' (U 678), 'liplapping loudly' (U 670), 'mangongwheeltracktrolleyglovejuggernaut' (U 580), 'Groangrousegurgling' (U 679) and 'Closeclutched swift swifter with glareblareflare scudding they scotlootshoot lumbering by. Baraabum!' (U 680).

Gender-bending

Bloom's preoccupation with gender and maternity is evident in his fantasies. As well as complaining of '[b]rainfogfag' at his time of the month, he fantasizes about motherhood in a line that I can only hear in SoCal Valley girl or Ross O'Carroll-Kelly-style Dublin 4 upspeak: 'O, I so want to be a mother' (U 614), before birthing eight children by simply being squeezed around the waist. If only it were that easy.

The casualness of Bloom's switch from male to female reminds me of Virginia Woolf's *Orlando*, published eight years after *Ulysses*. No stage direction announces Bloom is now a woman, the change in pronoun is the only hint: '*He taps her on the shoulder with his fan*' (U 644). Woolf's Orlando starts as a man, then wakes up a woman after a seven-day trance, and the change is dealt with similarly casually. 'It is enough for us to state the simple fact; Orlando was a man till the age of thirty; when he became a woman and has remained so ever since. But let other pens treat of sex and sexuality; we quit such odious subjects as soon as we can.' The fact of the gender switch doesn't matter, or the circumstances surrounding it, only the future as

337

a woman is relevant. In 'Circe', Bloom's change to a woman allows him the freedom to indulge certain fantasies and fetishes he has been suppressing, whereas Orlando is now restricted by gender, both physically with female clothes and with the loss of former wealth and freedoms. Molly's androgynous Turkish trousers in Bloom's dream ('Wore the breeches') turn him on. Mrs Breen wearing a man's coat and Mrs Dignam wearing her late husband's clothes and boots might not be about gender performativity but practicality: men's clothes are usually less restrictive and have more pockets. A few years ago, when the budget airline Ryanair announced carry-on luggage charges for anything over a small handbag, my mother sewed a 'Ryanair' jacket with eight book-size pockets, enough to hold a capsule holiday wardrobe with room for reading material.

Bloom's gender play brings to mind a contemporary novel, Andrea Lawlor's *Paul Takes the Form of a Mortal Girl*, about a shape-shifter who changes gender at will, using his power almost nonchalantly. Paul controls his body to morph into Polly, deciding on breast size and then penis size on the return transformation; he talks about the *story* he is telling with his gender and performance of gender. Paul chooses to switch genders by force of imagination – Orlando and Bloom are passively changed by forces larger than them.

Inanimate Objects and Abstract Concepts That Are Speaking Characters

Longhand and Shorthand, The Chapel of Freeman Typesetters, The Fire Brigade, The Soap, Sandstrewer's Gong, Wreaths of

Smoke, The Timepiece, The Quoits of a Bed (whose 'Jigjag, Jigajiga. Jigjag' (U 595) reminds me of the Spice Girls' 'zig-a-zig-ah' from their song 'Wannabe'), The Bells, The Kisses (from a brothelhouse), Midnight Chimes from Distant Steeples, Hollybush, Deadhand, The Buckles, The Gramaphone, The End of the World, The Beatitudes, The Fan, The Hoof, Singing Waterfall, The Sins of the Past, The Echo, Halcyon Days, The Button, The Orange Lodges and The Green Lodges, Morning Hours, Noon Hours, Twilight Hours and Night Hours, The Gasjet, Stephen's Cap, Doorhandle. The concrete nouns talking seem strange enough but when abstract nouns have opinions, things get weird. This fits with the sense that anything can happen in a dream.

Snacks

I am led by my belly. I want to know at all times where my next meal or snack will come from and how long I will have to go without eating. In my novel *Eggshells*, my protagonist, Vivian, spends a lot of time buying sweets in supermarkets, cakes in bakeries, stopping for buns in cafes, because this is how I punctuate my day. It was only when reviewers mentioned Vivian's sweet tooth – and one likened it to a childish arrested development – that I realized not everyone prioritizes food to such an extent. Bloom is a kindred spirit, however. His first thought when he gets off the train seems to be food. I can identify with the sense of snack-panic: 'On the farther side under the railway bridge Bloom appears flushed, panting, cramming bread and chocolate into a side pocket' (U565).

I have been on the opposite side of that panic – flushed and panting, cramming chocolate into my bag on the way *into* a train station. Bloom visits an ice cream shop followed by a butcher for pig's crubeen and sheep's trotter – I'm absolutely with him on the snack-preparation front, just maybe not on the choice of snacks. No journey, no matter how short, real or imaginary, is not made better with snacks.

Alice in Wonderland

At the risk of shoehorning all my obsessions into 'Circe', one of my favourite books is Lewis Carroll's *Alice's Adventures in Wonderland*. I collect versions of the book featuring different illustrators and currently host thirty-two copies. The more I read the 'Circe' episode, the more *Alice in Wonderland* comparisons hopped out at me. The rabbit-hole Alice jumps into is the portal to another world, like the hellsgates portal Bloom enters on the corner of Mabbot Street. Alice follows the White Rabbit into Wonderland the way Bloom follows Stephen into Nighttown; Alice finds herself in a long, low hall and tries various doors to see where the White Rabbit has gone; Bloom enters the Monto maze looking for the brothel Stephen has entered, 'Wildgoose chase this. Disorderly houses. Lord knows where they are gone' (U 579). Alice shape-shifts, growing and shrinking; Bloom ages, changes shape and gender. Joyce and Carroll use nonsense rhymes, wordplay and puns to test the limits of language: Alice and Bloom fall back on old songs and nursery rhymes, riddles and advertising jingles (Bloom) to keep a hold of their former reality in their new fantastical world. Both books contain a fan, a mundane prop with unusual powers: the White Rabbit's fan Alice holds causes her to shrink, and in 'Circe', Bella Cohen's fan has a riddle-speaking part and taps him on the shoulder as he turns into a woman. Also, a baby turns into a pig in *Alice in Wonderland*.

What struck me most was the similarity of the trial scenes in both texts. Both are farces, ludicrous show trials with a nightmarish sense of inevitability of guilt. The results in both cases seem to be a foregone conclusion. Both trial scenes are set in recognizable versions of the court, which twist and upend the usual legal jargon, but the content of the evidence is nonsense. The Queen of Hearts wants the sentence to be read first, the verdict afterwards. Georges Fottrell, clerk of the crown and peace in 'Circe', says, 'The accused will now make a bogus statement' (U 587). The Longhand and Shorthand characters in 'Circe', writing in their notebooks, remind me of the incompetent animal jurors in *Alice in Wonderland*, writing their names on their slates because they'll have forgotten them by the end of the trial.

Alice's sudden regrowth to full size coincides with her realization that the characters are nothing but playing cards and she wakes up. Bloom's back trouser button pops, causing him to straighten up and awaken from the fantasy. Both characters regain their courage: Alice defies the king's evidence, Bloom defies Bella and demands his moly back from Zoe. Both leave their fantasy land when they've stood up, literally and metaphorically, to the illogic; the enchantment is broken with their confidence.

Language Failing

In this episode, language often fails to convey intent, or unintentionally conveys intent by its failure. Bloom's sentences are short and stilted, sparse and bitty, full of staccato stop-start non-sequiturs. He uses the kind of out-of-context, unconnected speech you hear from someone sleep-talking in a dream that is so chillingly nonsensical you doubt the sanity of the speaker: to Mrs Breen, 'Don't give me away. Walls have hears. How do you do? It's ages since I. You're looking splendid. Absolutely it. Seasonable weather we are having this time of year' (U 572). He falls back on stock phrases and clichés when he's caught rotten by Mrs Breen in a red light district, but gets them that little bit wrong, malapropping constantly.

His excuses for being in Nighttown reveal a desperation to be seen as a righteous doer of good deeds: 'Rescue of fallen women Magdalen asylum. I am the secretary...' (U 573). Ellipses are used frequently to show the inadequacy of speech; when emotion is heightened, for example as Bloom is being cuckolded by Blazes, the ellipses run riot. His hesitancy is also reminiscent of dreams in which you're unable to scream or speak up for yourself.

The failure of language to spare him in the trial scene is used to darkly comic effect. Bloom is incapable of defending himself against the accusation of sexual misdeeds against his servant Mary Driscoll; he mumbles incoherently, talks inaudibly, gives long unintelligible speeches, becomes 'mute, shrunken, carbonised' (U 618) – a common nightmare in which we're unable to defend ourselves. His own rambling defence and his barrister J. J. O'Molloy's defence arguments are comically inadequate in their extensiveness: that Bloom is a baby, simple-minded, hallucinating, the victim of a conspiracy, has shipwreck and somnambulism in his family. O'Molloy's argument that 'there was no attempt at carnally knowing' and 'intimacy did not occur' (U 589) reminds me of Bill Clinton's hollow 'I did not have sexual relations with that woman' letter-of-the-law denial of sex with Monica Lewinsky, and I'm similarly uncomfortable with the bang of entitlement here. There seems to be an assumption that Bloom's class and status in comparison with his accuser's not only discredits Mary Driscoll's evidence but implies guilt on her part. The defence that Bloom didn't repeat his advances is probably the most damning; if O'Molloy was my barrister, I'd be looking for my money back.

Different Language Registers

'Circe' shows its author's sense of fun with language, using poetic stage directions, e.g. *'Bloom in gloom, looms down'* (U 700) like the children's phonics books *Mouse Moves House* or *Raccoon on the Moon*. Joyce references parlour games, ditties, riddles, hymns, advertising jingles (possibly his own earworms – the 'would Fleetwood would, would Fleetwood' ad slogan from years ago has permanently lodged in my brain), children's rhymes, myths and legends, legal jargon, political lingo, academic puff-speak, romantic babble, baby babble, farmer/pig-breeder jargon, newsboys shouting nonsensical headlines that read like April Fool's Day jokes ('Result of the rocking-horse races. Sea serpent in the royal canal' U 623).

343

Changeling Rudy

In the final scene, Bloom's son, Rudy, who died at eleven days, appears. He is '*a fairy boy of eleven, a changeling, kidnapped*' (U 702), given the same amount of years as days he actually lived. Dressed in an Eton suit with jewels for buttons and glass shoes, fairytale-style attire, Rudy has crossed the boundary between worlds. In the myth of the changeling, the fairy child must go back to the fairy world in order for the real child to return. There is something gut-wrenching about the vision of a child who is Rudy but not Rudy, self-contained and tragically unreachable. The stage direction ('*gazes unseeing into Bloom's eye and goes on reading, kissing, smiling*' U 703) took the wind from my lungs when I read it the first time: a stranger ghost-child returning from the dead, rather than providing comfort, would surely only increase the pain of loss. Like a benevolent version of the returned child in Stephen King's *Pet Sematary*, Rudy is resurrected by his grieving father's force of will, but Bloom can't bring back the child he wants. This is a quiet, tender ending to a riotous, tumultuous episode.

Eumaeus

Leopold Bloom, Master–Economist

DAVID MCWILLIAMS

David McWilliams is an economist, podcaster, adjunct professor at Trinity College Dublin, and a columnist with *The Irish Times*. He is the author of five books including the bestseller *The Pope's Children* and co-founded the Dalkey Book Festival and Kilkenomics. David is ranked fifth most influential economist in the world, with a knack for making economics digestible for the everyman.

On the Irish sea, the warmer it is, the bigger the waves. Winds from the South Atlantic blow upwards from the Caribbean. Hot easterly air, from the African equator, creates cyclones out in the Atlantic Ocean, which suddenly whip up, changing direction, driving a giant force towards Ireland. These south-westerlies rush vertically into the St George's Channel, through the gap dividing Cornwall from Wexford, between the larger and smaller island, making landfall in western Scotland. That's a lot of water churning around with no land breakers to sap its energy for thousands of miles. Between Ireland and Britain, millions of cubic litres of turbulent water are funnelled into the Irish Sea, a narrow briny bottleneck. If a vessel clings to the Irish coast, the island offers protection, but the further from land you go, the choppier it gets. It doesn't get much wilder or more exposed than the open seventy-mile stretch between Dublin and North Wales.

Citing Xenophon, the world's first economist, Buck Mulligan exclaims, '*Thalassa! Thalassa!*' (U 3) to Stephen as he marvels at the power of the sea on a calm Bloomsday morning. Dublin Bay in June can be deceptive; conditions in October are a different prospect. You wouldn't fancy sailing horizontally east to west into such vertical Atlantic winds roaring their way up the channel, yet on an unseasonably warm October, a lanky twenty-seven-year-old in tennis shoes did just that. He staggers along the galley of the Holyhead to Kingstown mail boat, and pukes violently overboard. James Joyce is coming home. But why?

* * *

Five weeks earlier, in September 1909, Joyce's younger sister, Eva, visiting him in Trieste, was feeling homesick. She did however like the fact that Trieste was full of cinemas. Cinemas were all the rage. The entertainment technology was changing the world. Europeans flocked to picture houses and the theatres outdid themselves in terms of luxury, seat size and the number of movies shown each day and night. Travelling affairs initially, the first permanent cinema opened in Trieste the year Joyce arrived, in 1905. By 1909, there were twenty-one cinemas in Trieste and the port city had become a major film distribution hub, servicing the entire Austrian empire, pumping out hundreds of films. As is the case today, when a new technology hub emerges in a city or a region, it attracts all sorts of entrepreneurs willing to take their chances, and plenty of speculative finance. Operating on the Ryanair model that a plane is only making money when it is in the air and therefore the more planes flying the more profitable the business, in the highly competitive world of early movies, Trieste's cinema owners opened their doors early in the morning and didn't shut until late at night.

Eva casually mentioned she thought it odd that Trieste had so many cinemas yet there wasn't one in Dublin, a far bigger city with a larger potential audience. Joyce, himself a cinema buff, saw his opportunity: he'd open the first cinema in Ireland and make his fortune. But he had no money; he must find backers. Today, they'd be called private equity or 'early-stage' investors. The fusion of new technology with changing social behaviour has always provided opportunity for profit and Joyce saw a gap in the market. Opening a cinema in the

early twentieth century is today's equivalent of launching an
Internet start-up; it was cutting edge, modern and, as punters
were lapping it up, movies were sucking in some of the best
and most recognized actors from the old-fashioned art form
that was theatre. Culturally, cinema was the future and Joyce,
ever the technologist, saw himself as part of the revolution.

Luckily for our thrusting young entrepreneur, Trieste,
cosmopolitan and commercial, was an ideal spot to raise
money. Joyce quickly found a syndicate of businessmen who'd
taken an early punt on the cinema game and had done so well
that they'd opened cinemas all around the Austrian empire and
as far away as Bucharest. They were called the Volta cinemas,
and Volta appealed to Joyce, not least because the cinema
seemed to be ahead of its time, fusing new technology with
an old art form, allowing the viewer to travel through time
and space.

Playing a blinder at the critical elevator pitch, Joyce whetted
investors' appetites with the opening gambit: there is a city in
Europe with a bustling population of 350,000 and not one
cinema; it's ready for the taking. He then added the extra spice:
there are two more cities on the same island, Cork and Belfast,
without cinemas. Ireland had close to a million urban dwellers
yet not one cinema. Joyce contended Ireland was virgin trading
soil ripe for far-sighted operators like themselves. If they moved
quickly, enthused the start-up kid, a profit bonanza was theirs.
With their money and Joyce's contacts, a fortune was abegging
with more than enough loot to go around.

The Trieste syndicate, buoyed up by their previous successes
in the field, bought his schtick. Presumably their long game

was to set up a few theatres in each city and then flip onto a local buyer, trouser a rake in the process, and move on. Buying low, selling high was Joyce's plan too, as he had no intention of staying in Ireland for long. The contract was signed on 16 October – amazingly quickly. Joyce proved to be a shrewd negotiator. For a man who was a better spender than saver and purportedly couldn't handle money, the contract he negotiated reveals a canny financial operator, and a true salesman. He convinced the partners, all strangers, to give him 10 per cent of the equity and profits, although he didn't invest a penny. On top of this, he was to be paid expenses and a wage. He was given an advance and negotiated a clause stipulating that he would be the exclusive operator in August and September, thus allowing him to take paid holidays in Ireland every year, when the language schools in Trieste shut due to the heat. For a man who came to the negotiating table with nothing but an idea and a sales patter, the contract revealed a hustler with an acute sense of a deal. No longer a disinterested commentator, James Joyce was now in business. Hands were shaken, the deal was done, Joyce was off. The portrait of the artist as a young entrepreneur.

The Artist as Entrepreneur

With a material upside if things worked out, Joyce went about his business with uncharacteristic freneticism, negotiating property with landlords, discussing colours with painters and decorators, selecting films with distributors, talking to newspapers' admen about publicity, buttering up journalists for flattering reviews, becoming expert in all classes of fields from seating and upholstery to lights, technical projector operation and pricing structure for his various shows – cheaper for matinees, more expensive for the flagship evening headliner. He mastered ticket-selling tricks, bundling tickets at a discount, creating panic-buying moments where punters would stump up more, thinking seating was scarce. For a perennial bankrupt, Joyce figured out cash flow management, balancing his outgoings with his revenues. In terms of marketing and publicity, something he took to naturally, our man had to create enough hype to ram the opening night to the rafters, generating what would now be called a FOMO event. Joyce designed the posters, interviewed the staff, oversaw the interior design of the theatre and got the place ready for the grand opening on 20 December 1909.

Any new venture in Dublin can count on half the city waiting for you to fail, particularly if you're a returned local, made good, showing up the inactivity of the left-behinds. How many peers must have spat into their pints when they read the *Evening Telegraph*'s fulsome review of the Volta?

Remarkably good...
Admirably equipped...
Large numbers of guests...
No expense spared...
Particularly successful...
Excellent string orchestra...
Mr Joyce has worked apparently indefatigably and deserves
    to be congratulated on the success.

Having acquired the finance and the venue, and successfully established the brand with a grand opening, full programming and gushing reviews, in January 1910 Joyce headed back to Nora, leaving a manager from Trieste to run the shop in Ireland.

It should not surprise anyone that Joyce the artist and Joyce the entrepreneur were the same person. Artists and entrepreneurs are blessed with similar mindsets. The type of minds who make great art are also the type of minds that create great businesses. Both the artist and the entrepreneur are innovators. They both have skin in the game. As distinct from the critic or reviewer, the artist is exposed. Their work is on show. Likewise the business innovator. Failure in both the arts and business is quick, brutal and unforgiving; success is merely a prelude to the possibility of failure. Both artists and entrepreneurs live in the theatre of risk, performing on the public stage of jeopardy. Yet they do it because they must. It's in their DNA. These independent, slightly unreasonable, regularly difficult and cussed mindsets have no alternative. Both the artist and the entrepreneur die when shackled. Neither wants a boss, a wage or an insurance premium. Both need to know that they are making something new, figuring out not only a novel way of doing things, but better, more inventive ways. Self-expression drives them.

Born disruptors, truly great artists and entrepreneurs are modernists. From a macroeconomic perspective, both artists and entrepreneurs create demand where no demand existed previously. They are magicians, conjuring up something out of nothing but their imagination and their courage. Unlike the critic, the artist is eternally optimistic; likewise the business innovator. They must believe in the future, otherwise what's the point? The energy of innovation drives them on, when it would be far easier at times to get a job, take orders and clock in and out. However, taking instruction is not in their nature. These characters are hardwired differently. The optimism of their will overcomes the pessimism of their intellect, making them exciting. Originality is their currency and constant adaptation their tool.

The artist and the entrepreneur, so often pitted against each other in the lazy bohemian versus bourgeois undergraduate framework, are in fact on the same side. These types of characters drive the economy and culture, generating ideas, new interpretations, new products, new companies, breeding wealth and opportunity for others. Historically, societies who welcome these dissenters and dignify their efforts, are rewarded with the most dynamic economies. Healthy economies, like healthy artistic cultures, thrive on dissent. As the economist Joseph Schumpeter noted, the essential fact of any economy is innovation, or what he termed the 'relentless gales of creative disruption'. The artist or entrepreneur is a born rebel, sometimes uncompromising, often awkward, but always pushing the boundaries. When they are comfortable, they are not doing their job.

While Joyce was haggling over the price of a projector for the Volta, that same mind was trying to get *Dubliners* published, writing his infamous letters to Nora and walking around Mary Street, imagining Blazes Boylan or Buck Mulligan and, of course, Bloom.

Creative people have an opinion, and they are courageous enough to risk the ridicule of the crowd for that opinion to be heard, to be on the page or the canvas – or to be on the shelf. A similar courageous process pushes the artist and the entrepreneur. Intriguingly, success can only come after the effort has been made, making their entire existence inherently risky. Success is never predictable. The magic of great art, music or great business beguiles us maybe because it is often impossible to figure out where the inspiration came from. Who gave the artist or the entrepreneur permission to go down a particular road? In fact, neither seek permission, they just do.

From a societal point of view, being open to these discordant types is an essential prerequisite for economic and cultural blooming. Commercial self-expression, as well as artistic self-expression, are influenced by what the societies believe in, the norms and principles the country or region espouses. Although rarely acknowledged by commercial commentators, values like acceptance, dignity, hope and even love drive economic activity. Setting up a company on your own, as much as writing a book, is an act of defiance, expectation, endurance and creative resilience. The process, whether it is the bohemian artistic urge or the bourgeois business impulse, starts with a little mutiny inside the head of the innovator, the person who makes the world dance, both in a commercial and artistic sense.

Backing yourself is part of everyman's desire to make a difference, to leave a mark, fuelled by our everyday traits, curiosity, imagination, anticipation and individual human grit. These are not the characteristics of Homeric heroes; they are the personality traits of the everyman. The can-doer or game-changing innovator of Joyce's imagination is not the standout genius but the quiet outsider, the dissenter in the crowd. Who is likely to be this dissenter, a fully paid-up comfortable member of an established class following an established dogma, or a slightly out-of-kilter outsider aware that they don't fit in? The outsider is the alchemist of economic change. A country that dignifies these interlopers, bequeathing self-esteem on their efforts, encourages independent thought and venerates dissent is also likely to generate innovative energy. These are the traits of a liberal society: open, non-judgemental, preferring rationality over superstition, science over falsehood, proof over conjecture, reason over religion, and questioning over dogma. This is what Joyce saw all around him when writing *Ulysses* in multi-ethnic, mercantile, savvy, innovative, tumultuous Trieste, a thriving, bustling city in the centre of Europe, yet on the edge of everything. Dublin was not such a place. Bloom may have been at home in Joyce's Trieste but by placing him in Dublin, Joyce invented the ultimate outsider.

Enter Bloom

Bloom's weakness for offal, well advertised now, anchors his introduction but so too does his economics. Mr Bloom's economics, although often overlooked, are central to the character and ultimately reflect those of his creator.

In Dublin, Bloomsday breakfasts have become an exuberant embarrassment of innards, suitable only for those of a certain constitution, unlike our man. His dietary anxieties are well appreciated, but Bloom's sophisticated economic mind is sometimes forgotten. In the 'Calypso' episode, Bloom's opening concerns rest squarely in the realm of the economy – and economics remains an ever-present matter. With a combination of engineering exactitude softened by a profound understanding of human emotions, Bloom displays the foundational elements for what John Maynard Keynes, Joyce's contemporary, suggested is the basic chemistry of the master-economist:

> The master-economist must possess a rare combination of gifts [...] He must be mathematician, historian, statesman, philosopher—in some degree. He must understand symbols and speak in words. He must contemplate the particular, in terms of the general, and touch abstract and concrete in the same flight of thought. He must study the present in the light of the past for the purposes of the future. No part of man's nature or his institutions must be entirely outside his regard. He must be purposeful and disinterested in a simultaneous mood, as aloof and incorruptible as an artist, yet sometimes as near to earth as a politician.

Does this remind you of anyone?

In the opening pages of the 'Calypso' episode, Joyce introduces us to Bloom. Critically, he is non-ideological. In time, we will see him support some contemporary economic ideas identified with both the Left and the Right, such as the universal basic income, public investment in utilities, municipal reform and annuities to minimize inequality at birth. Bloom values hard work and innovation, displaying an acute dislike for casino capitalism with its speculation and easy gains. Standing for rational discourse, scientific proof and individual freedom which fosters creativity, Bloom is an economic centrist, sometimes Left, often Right, but ultimately in the tolerant centre.

He leaves home early, noticing the precise mechanical way the hall-door flap drops limply. From that moment, Bloom is revealed as an acute observer of minutiae, a watcher, a note-taker, a number-cruncher, the ultimate Edwardian details man. Our first glimpse hints at the extraordinary scientific chronicler, the technical obsessive and reforming civic tinkerer who is later unmasked. Displaying the essential traits for the economist with our measuring, computing and comparing, Bloom differs from the academic because, unlike most economists, he is also a financially astute hustler, flogging his wares in the market, involved in the extreme end of the commercial world, where value is created out of nothing.

Living off his wits, Bloom has skin in the commercial game and earning his crust as an advertising copywriter, Joyce makes Bloom the scourge of all Marxists and assorted materialist dialecticians. Preferring reason to rules, he doesn't fit neatly into any ideological box. Even in his tug of war with Stephen, our flexible hero seeks compromise, the middle ground, some sort of peaceful resolution. Bloom owes more to messy Hegelian synthesis than absolutist ideological brutalism. Ultimately, the bohemian Bloom who seeks out the darker side of the city and the bourgeois Bloom who wants the steady family life come together, synthesizing in the streets of Dublin.

Bloom is close to the liberal, civically minded, engaged citizen economist, involved in what the Greeks termed 'polis', that social and economic community organized within an urban environment. The alleys, shops, bars and brothels were to Bloom's Dublin what the agora was to Socrates' Athens, a living social organism teeming with ideas, people, opinions, products, sex and stances. Bloom is everyman in the Socratic sense. Socrates sought out the everyday, the traders, the seedier end of town; so too did Bloom, and underpinning this is a fascination with the dynamic economy.

The Citizen Economist

Written in a period of dramatic social, political, technological and economic change, against the backdrop of huge unemployment as well as constitutional chaos in Europe, the dilemmas thrown up in those post-war, pandemic-scarred years are not dissimilar to today's, rendering Bloom's economics remarkably fresh. These massive changes would have profoundly influenced Joyce and they are evident in the worldview of Bloom, the self-employed citizen-economist.

In the opening pages of 'Calypso', we see a furtive economic imagination at work. Once outside the Eccles Street home, at 8 a.m. on 16 June 1904, Bloom's first calculation is a purely commercial one. Can he flog an ad? The sun is rising, he's daydreaming of Arabic markets, stale turnover bread, his father-in-law's moustache and Molly's new scarlet garters. Bloom sizes up the money-making potential of corner publican Larry O'Rourke, before quickly deducing there's 'no use canvassing him for an ad' (U 69). In Bloom's head he has already totted up Larry O'Rourke's balance sheet and concludes that Larry won't spend any money on an ad, so better walk on. This is Bloom the hustler.

But he's a hustler with a civic worldview. Next thought has Bloom contemplating an imagined map of the city that allows a walk across Dublin without meeting a pub. Surveying the street down to McAuley's pub then, known now to Dubliners as 'The Big Tree', he muses in the same breath that if the council would ever run a new tramline up the North Circular Road to McAuley's, 'value would go up like a shot' (U 69). In one half-thought, Bloom captures the essence of the argument outlined in the most popular economics book written during Joyce's lifetime: Henry George's *Progress and Poverty*. With admirers as diverse as George Bernard Shaw and Leo Tolstoy, this book was a huge bestseller in America. Central to George's work was the notion that public investment, such as a tram for example, enriches private owners rather than the general citizenry, and this is precisely what concerned Bloom.

We are still having this argument today. Take the building of a metro or a tram stop in our crowded cities with overvalued property. The value of the land around the new tram stop goes up automatically as it is more desirable. Estate agents hype it up in their blurb but the people who live near this tram stop, whose houses prices have gone up, have done nothing to deserve this bonanza, yet they benefit enormously from the taxes of the general population who pay for the tram. The issue – considered by Bloom – comes down to who finances public investment and who should benefit: the taxpayer or the property speculator? Profoundly undemocratic, this type of speculative profit annoyed Bloom as it breaks the connection between creativity and value, instead lining the pockets of an opportunistic class of gamblers with windfall gains paid for by others. Speculation and this type of 'easy money' didn't sit well with the creative and workman-like instincts of Bloom. (Of course, his antipathy to the gambler may also have been influenced by his nemesis, Blazes Boylan, who was fond of a flutter on the horses.)

Landlordism was rife in Bloom's Dublin, and anyone interested in the average citizen's welfare would have been acutely aware of the fact that public infrastructure, while benefitting commuters, enriched the landowning class immeasurably more. Joyce's and the Joyce family's constant hassles with landlords can't be too far from the surface here. Bloom views enrichment by landownership as rent-seeking feudalism, something which is profoundly anti-modern. Nor does he believe in the basic Marxist interpretation of value (fashionable at the time), which argues that the foundation stone of value is the amount of labour that goes into making something (the Labour Theory of Value). Bloom is a much more sophisticated thinker who understands that value means something different to different people; value is ephemeral and mercurial. Bloom is a modernist who believes the essential alchemy of economics happens in the everyday human mind.

Bloom walks on in search of his breakfast. On Dorset Street, he observes the notices in the Zionist newspaper in which his morning kidney has been wrapped by the Jewish, but non-kosher, butcher Dlugacz. As an advertising copywriter, Bloom understands economic value resides in the brain, where yearning creates demand and economic value is as much perceived as real. Value is highly subjective, open to persuasion and always changing. Bloom lived in the weightless economic world of the future where profit and innovation come from inspiration and mental agility rather than the perspiration and grunt of the worker. As such, like Joyce, Bloom would have been very much at home in the future. Bloom's advertising mind was perfectly suited to the Instagram age, rooted in the power of persuasion, emotion and the irrationality of humans when it comes to buying, parting with money and dreaming of future returns.

As an economic thinker, Bloom was, by instinct, of the behavioural persuasion, understanding that people value meaning. A profound but simple notion, the economics of meaning, memory, experience, either realized or hoped for, is one of the most powerful forces in the modern economy, but in 1904 it would have been decidedly avant-garde. Bloom wouldn't have landed there without a good grasp of Freud and the psychological breakthroughs of the time. As an arch commercial manipulator, he discloses a keen grasp of the power of dreams and the economics of the crowd.

Having assessed O'Rourke's commercial worth, noted the anti-democratic way public wealth accrues to private property owners, Bloom then (on the same page) muses on the profitability of dreams, experiences and collective urges that drive the economy. A Jew by his father's name, yet baptized three times, once Protestant, once Catholic and once for the craic, our conflicted, cosmopolitan hero understands how the attachment to the tribe, either real or invented, can overrule our individual rationality.

The economics of meaning is perfectly captured in the ad in the Zionist paper 'Agendath Netaim' (U 72) selling the dream of a new life in what (spoiler alert) will become Israel. But we are talking 1904 not 1948 here. Bloom reads the ad. It promises orange groves, almond trees and citrons. Bloom sees what is going on: a property business, where owners of land, in what was the Ottoman empire, are persuading European Jews to buy into a dream of living on the side of Lake Tiberius. As Trieste was one of the main ports for European Jews heading to Palestine, Joyce was well versed in the Zionist arguments of the time. Theodor Herzl, the father of Zionism, lectured in Trieste just as Joyce landed there. A major Zionist influencer in Trieste was Moses Dlugacz, who from 1912 to 1914 was also a student of Joyce's, and the two men spent long evenings chatting about philology, politics, economics and literature. When Bloom reminisces about evenings spent in the house of his Jewish friend, Citron, we can imagine the author is recalling his time with the real-life Dlugacz. In the end, Joyce honours Dlugacz by naming the Zionist pork butcher after him.

For Bloom, the Zionist ad flogging land to Zionists is the commercial equivalent of turning water into wine. Since this is what he does every day, he appreciates the difference between the real nuts and bolts value of the real estate and the perceived value, the price in the heads of middle-class German Jews. The gap between real and imagined value is the elixir of profit.

The Bourgeois Outsider

This encounter with Dlugacz gets Bloom, no Zionist, thinking of his old childhood Jewish friends, Citron and Mastiansky, over on the other side of the city in Little Jerusalem, where Bloom was born and grew up before he fled, seeking the less claustrophobic atmosphere of the city centre. Assimilation, adapting and innovating are the key elements of Bloom's economic worldview, coming together in tolerant urban environments. Urban cosmopolitanism, with people coming and going and acceptance of foreigners with their different ideas, goods and products, is central to Bloom's tolerant bourgeois views of commerce and economics. The elixir of economic growth and wealth creation for Bloom is human innovation. Before a country can redistribute wealth (something Bloom cared about), a society needed to create wealth (something Bloom thought about), and the process of wealth creation is innovation, getting more out of less. Bloom saw innovation stemming from free people, dissenting from the typical world-view, opposing dogma, and having both moral courage and the financial incentive to take a risk. Essentially a bourgeois thinker, Bloom's vision for economics had its political roots in the centre. Neither of the Left nor Right, Bloom occupied the vibrant centre where people mix, tinker about with things and ideas and generally make things up.

The link between the bourgeoisie and economic innovation is an old one. The word bourgeois comes from the German word *burgh*, meaning fortress. In Anglo-Saxon England, the

363

burhs were armed trading settlements on the coast built to defend against the Vikings, which is where the English word 'borough' derives from, giving us derivations of brough, burgh and bourg, as in Middlesbrough, Edinburgh or Strasbourg. If you were bourgeois in the Middle Ages, you lived in an urban environment, usually a free city, normally part of a self-governing community, quite distinct from a peasant on the land, beholden to some hereditary knight or baron. Curious people flocked, Dick Whittington-style, towards the freedom of the city. Urban and rural were poles apart in terms of quality of life, exposure to ideas, commerce, opportunity and money. The merchant, a free-trading, free-thinking creature of the city, emerges in the Middle Ages, giving substance to the German expression *Stadluft macht frei*, the city air makes you free. Floating in the air of the city are radical ideas of freedom and notions of individual sovereignty, comforting for the dissenter and the outsider. Places where tradition, family and pedigree are far less important, cities favoured ability, smarts and grit. A bourgeois artisan and merchant making their way in the world acted as a counterbalance to the old order and power base of inherited family fiefdoms bolstered by religious dogma. The revolutionary force that upset the powerful stranglehold of church and squire was money – and the merchant. To Bloom, the city that is accepting of outsiders, minorities, foreigners, non-believers is also likely to release the energy of its own mutineers. Such thoughts bring him back to his own tribe, the Jews, the ultimate European outsiders. His economic philosophy is elaborated in his conversation with Stephen in 'Eumaeus', when Bloom states:

History, would you be surprised to learn, proves up to the hilt, Spain decayed when the Inquisition hounded the Jews out [...] In the economic domain, the priest spells poverty. Spain again, you saw in the war instead of the go-ahead America. It's in the dogma. Because if they didn't believe they'd go straight to heaven when they die, they'd try to live better, at least so I think.

As Christian Europe's only real outsiders, how Jews are treated, Bloom claimed, is an accurate indicator for other internal prejudices within a society. He uses Jews here as shorthand to tell a greater story. A society or city that embraces Jews and confers dignity upon them will also be more accepting of internal dissent and more likely to favour commerce over inheritance as the path of economic growth. Deploying Christian Spain as his example, once the Spaniards kicked out the Jews (and the Arabs) and turned itself into the sixteenth-century religious fanatical warlord state (the European equivalent of the Japanese Shogunate), Spanish society morphed, eschewing commerce, trade and enquiry, wrapping itself up in religious purity and dogma. Spain, despite plundering America of all its gold, stagnated intellectually, politically and economically. American gold flowed through Spain, as the religiously pure but economically stultified Spaniards spent their South American windfall like a modern-day Lotto winner.

The country that took many of those Jewish refugees, the Netherlands, and its capital Amsterdam, gladly accepted Spain's money. A hundred years after Columbus landed in

America, Spain ruled most of the New World, yet by the late sixteenth century Amsterdam was the richest, most sophisticated city in the world. Dissent not dogma makes the economy dance. As Bloom points out, the priest with his dogma spells poverty. Rules, rituals and traditions suffocate effort, enquiry and curiosity. Bloom, the adman innovator, stood for bourgeois enterprise, freedom of thought, respect for scientific discovery; Bloom, the liberal social reformer, believed in the distribution of wealth, easing of poverty and the brotherhood of man. Bloom, the citizen-economist, a follower of Georgian economics, believed that land is a dead asset which is only made valuable by other people's money.

The Radical Centrist

In Bloom's head there was a sequence: you create wealth first and then you redistribute it. With wealth created, Bloom the entrepreneur yields to Bloom the social reformer. Universal basic income is an idea beloved of twenty-first-century progressives. By giving a basic annual income to everyone, as an alternative to weekly welfare to those in need, it allows the market to operate vibrantly with a safety net for those who might otherwise fall through the cracks. Bloom was onto it 100 years ago. In 'Eumaeus', Bloom outlines his vision for the universal basic income:

> I want to see everyone, concluded he, all creeds and classes *pro rata* having a comfortable tidysized income, in no niggard fashion either, something in the neighbourhood

of £300 per annum. That's the vital issue at stake and it's feasible and would be provocative of friendlier intercourse between man and man. At least that's my idea for what it's worth. (U 747)

Bloom isn't talking about giving the poorest people constant top-ups but giving everyone the same amount so as to liberate people from the hassle of making ends meet and allowing them the luxury of going out and trying their hand in the bourgeois world. He is also implicitly saying to the bohemian Stephen that artists too would qualify, thereby having a basic income, allowing them to concentrate on their art, free of having to worry about mundanities such as paying the rent – a perennial concern for the artistic Joyce.

Today the case for a universal basic income hinges on the encroachment of labour-saving technologies like automation and AI. The period 1918 to 1920, when Joyce was writing *Ulysses*, was also a period of great upheaval as technologies that had been fast-tracked by the war effort were decommissioned and put to use in the economy, from electricity to cars, washing machines, electric ovens, radios and talking films. Here's the great reformer Bloom, imagining himself as the reformist Lord Mayor of Dublin, addressing the perils of mechanical fetishization, a well-known weakness of the wealthy. Its twenty-first-century equivalent can be seen in the regular exhortations about the transformative power of Big Tech by very rich people.

Machines is their cry, their chimera, their panacea. Labour-saving apparatuses, supplanters [...] manufactured monsters

for our mutual murder, hideous hobgoblins produced by
a horde of capitalistic lusts upon our prostituted labour.
(U 602)

Bloom's solution isn't to eat the rich, but a much more
modern, less dogmatic universal basic income. Why? All this
technological disruption of the old world created economic
anxiety and fear. The favoured political alternative at the time,
outlined by Lenin, was Soviet communism but, for Bloom,
communism – with its attendant dogma and strictures – would
have the same effect on innovation as the priest-run church.
After all, to free-thinking liberals, political commissars were
only priests with better uniforms.

Even in his more utopian moments, Bloom held fast to the
centre. The tolerant centre is where the outsider feels most
comfortable or maybe least uncomfortable. The extremes held
no attraction – be they the nationalist extremes of the Citizen
accusing Bloom and his tribe of killing Christ or his own
introverted Jewish community who had no time for a 'marryer-
outer' like Bloom. Like Joyce in Trieste, Bloom preferred
the mixed-up cosmopolitanism of the vibrant metropolitan
streetscape, which he made his own and where he derived his
inspiration, which came from the great waltz of civic urban
streets, as the urban designer Jane Jacobs termed it.

Think about what Bloom saw and celebrated. The key word
is diversity. On the street, in the bar, at the funeral, down in
Nighttown, in the cabman's shelter, in the shops, in the parks.
It's all about difference, diversity and serendipity. As he strolls
Dublin's streets, he bumps into all sorts, some by accident, some

intentionally, rich and poor, Dubs and culchies, young and old, spoofers and savants, nationalist and unionist, whores and coppers, lame Christian and dissenter, artists and entrepreneurs, and, yes, bohemian and bourgeois. Bloom's Dublin was that diverse ecosystem, fragile and strong at the same time, interdependent and complex, but ultimately alive and diverse. Diversity loves freedom, liberalism and acceptance, and Bloom the outsider revelled in it, becoming its spokesman with his musings on its sanitation, water pressure in the sewers, tram timetables, use of the river and the canals, housing, electricity, rates, politics, sex, music and everything in between.

Diversity was his thing, diversity in residential and commercial buildings, diversity in transport, racial and social diversity, diversity in the public and private economy, diversity in architecture, where density is strength, the font of ideas, rows and reconciliations in a future-orientated city that embraces science, progress, movement and difference, turning its back on fundamentalism, nostalgia, mythology, sexual strictures, opening itself up to the adventure of the day and, of course, the night which all proper cities promise. Above all, the city is somewhere where synthesis can occur, common ground can be found and the great revolution of economic innovation turns.

The Entrepreneur as Artist

At its heart, *Ulysses* is about the unlikely friendship between an erratic, volatile, bohemian, young artist Stephen and an older, wiser, bourgeois, empirical reformer Bloom. The novelist son with the adman father; the poetry with the prose.

In the small hours, bourgeois, sober Bloom takes bohemian, brothel-weary Stephen under his wing. Dedalus has been out on the tiles in Nighttown and needs guidance. It's time to sober up and get serious. Fatherly Bloom wants to navigate the younger man through the obvious pitfalls of Dublin, both the source of creativity and (as my own mother warned me) the graveyard of ambition. Both men are knackered and haven't much to say to each other as they head to the sanctuary of the cabman's hut under Butt Bridge. Bloom is trying to get Stephen away from Dublin's numerous temptations and, psychologically, he is trying to get Stephen to face up to the reality of hard work, commitment and application to maximize his talents. Joyce knew that Dublin, then as it is now, is full of the 'what might have been', the great talents unrecognized, dragged down by the insane immaturity of the artist waiting for something to happen. Opportunity doesn't wait. This is Stephen's Eminem 'Lose Yourself' moment. And Bloom knows it. Bloom, ever pragmatic, insists that theory and practice, brain and brawn must be reconciled: the bohemian can only reach his full potential by succumbing to the discipline of the bourgeois.

Picture the lanky Joyce of October 1909 puking on the mail boat, returning to Dublin. The moment the artist and the entrepreneur merge, combining the best of both impulses. The brothels and the carousing pubs of Dublin are faux bohemia, swamps of bitter mediocrity, places that will sap Stephen of his genius. It's now time to get real and knuckle down. As Declan Kiberd maintains, 'Stephen accepts the clear implication of what Bloom is saying that the bourgeois and the bohemian should be one and the same thing.' This is something Joyce himself understood when he opened the Volta. The creative business mind and the creative artistic mind are one and the same type of machine: iconoclastic, irreverent, innovative but ultimately liberated by work, hard work. Both live in the world of risk and are prepared to back themselves, even when – or especially when – no one else sees the vision, the end-product, the big picture. These visionaries make the economy run, taking on the responsibility, and risking the chance of failure. Risk is their design.

Bloom, like Joyce himself, is juggling the bohemian and the bourgeois. Joyce wanted the family life, but also the excitement. Bloom wanted the stable marriage – which he couldn't achieve – and the bohemian street life. Both realize that bohemian brilliance can only be fashioned by bourgeois discipline. Joyce, through the older more experienced Bloom, is trying to lead Stephen towards the sunlit uplands of application and grit.

* * *

We are now at the moment of commercial fusion: when inspiration meets perspiration, when innovation and human ingenuity fuses with mercantile determination, leading to new products which replace what went before in a Schumpeterian gale of 'creative destruction'. The old is destroyed but in the very act of destruction, something new, something better, something original is created. Modernism incarnate.

Great art, great literature and great economies are fashioned, designed and completed in the same way, on the same road; and Bloom knew all the signposts.

Ithaca

Reading as the Police

ERIC A. LEWIS

Eric A. Lewis has written on Joyce, Zoë Wicomb, and Nuala Ní Dhomhnaill. He has a BA from William Jewell College and a doctorate from Notre Dame. He has written about the cultural politics of South Africa, and he has learnt Irish in the Connemara Gaeltacht. He is currently a post-doctoral fellow at the Georgia Institute of Technology and, along with fellow contributor Shinjini Chattopadhyay, hosts the podcast *tipsyturvy Ulysses*.

urveillance makes subtle appearances throughout James Joyce's life and work, but especially in *Ulysses* (1922). The novel was composed from 1914 to 1921, during which the First World War and multiple insurrectionary nationalist movements increased both the practice and experience of surveillance throughout Europe. In Ireland alone, this time span encompasses the Easter Rising and War of Independence, military conflicts in which informants and intelligence agents played key roles. Even outside of Ireland, on the Continent, where Joyce lived in voluntary exile, he became an observed subject of multiple governments in multiple countries. *Ulysses* itself is set in Dublin in the recent past of 1904, at the seeming height of unassailable British colonial authority in Ireland. In this representation of colonized Dublin, police feature prominently: they are seen on patrol, spoken with as friends and implied by the many police barracks characters pass on their walks through the city. They and other elements of colonial Ireland's surveillance regime, such as informants, are present in Leopold Bloom's mind, too. For instance, he remembers being chased by a mounted policeman after joining a protest in anti-colonial solidarity with the Boers resisting British imperial ambitions in South Africa and fears being watched or having his belongings searched.

For all of Bloom's fears, though, nothing comes of the novel's surveillance subplot. Bloom is never followed, apprehended or searched. Even Corny Kelleher, the seemingly obvious police informant that Bloom identifies, does nothing sinister in the novel. In fact, Bloom and Kelleher meet up multiple times, and when they do, Kelleher is nothing but helpful. Martin

Cunningham, an official in Dublin Castle who explicitly cites intelligence files on Bloom, is Bloom's somewhat friendly acquaintance. To the extent that he is less than friendly, it is not because of tensions related to his and Bloom's respective places in a surveillance regime, but instead because of Cunningham's participation in the general anti-Semitism shared by just about every resident of the Dublin of *Ulysses*.

So, instead of culminating in any relevant climax in the text of the novel, this surveillance subplot is resolved in the reading of *Ulysses*, specifically episode seventeen, 'Ithaca'. By reading the episode's inventories of Bloom's possessions, readers come to resemble just the sort of home intruder and intelligence agent Bloom explicitly fears. Bloom passionately defends the privacy of his home, specifically the contents of the locked drawers in the sideboard in his front room, but 'Ithaca' lays these contents bare to readers. The novel's surveillance subplot therefore depicts the relationship between readers and Bloom as much as it depicts Bloom's experience in a colonized, heavily policed city. By evoking surveillance to the extent that it does, *Ulysses* provokes a comparison between the colonial surveillance exercised in the novel's setting and the practices of Joyce's readers. Furthermore, by carefully delineating the information it shares with readers – cataloguing the contents of drawers, cupboards and bookshelves, to the exclusion of more typical, novelistic content, such as the specifics of characters' interactions or feelings – 'Ithaca' in particular positions its readers as intelligence agents in its fictional Dublin and manipulates them into acting the part. Like the intelligence agent, readers must use limited observable behaviour and accessible evidence to make judgements about the subject of observation – whether a character or criminal suspect, as the case may be. Police executing a search of a suspect's home rifle through someone's belongings and compile a list for investigators to review in hope of gaining new insights. *Ulysses* provides readers with such a list and little else, prompting them to adopt the role of such investigators, consciously or not. Like the Castle official Cunningham, the novel's readers use the scraps they are able to access to infer Bloom's inner truth, but in contrast with the novel's fictional surveillance regime, they have access to more scraps. Specifically, readers violate Bloom's most fiercely protected privacy – that of the secrets of his bottom drawer – and thus become the very intruders he fears and otherwise never confronts.

In this way, this book about everything is about surveillance. This theme is yet another way in which *Ulysses* is timely. Decades before everyone carries GPS-enabled devices in their pockets and uses them constantly to navigate, *Ulysses* delights in recording characters' movements across Dublin turn-by-turn. Decades before big data began aggregating customers' purchases and searches in order to target ads, *Ulysses* records what characters possess, where they bought it and for how much. The novel's representation of British colonial surveillance anticipates the diffuse, corporate surveillance of today.

My focus in this chapter, however, is the novel's treatment of surveillance as an analogue for reading. Such an account of reading is significant because it departs dramatically from typical understandings of the practice. Through the surveillance subplot in which readers are encouraged to participate, *Ulysses* suggests that reading is not the innocent, perhaps even morally upright practice it is often considered. According to this surveillance subplot, readers do not necessarily identify with the characters about which they read. They do not exercise their empathy and thus become more moral people. Instead of just innocently looking in from the outside, perhaps with a kind disposition, readers become implicated in the novel's plot in roles they would likely neither recognize nor appreciate. In the case of *Ulysses*, they are implicated as participants in the very colonial police regime that Bloom fears.

Surveillance in *Ulysses*

Ulysses represents surveillance throughout its length, both explicitly and implicitly. Police are ever-present, and informants are often evoked. According to Enda Duffy, the novel 'relentlessly pinpoints the mechanisms of the colonial regimes of surveillance and the panoptic gaze'. *Ulysses* is, as K.J. Devlin put it, 'a police novel' – that is, 'a novel that engages the issue of scopic surveillance, regulation, and punishment.' Through this emphasis, *Ulysses* establishes a prominent surveillance subplot. Police are in search of malcontents and dissidents, and Bloom, given his interest in Irish home rule and (admittedly more casual) in socialism, could be read as such. Therefore, Bloom frequently notices and reflects upon police presence and action. In a more plot-driven novel than *Ulysses*, a reader might naturally expect this paranoia to lead to something, some climactic encounter between Bloom and the surveillance regime he fears. Instead, the novel unfolds in a series of anti-climaxes in which the police are either indifferent or even helpful to Bloom.

For instance, passing a squad of constables in the street prompts Bloom to reflect on his fear of the subtler intelligence regime supporting such outward signs of British colonial authority in Ireland. Recalling his previous encounter with a protest-dispersing mounted policeman, Bloom watches the constables disperse on their beats and thinks, 'Nasty customers to tackle' (U 206). However, what Bloom fears more than physical confrontation is police surveillance and intelligence-gathering – an abstract idea best represented by the infamous Irish figure of the police informant. Dwelling on the topic after the constables have departed, Bloom cautions himself, 'Never know who you're talking to. Corny Kelleher he has Harvey Duff in his eye. Like that Peter or Denis or James Carey that blew the gaff on the invincibles. [...] All the time drawing secret service pay from the castle. Drop him like a hot potato' (U 206–7). It is not the uniformed constables that scare Bloom most, but instead the harder-to-recognize intelligence-gathering forces that support them. Bloom thinks he recognizes one such informant to be held at arm's length in Corny Kelleher, but he generalizes his fears beyond Kelleher to other, less easily recognized threats: plainclothes policemen who seduce and question servants, Peeping Toms who spy through keyholes, false lovers, 'barmaids too. Tobacco shopgirls' (U 207). Essentially, Bloom imagines a diffuse surveillance regime that is inescapable. Even if you manage to recognize and avoid one representative, as Bloom believes he has done with Corny Kelleher, there is always another, occupying some innocuous position in your everyday life and ready to report on you to Dublin Castle.

The figure of the informant features prominently throughout Joyce's work. For example, in his article on 'Fenianism' (1907) for the Triestine newspaper *Il Piccolo della Serra*, Joyce explains that the secret revolutionary Fenian movement collapsed 'because in Ireland, just at the crucial moment, an informer appears' in a national tradition of betrayal. In light of this tradition, Joyce praises James Stephens's innovative organization of Fenians into isolated cells to minimize the harm a potential informant could do and puts the same opinion in Bloom's head: 'James Stephens' idea was the best. He knew them. Circles of ten so that a fellow couldn't round on more than his own ring' (U 207). In the *Dubliners* (1914) story 'Two Gallants', Corley resembles the informant Bloom fears; not only is this police inspector's son 'often to be seen walking with policemen in plain clothes, talking earnestly', but he also seduces servants, like Bloom's imagined plainclothes officer. In *A Portrait of the Artist as a Young Man* (1915), Stephen jokes about 'the indispensable informer' when his fellow university students chide him for his lack of nationalism. *Finnegans Wake* (1939), of course, centres on just what crime Earwicker committed in Dublin's Phoenix Park and who witnessed it.

In addition to its significant role in Irish history and Joyce's fiction, surveillance impacted Joyce's own personal experience. While living in Trieste, a city that resembled Dublin in being part of the Austro-Hungarian empire but populated by passionate Italian nationalists, Joyce frequented socialist bars that were under regular police surveillance. According to

Franz K. Stanzel, when Joyce spent much of the First World War in Zurich, he was under surveillance by both the Austrian and British secret services. John McCourt even notes that the Austrian secret services 'actually went to the trouble of sending a spy to take English lessons with [Joyce] in an attempt to extract information'. Even though Joyce faced little police repression resulting from such surveillance – he 'was seen as a quiet person without any criminal record, certainly not as an agitator' – he still became obsessed with the police intelligence-gathering that he experienced.

Bloom's experience in *Ulysses* resembles Joyce's own: his fears of a colonial intelligence network are confirmed – but his fears of its harmful impact on him are not. Bloom's suspicions of Kelleher are supported by the latter's frequent, casual interactions with police. In 'Wandering Rocks', Kelleher briefly steps outside of his workplace and starts a conversation with Constable 57C, who is passing by on his regular beat:

> — What's the best news? [Kelleher] asked.
> — I seen that particular party last evening, the constable
>   said with bated breath. (U 288)

Ulysses briefly represents its suspected informant in conversation with an explicit member of Dublin's colonial police regime but cuts away to other characters and another scene once their conversation starts to become interesting. Instead of learning whom exactly this informant and constable are discussing, readers are directed to the next of the episode's many vignettes centred on yet another of the many minor characters of *Ulysses*. The unidentified 'particular party' Kelleher and the constable discuss could be the subject of state surveillance, and this conversation could thus confirm Bloom's suspicions, or they could merely be the subject of gossip between friends. Furthermore, since the constable reports on what he has seen to the potential informant, Devlin suggests that Kelleher may even be an anti-colonial intelligence agent to whom an informer in the police is reporting. In any case, a suspected informant's mysterious conversation with a constable contributes to the novel's depiction and evocation of surveillance, even if the novel withholds the specifics of their conversation from readers. In 'Circe', Kelleher uses his connection to the colonial police regime to keep Bloom out of trouble. A drunken Stephen starts and promptly loses a fight with two soldiers, and the night watch begin to write him up as he lies unconscious in the street. Bloom waves down a passing Kelleher, who talks the night watch down: 'That's all right. I know him. [...] Leave it to me, sergeant. [...] Come and wipe your name off the slate. [...] (*winking*) Boys will be boys' (U 698–9). The informant appears, and rather than betraying Bloom to the police, he helps him out. Kelleher even uses intelligence gathered via Dublin's rumour mill – the very weapon of the informant – to do so, referring to Bloom's rumoured gambling windfall as an explanation for his innocent, apolitical misbehaviour: 'Won a bit on the races. Gold cup. *Throwaway*. (*he laughs*) Twenty to one. Do you follow me?' (U 698). In *Ulysses*, Joyce's prediction is realized, and an informant appears at the crucial moment; however, when he does so, he helps the novel's protagonists get out of trouble. Of course, Stephen and Bloom are not revolutionaries, and lenience toward them says nothing about police treatment of more active discontents. Still, this is a strikingly benign depiction of colonial surveillance.

Similarly, even though Martin Cunningham is a colonial intelligence agent with information on Bloom, he functions in the plot as a help rather than a hindrance or antagonist. Throughout his appearance in multiple texts, Cunningham is consistently associated with intelligence work. For instance, in the *Dubliners* story 'Grace', Cunningham is described as 'well informed', possessing 'secret sources of information'. In *Ulysses* itself, Cunningham casually cites these secret sources in reference to Bloom. When asked to weigh in on Bloom's suspect Irishness and nationalism, Cunningham asserts that Bloom is involved in the Irish nationalist group Sinn Féin: 'it was he drew up all the plans according to the Hungarian system. We know that in the castle' (U 438). There is no evidence in *Ulysses* that Bloom is actually involved in Sinn Féin, and Cunningham also incorrectly states that Bloom was born in Hungary rather than Ireland, but what matters in this scene is the presence of surveillance and its impact on Bloom. Bloom is a suspected nationalist agitator, but the Castle agent Cunningham is still a friendly acquaintance. Further corroborating the seemingly benign nature of the surveillance Bloom is under, Cunningham cites this intelligence about Bloom to argue in Bloom's favour. Cunningham is asked to share what he knows about Bloom to weigh in on a debate about whether or not Bloom is Irish. On one side of the conversation, a group of barflies draws from the anti-Semitic trope of the Wandering Jew to argue that, because he is Jewish, Bloom cannot be Irish. Instead, says the Citizen, the most violent of them, 'Saint Patrick would want to land again at Ballykinlar and convert us [...] after allowing things like that to contaminate our shores' (U 439). On the other side, another bar patron asks, 'Why can't a jew love his country like the next fellow?' (U 438). Cunningham's evidence suggests that no matter Bloom's religion, ethnicity or place of birth, he is indeed Irish – so Irish that he's under colonial surveillance. Similarly, when the Citizen begins to threaten Bloom, Cunningham quickly spirits Bloom away. Cunningham does not challenge the Citizen directly, sharing some of his anti-Semitic suspicion of Bloom, but he does help Bloom escape.

Bloom fears the surveillance regime that Joyce takes care to depict in detail in *Ulysses*, but his fears are not realized in the text. He encounters an informant and an intelligence agent multiple times and suffers no harm as a result. In fact, those very agents come to his rescue, helping him escape other officials or violent individuals. Bloom's escape only extends so far as the world of the text, however. When readers take up *Ulysses*, they end up carrying out the surveillance actions that Bloom specifically fears. In this way, the novel's surveillance subplot becomes an argument about the nature of novel-reading. In contrast with conventional ideas of reader identification with characters, reader–character relationships are more complicated and prone to conflict. No matter how much readers love a character, that character may not love them back. That character may fear and hate them instead because of the fictional role – such as a member of a colonial police regime – that novels assign them through framing and style.

Readers' Surveillance of *Ulysses*

Readers of *Ulysses* pick up where its characters leave off and subject Bloom to the sort of intelligence work he fears. 'Ithaca' is structured as a series of detailed questions and answers about the world of *Ulysses*. In the novel's seeming climax, when Bloom and Stephen retire to Bloom's home, the present action is derailed by the episode's many strange questions and answers, which range in content from Bloom's and Stephen's pasts, to the nature of Dublin's water infrastructure, to the contents of Bloom's home. Duffy compares the style of 'Ithaca' to the 'question-and-answer of the police interrogator and suspect', but given its minute attention to the many items in Bloom's home, parts of 'Ithaca' as much resemble the documentation resulting from a police search. Furthermore, 'Ithaca' not only imitates a police search but also prompts readers to participate by investigating the resulting inventories in order to learn yet more about Bloom. It is, of course, perfectly normal for readers to read about and attribute significance to a fictional character's possessions, but *Ulysses* renders this relationship troubling by both providing readers an unusually comprehensive inventory of Bloom's household possessions and having Bloom passionately defend the privacy of those very possessions. Even after suffering adultery, public humiliation and anti-Semitism all day, the offence that most angers Bloom is the threat of violation of the privacy of his home and the security of his possessions. By ending in a surface-level anti-climax but rendering the novel's readers as the climactic antagonists the novel lacks, the surveillance subplot of *Ulysses* reaches beyond the book's covers and becomes a book about its readers. When they follow the novel's prompts, interpreting the information that 'Ithaca' provides them, readers become feared intruders who would be at home in Dublin's colonial police regime – members that actually carry out the more sinister intrusions that the novel's informants and police do not.

Bloom is threatened with and takes up arms against the invasion of his domestic privacy during the 'Circe' episode. 'Circe' resembles a pantomime. It is structured as a playscript, complete with play-formatted dialogue and stage directions. There are frequent on-stage costume changes that establish a dream logic in which characters transform in response to events and their own emotions. In a key scene in this episode, Bloom is subjected to a series of imagined taunts and humiliations in Bella Cohen's brothel. Of the many scenarios with which he is threatened, Bloom takes particular offence at the violation of his possessions. Bella, temporarily transformed into the domineering Mr Bello, taunts him with a vision of 'a man and his manfriends' who will wander around Bloom's home, break some of his possessions and 'violate the secrets of [his] bottom drawer' (U 653–64). Bloom's response is uncharacteristically violent: he '*clenches his fists and crawls forward, a bowie knife between his teeth*', and swears vengeance (U 654). Such behaviour from Bloom is a noteworthy departure. He considers knife-wielding political and marital violence elsewhere in the novel but dismisses it out of hand. When recalling the Phoenix Park Murders, an infamous 1882 assassination of British colonial administrators by Irish nationalists, Bloom 'certainly did feel, and no denying it [...] a certain kind of admiration for a man who had actually brandished a knife, cold steel, with the courage of his political convictions though, personally, he would never be a party to any such thing' (U 744). Thinking of his wife's infidelity, he also reflects upon 'love vendettas of the south' in which a typical cuckolded husband 'inflicted fatal injuries on his adored one as a result of an alternative postnuptial *liaison* by plunging his knife into her' (U 744), but Bloom betrays no interest in pursuing such a strategy himself. He weighs many options regarding his marriage in the aftermath of Molly's infidelity, including divorce, exposure and a cover-up, but confidently confirms, 'Assassination, never' (U 866). When the barflies in 'Cyclops' encourage Bloom to take up arms in response to global anti-Semitism, Bloom is similarly dismissive: 'But it's no use [...]. Force, hatred, history, all that. That's not life for men and women, insult and hatred' (U 432). In contrast with such restraint, the threat to his secreted-away private property inspires uncharacteristic violence.

Depending on one's interpretation of the phrase 'bottom drawer', the violation Bella Cohen describes may not occur within the pages of *Ulysses* itself, but instead be perpetrated by the novel's readers. Bloom's bottom drawer may be his wife Molly's bottom drawers. In that case, Molly's lover Blazes Boylan is the violator against whom Bloom takes up imaginary arms. However, given Bloom's explicit 'equanimity' about Molly's adultery (U 865), his violent reaction likely regards a different bottom drawer. Only one party violates the secrets of the literal bottom drawer in Bloom's front room sideboard: readers of 'Ithaca'. After Stephen leaves, Bloom goes to the sideboard, where he keeps all of his most secret possessions, to add the most recent letter in his ongoing epistolary affair, which he picked up earlier in the day. As Bloom goes about this simple task, the episode takes the time to lay the contents of these drawers bare for readers. The questioner asks, 'What did the first drawer unlocked contain?' and 'What did the 2nd drawer contain?' (U 848, 852), and the episode proceeds to detail the contents of each for over 100 lines, across multiple pages: 'A Vere Foster's handwriting copybook [...] 2 fading photographs of queen Alexandra of England and of Maud Branscombe, actress and professional beauty: a Yuletide card [...] a butt of red, partly liquefied sealing wax' (U 848–49), etc. 'Ithaca' provides similar inventories elsewhere: of the contents of the Blooms' kitchen cabinet when Bloom opens it while preparing hot cocoa for Stephen and himself (U 790); of the furniture in Bloom's front room, rearranged since that morning, when he first enters the room; and of the books on Bloom's bookshelf after he sits down in the front room. This last inventory both lists the books and describes each book's condition and the type and location of bookmarks. A police search might produce just such inventories for the use of investigators or intelligence agents interested in the resident in question.

Readers thus find in 'Ithaca' a chance to dig deeper into Bloom in a way that makes them resemble the police, informants and intelligence agents Bloom fears. This episode's inventories of Bloom's possessions, especially the secrets of his bottom drawer, enable readers to thicken their own intelligence files on Bloom with greater understanding of his past, interiority and present condition. Furthermore, many of the specific contents of Bloom's drawers, such as pornographic photos, financial records and nationalist political statements (specifically, 'a sealed prophecy (never unsealed) written by Leopold Bloom in 1886 concerning the consequences of the passing into law of William Ewart Gladstone's Home Rule Bill of 1886 (never passed into law)' U 849), are things that Bloom likely would prefer remain private.

However, even as 'Ithaca' tells readers yet more about the novel's central three characters, particularly Bloom, it tells them little that they are eager to know. Central questions of plot are ignored and left unanswered. Instead of representing the present, climactic scene of the novel and clarifying the nature of Bloom and Stephen's interaction and the likelihood of future interactions, 'Ithaca' details minutiae of the setting or Bloom's and Stephen's past, when it does not go further afield into irrelevancy. It substitutes banal material detail for the sort of insight into psychology and relationships to which novel-readers are accustomed and that they typically desire. However, readers are left with the private contents of Bloom's locked drawer from which to make inferences, as might the intelligence agent. Even if these contents do not tell them much, readers have still violated Bloom's precious privacy by merely reading the inventory the text provides.

'Ithaca' transforms characters into lists of facts that are irrelevant to typical novelistic concerns – not only the inventories of possessions that correspond to police and intelligence reports, but also more straightforwardly parodic lists, like the catalogue of preposterous mathematical relations between Stephen's and Bloom's ages (U 794). In 'Ithaca', the unusual content of *Ulysses* denies readers the sort of information and reader–character relationships to which they are accustomed and prompts them to adopt reading strategies that resemble surveillance and thus to occupy the role of the intelligence agent Bloom fears. 'Ithaca' casts its readers as the domestic intruders Bloom fears and invites them to carry out yet further surveillance work in their use of that information – an invitation many of Joyce's readers accept.

'Ithaca' is thus a prime example of *Ulysses* as a book about everything. The episode not only represents the novel's fictional world in detail irrelevant to typical novelistic concerns, ranging from attention to microscopic bacteria to the movement of heavenly bodies, but also – pointedly – reaches beyond the bounds of its covers and is in part about its readers. *Ulysses* depicts its readers as members of the police regime Bloom fears, both making more visceral the novel's depiction of early-twentieth-century surveillance and challenging typical understandings of reading.

Conclusion

The resemblance between the reception strategies *Ulysses* encourages and contemporary technologies of colonial surveillance and policing reaches beyond the bounds of *Ulysses* itself and reorients readers' relationships with Bloom. Bloom is the clear human heart of *Ulysses*, and readers generally feel affection for him. At the same time, however, the style and content of 'Ithaca' – digressive questions that leave readers with inventories of possessions instead of a recognizable novelistic narrative – implicate them in one of the conflicts troubling

Bloom and driving the novel. To access Bloom during the novel's climax, readers must act like an investigator following up on a police search of his home. This framing makes them the very figure Bloom most fears and otherwise never confronts. Readers, both Joyce's contemporaries and their successors today, may not share in the anti-Semitism or chauvinism of, say, the Citizen and the others who confront Bloom in Barney Kiernan's pub, but they perform the police work he fears by following the limited interpretive avenues *Ulysses* provides. The colonial surveillance subplot is a particularly strong example of *Ulysses* as a novel in which little happens: Bloom fears that Corny Kelleher is an informant, and the novel neither confirms nor denies Bloom's suspicions, because nothing of interest happens. Despite Bloom's direction to himself to avoid Kelleher, they meet, and when they do, the suspected informant is nothing but helpful. Martin Cunningham is a colonial intelligence agent in Dublin Castle, but that fact becomes relevant only in private conversation about Bloom, in which Cunningham weakly pushes back against the Citizen's anti-Semitism and gets Bloom out of there when things become violent. Whereas Molly's adulterous tryst with Blazes Boylan does occur, and Bloom does confront the Citizen about the hypocrisy of his ideology of national purity, no intelligence agent makes a difference in *Ulysses* – until the novel is read, at least. Readers pick up where the novel's abortive surveillance plot left off, and their responses to the novel fulfil Bloom's otherwise paranoid fears. No fictional character violates the secrets of Bloom's bottom drawer, as Bella Cohen threatens, but the novel's readers do.

All of these considerations demonstrate one particular way in which *Ulysses* is a book of everything. Joyce writes with an eye towards his audience and makes readers part of the novel's plot. Joyce shows how reading resembles surveillance and does so by spying on readers in action and manipulating their responses. Rather than invite readers into a fictional world, Joyce's style pushes them into the role of villainous intelligence agents. In his biography of Joyce, Richard Ellmann writes, 'Some temperaments demand the feeling that their friends and sweethearts will deceive them'; Joyce had such a temperament, and his 'conversation often returned to the word "betrayal"'. This personal paranoia carried over into Joyce's fiction and his characterization of readers' relationships with his characters. Just as Joyce suspected everyone in his life of being ready to betray him, so *Ulysses* represents readers as betraying the very characters with whom they identify and for whom they read.

Penelope

MARINA CARR

Marina Carr is one of the foremost playwrights in the English language and Associate Professor of Creative Writing at Dublin City University. Among her plays are *By the Bog of Cats*, *Marble*, as well as versions of Greek tragedy with emphasis on the cultural confusions, pain and comedy of transitional societies.

Dear Mr Joyce,

Though this greeting is far too polite and respectful given the outrageous gall of the way you have drawn my character in your smutty Romance. 'Sweets of Sin' wouldn't be in it with your innuendo and bare faced lies. I suppose a book is worth nothing without a woman in it and you poets have to be endlessly whining and swooning and lying about and parsing a poor woman to flitters. Indeed you have to be right there in the bed beside her imagining her farting and scratching and praising her own bosoms and thinking dirty thoughts about men to take her right down to your own pigsty level. What sort of a man traduces a woman like that? And for your information I have not farted since I reached the age of reason. I am not responsible for when I was a squalling babe in nappies. And for you to devote divers paragraphs on the eructations of my person is beyond the beyonds and drives me to madness here in the purple fields of Hades. Yes the fields are purple here during the day and black at night. I've asked about for you so I could confront you to your face and give you the dressing down coming to you but not a sign of you in Plouton's caverns though there are writers aplenty here. Your man Shakespeare is Plouton's scribe. Drives everywhere with him in his chariot, writing down every bit of nonsense that falls from the King of the Dead's cracked mouth. You've made me infamous here Mr Joyce, a holy show you've made of me. Plouton himself called me out the other day on his progress, Master Shakespeare perched beside him on the cushions, quill in his hand, poised to record for all the dead the bon mots that fall from the Royal mouth.

Molly Bloom, says he the other day, we all have to line up outside our houses when Plouton goes by, all respectful like.

Molly Bloom, says the bould Plouton, step forward and sing one of them ditties of yours. And I says, bowing of course and craw thumping the way he wants it, my Lord of the Dead, says I, I'm not her at all, I'm not the Molly Bloom you think I am. That's only the figary of a mad poet's festering mind. I'm Molly Bloom, respectable wife of Leopold Bloom, and if I do sing it's in the professional manner on a stage and I won't be ogled and tittered at by every wide boy just because a parcel of lies was written about me back in the day by one James Joyce esquire. I'll esquire him when I get my hands on him. And the King of the Dead harrumphs and consults with Master Shakespeare who's giving me the smirk with his boiled eyes as if to say, I have the measure of you missus and I know by the gatch of you you'd like a good wrangle in the feather bed come dusk. Well let him dream on. You'd think a poet of his calibre would have a fligget of intelligence and understanding about the human condition and about women and their predicament in this world, in any world, not a bit of him, sniggering like a schoolboy at me as they gallop off to taunt the next poor woman lined up in front of her garden, making their infra dig remarks and me standing there helpless for the whole population to look down their noses at. You sent me down to Hades with a past, Mr Joyce, a past I had none of and it follows me here and has my good name in tatters so every ghoul thinks I'm easy for it and will lie back in the fields of asphodel without a murmur and let them have their way.

I went to Paris to haunt your sleep. Your dreams. I was attempting a visitation but not a budge out of you though I knocked over the kettle and ran the cat. But there you were stewing in drink and your poor wife trying to sleep beside you. And you know what struck me, you were upside down in the bed, your feet in the poor woman's mouth. Lord Almighty how she puts up with you. Is that the way you think you should sleep beside a woman? Your mouth to her arse? Your big spawgs in her gob? Then word came to me that you died so I went looking for your grave to have it out with you there. Cementerio de Fluntern. Wouldn't you think your own would want your bones in with themselves but of course the Irish government wouldn't hear tell of your carcass laid to rest on the consecrated sod. Beautiful cemetery, Fluntern, but not a peep out of you after all your smart-alecky drivel about flashing eyes and flashing busts and mandolins and lanterns and sparrowfarts and petticoats and garters and women's drawers. Sweet God the impudence of you when you were alive and not a gig to be heard from your grave and you clattering the brains out of your head all your days to come up with one more outrageous sentence than the last. Your poor wife must've been a saint to put up with your glooms and the deepdown torment that must be in you, having to be out looking for it from first mass till the last hoor house closes shop for the night.

I'm sending this letter with Acheron because you were spotted the other side of the Styx waiting for your papers to enter Hades. Lazing under a pomegranate, I was told. And still writing, a flask of wine propped up against a stone. Well you better not be writing about me or I'll lodge a complaint with His Lordship's scribe and have you refused entry. We don't need your sort of man in our midst for all Eternity and beyond.

But I want to keep this brief and to the point. This is what I want you to do. I want for you to retract everything you thought, said and wrote about me and I want it in writing so it can be read out loud and clear as a proclamation by Master Shakespeare to the population here. It's the least you can do to unsmirch my reputation. I'm not going round with my head down like that dotty Penelope and her blagguard of a husband who makes her walk ten steps behind him, giving the once over to every woman who crosses his path. She's under the impression that I'm related to her in some way. I had to tell her I haven't a drop of Spartan blood in me or any Asia Minor for that matter. But she kept insisting, blathering on about suitors and Ithaca and Jammess Joysa and Omero and it only dawned on me after she was talking about you and that lad Homer. Have you done a nut job on her too? Oh you twattering bards with your shipwrecked minds spewing your silage

and sewer over the flower of noble womanhood, your
slavering deranged fantasies dreepin all over us, wanting to
make trollops of us all and not one of ye'd know a woman
from a cabbage. Good for nothin's that wouldn't be in the
world only for us and not a particle of love in your nature
if it isn't serving the lust of your eye and the lust of your
heart. I see ye coming, that determined vicious swagger,
like lions only a lion'd have more to say for himself in
the leaba. No, your minds always on thirsty titties and
imagining every unblemished woman with the coal man
and the bishop and the gypsy and the German Emperor
if you don't smile. Seafoid and blatheration, the bitten of
Greek and Latin thrown in as if that impresses us and all
you're really doing is disgracing yourself while leaving the
rest of us no wiser as to the real nature of womankind.
It's not right, Mr Jammess Joysa, to take from women the
dignity and privacy you guard so jealously for yourselves.
Supposing I was to write down the lavatory of your mind
and call it Joyce's soliloquy of the chamber pot, farting
and wanking and admiring your scrotum and feeling your
own balls and genuflecting over your jouncing unbiddable
mickey as you croon Mother Machree or Love's old sweet
song. How would you like that? I think you'd have the
highest magistrates in the land on top of my head for the
infringement and assault on your salient right to keep
private what is private. If civilization has anything to offer,
it is, as I believe the Jesuits called it, custody of the tongue,
if not custody of the wild seething mind and who knows
what that is in all its glorious reptilian jungle swill? I'll give

399

you that, you got the swill part right. But decorum, Mr Joyce, decorum. And a woman's dignity. After all she has to walk down the street with her hat on and at least hope every male she passes by is not instantly thinking about the size of her bosoms and the shape of her you know what.

Yours,
Molly Laredo Bloom.

Westbank,
River Styx and
Environs
Date?

My dear Mrs. Molly Laredo Bloom,

You can imagine my consternation and delight at the receipt of your scorching missive. There was I thinking I had made you up out of the squalor and confusion that some call the imagination but here is your letter in my hand, ghostly though it be. There is after all, as the prophets tell, a vague something behind everything, design might be too commodious and ambitious a word to describe it, but an everything behind the veil of something at any rate. How else to explain the fact of your letter or indeed my continued existence and your existence at all.

I was flummoxed before the arrival of your letter but am now in a complete reel and don't know which side of me is up in this strange place I find myself. Five rivers, I'm told, run through these lands. I believe I sojourn on the banks of the Styx, as you surmised. And yes, I'm waiting for the blasted paperwork to be completed before I am permitted to embark on the next leg of the journey, though I am as confused as to where that will be as I am as to where I am right now. My last sane memory is lying in an operating theatre about to go under the ether for stomach pains. And when I woke I was soaring like a wild gull over the dear old land of the shamrock. I wanted to alight but some wind or stronger will than my own forbade me until I was dropped here like a stone among all the new dead. There are thousands of us, every race you can imagine and some you can't. The trees sing and the river whispers but then didn't I always know that in my heart of hearts? I hang mostly with the Greeks. I'm superstitious about them. They've always brought me luck. And they have endless supplies of the grape, wherever they get it, and part freely with it and sing their melancholy songs come dusk.

But let us talk of you, Molly, in this post human place we find ourselves. Lord, the wonder of it all, Molly. My dear Molly, is it really you? Or some prank set up by fat-backed Gogarty and the sly Cosgrave to try and rise me again as they did back when I walked Dublin in second-hand trousers and torn shoes, my heart full of dreams and rage at the perfidy of the tribe and my poor naked land with its broken music and its dripping gardens and the eternal odour of scutter and ashpit. The tribe that made me a vagabond, wandering the earth with one arm longer than the other. Paddy Pig and Micky Muck, their grandiosity and degradation slinging it out as no doubt they are still and will be for a while to come yet. But don't get me started on the Gael. Haven't I said enough on him to last me several lifetimes.

Molly, my dearest Molly, may I call you that? The one true woman born, though I know I made you up, or at least I thought I did until your letter arrived in my lap. My dear Molly, you scalded the heart out of me when I read your angry words at what I wrote about you. I can imagine the eyes blazing in your head as you write down all your rage at my presumption in attempting to give song to the inner workings of a woman's mind and the poetry of a woman's body. Molly, you were my clou, the star turn of that tiresome book and your wisdom alone salvaged it. What can I say in my defence? It was the only book I could write at the time and it upsets me that I have offended you in the writing of it. You probably think me a bowsie, a peeping Tom, a sloothering and slavering miscreant of the first perversity, but Molly, let me tell you something, I may be a bad writer, even a very bad one, but I have never used obscene language in my speech. Ask anyone who knows me, knew me, and they'll tell you they've never heard me utter an unfit word before a woman. And when men told filthy lecherous stories in my presence I would turn away in disgust and yet you seem to think me a beast.

So much for speaking and the decorum you accuse me of lacking and the basic manners I learnt at my mother's knee. That is one thing Molly. Writing is entirely another. Words for me are never just words. They are electric, wild, free, thrilling keys to the untrammelled soul, the mysterious scripture and golden ogham that ever expand the visible and the divine made human in all its magnificent tortured slow sad evolution.

And Love, Molly. What I tried to capture with Molly Bloom was the majesty of Love. Love as Art's true source and best subject. And for better or worse, in my soul of souls, all my life I have equated the two. Art and Love. And the highest love for me is the love a woman has for a man and a man for a woman. It is the only thing that makes sense in this everlasting round of birth, copulation, death. Love was my modus operandi, my one and only sacred principle to help me withstand what the world and its mother calls living. Human existence cannot be borne without the rapture of love, love as Tristan had for Isolde, Juliet for Romeo, Dante for Beatrice, Shakespeare for his dark lady. I was fortunate in finding that love in an unprepossessing girl out of the west. And forgive me Molly if I seem too familiar, but as I write to you it seems it is Nora who is listening. Have you seen her or heard any word of her your side of the river? If so, please inform me at once. I don't know how she'll get on without me. When we first went abroad, I had to hold her hand like a child, so terrified she was of all the strange smells and the markets and the foreign tongues. I had to buy her clothes, her hats, her shoes. She'd be struck dumb once we left our room, hiding behind me if anyone spoke to her, blushing like a cart of apples till the tears streamed down her cheeks. But I knew the first day I clapped eyes on her on Nassau Street, knew before I spoke a word to her that if I was to write anything worth reading I would only do so if I kept her near. It was her I was trying to capture, Molly, when I created you. And I can see your eyes blazing again as you read these lines, I can hear you thinking, Don't I exist in my own right? I, Molly Laredo Bloom, without being pilloried and plastered across a bed at four in the morning at the whim of your pen Mr James Joyce esquire? Yes you do Molly, yes you do, but let me explain myself before I lose the thread of my thought. In writing you I was writing Nora. Nora with bits thrown in from hither and yon as writers do. My mother, my sisters, the cousins, the arthritic old aunts, the washerwoman, the tinkers, the hoors, you name it, all food for the flame. If anyone really saw the inside of a writer's mind they'd be less than underwhelmed at the demented sorcery, the garbage fossicking, the snapping up of unconsidered trifles that goes into the stinking seething cauldron that others less demented and better informed call Art and Literature.

But Molly, Nora, you are becoming interchangeable for me as you were when I wrote you down, I have loved in you this image I have of the beauty of the world, the mystery of life itself before the heart ages and hardens, the doom of the race of whom I am a child, your soul, your name, your eyes seem to me strange blue wildflowers growing in some tangled rain-drenched hedge. I speak your name here, softly to the river and the night, and weep to remember the beauty of the world that passed like a dream behind my eyes. When I lived and watched her breathing beside me, I prayed to a God I didn't believe in, prayed that when I died he would allow me to hover forever in some dark blue rain-drenched flower in a wild hedge at Aughrim or Oranmore. But it appears it is not to be. Nothing will remain of Nora or of me, our little human passion and driven bodies beneath the reign of uncouth stars. We lived and laughed and loved and left. How sad life is. How sad death too, though I'm new to it. At least I think I am. Did I die yesterday or a thousand years ago? Was I ever above at all? What does that even mean from here, the wrong side of the Styx? From one disillusion to another. But I can hear you saying, enough of your auld palaver Jimmy Joyce, you're a brute and in the pages of your dirty book you've made a brute of me too. All I can answer, Molly, is all men are brutes with their wild beast cravings for every secret and shameful part, every odour and act of a woman's body and soul. And all our depravities and chittering and scribbling and bog talk on the subject are only a vain and crude attempt to capture and own something pure, something sacred, to find an altar to worship at, to take our eyes away for a second from the nullity, the nothing of it all and turn that gaze with languor and longing towards the one true object of our desire. Love. Ravishing Love. Woman. I done me best on that score when I was let and loathe to me in guilt and glory. I accept your ire with bowed head and all that is left is to ask your forgiveness for laying the burden of my tortured mind on your unblemished soul. But Molly, you erupted from my pen like ten volcanoes, turning the ink to lava, incinerating the pages with the heat of your desire and loathing, like a Queen riding in triumph through Persepolis or Thebes or Argos, dispensing to us poor beggars of the realm the alms of grace, freedom, eloquence and I will retract whatever you command me to retract as soon as I am permitted to cross the river.

I await your reply and won't rest until we are on better terms. On another matter, might I impose on you to enquire if there is a room to be had your side of the river, assuming I will be furnished with my travel documents soon. I don't know what they use for money here. No doubt there is currency of some sort. Nothing free in the last world and I begin to suspect, nothing free here either.

With kindest regards,
Sincerely yours,
James Joyce.

Works Cited

Telemachus – Joyce and the Greeks

Aristotle, *De Anima* (*On the Soul*) (Penguin Classics, 1987)

___. *Poetics* (Penguin Classics, 1996)

___. *Metaphysics* (Penguin Classics, 1998)

___. *On Sense and the Sensible* (University of Adelaide Library, 2000)

Bérard, Victor, *Les Phéniciens et l'Odyssée* (A Colin, 1902)

___. *Les Navigations d'Ulysse Tome I: Les Iles de la Très- Verte. Tome II.* (Mer Rouge et Méditerranée, 1927)

Homer, *The Odyssey* (Penguin Classics, 2009)

Milton, John, 'Lycidas', *The Complete Works of John Milton* (OUP, 2019)

O'Hehir, B. and J. M. Dillon, *Classical Lexicon for Finnegans Wake* (University of California Press, 1977)

Rouse, W.H.D. *The March Up Country: A Translation of Xenophon's Anabasis Into Plain English* (Nelson, 1947)

Nestor – Ulysses, *Race and the New Bloomusalem*

Bauman, Zygmunt, 'Allosemitism, Premodern, Modern, Postmodern', in *Modernity, Culture, and 'The Jew'*, Eds. Bryan Cheyette and Laura Marcus (Polity, 1998)

Cheng, Vincent J., 'Catching the Conscience of a Race: Joyce and Celticism', in *Joyce in the Hibernian Metropolis*, Eds. Morris Beja and David Norris (Ohio State University Press, 1996)

Cohen, Stanley, *States of Denial: Knowing about Atrocities and Suffering* (Polity, 2001)

Deutscher, Isaac, 'Who is a Jew?', *The Non-Jewish Jew and Other Essays*, edited by Tamara Deutscher (OUP, 1968)

Goldberg, David Theo, *The Racial State* (Blackwell, 2002)

Ignatiev, Noel, *How the Irish Became White* (Routledge, 1995)

Lentin, Alana, *Why Race Still Matters* (Polity, 2020)

Lentin, Louis, 'I Don't Understand. I Fail to Say. I Dearsee You Too', in *Joyce in the Hibernian Metropolis*, Eds. Morris Beja and David Norris (Ohio State University Press, 1996)

McVeigh, Robbie and Ronit Lentin, *After Optimism? Ireland, Racism and Globalisation* (Metro Eireann Publications, 2006)

Rolston, Bill and Michael Shannon, *Encounters: How Racism Came to Ireland* (Beyond the Pale, 2002)

Rolston, Bill and Robbie McVeigh, *Ireland, Colonialism and the Unfinished Revolution* (Beyond the Pale, 2021)

Wolfe, Patrick, *Traces of History: Elementary Structures of Race* (Verso, 2016)

Proteus

Aristotle, *De Anima* (*On the Soul*)
(Penguin Classics, 1987)

Eriugena, John Scotus, *On the Division
of Nature* (*De Divisione Naturae or
Periphyseon*) (Bellarmin, 1987)

Joyce, James, *A Portrait of the Artist as
a Young Man* (Penguin, 1992)

Kearney, Richard, *Touch: Recovering
our Most Vital Sense* (Columbia
University Press, 2021)

Lotus-Eaters – Turn on, Tune in, Bloom out

Canetti, Elias, *Crowds and Power*
(Continuum, 1978)

Dick, Philip K., *The Divine Invasion*
(Vintage, 1991)

Fisher, Mark, *K-Punk: The Collected
and Unpublished Writings of Mark
Fisher (2004–2016)*, edited by

Darren Ambrose, with a Foreword
by Simon Reynolds (Repeater Books,
2018)

Lilly, John C., *The Center of the
Cyclone. An Autobiography of Inner
Space* (The Julian Press, 1972)

Aeolus – Inside 'Aeolus' and The Irish Times, *Everything is Copy*

Homer, *The Odyssey* (Penguin, 2009)

Kiberd, Declan, *Ulysses and Us. The
Art of Everyday Living* (Faber, 2009)

Lestrygonians

Ellmann, Richard, *James Joyce* (Oxford
University Press, 1982)

Scylla & Charybdis – Homer... Shakespeare... Joyce... Borges

Alighieri, Dante, *The Divine Comedy*
(Penguin Classics, 2012)

Bloom, Harold, *The Western Canon*
(Penguin, 1995)

Borges, Jorge Luis, 'The Approach to
Al-Mu'tasim' and 'Pierre Menard,
Author of the Quijote', and 'Theme
of the Traitor and the Hero' and
'Kafka and his Precursors' and

'Shakespeare's Memory' *Collected
Fictions*, trans. Andrew Hurley
(Penguin, 1999)

Cervantes, Miguel de, *Don Quixote*
(Penguin Classics, 2018)

Césaire, Aimé, 'Une Tempête.'
Collection Théâtre, 22. (Éditions
du Seuil, 1969)

Fernández Retamar, Roberto, *Calibán and Other Stories* (University of Minnesota, 2002)

Friel, Brian, *Translations* (Faber, 1981)

Homer, *The Odyssey* (Penguin Classics, 2009)

___. *The Iliad* (Penguin Classics, 1992)

Milton, John, *Paradise Lost* (Penguin Classics, 2003)

Shakespeare, William, *The Complete Plays* (OUP, 2005)

Wilde, Oscar, 'The Decay of Lying' and *The Picture of Dorian Gray*, in *Complete Works* (Collins Classics, 1999)

Wandering Rocks – The 'Retrospective Arrangement' of Dublin in 'Wandering Rocks'

Baudelaire, Charles, *The Painter of Modern Life and Other Essays*, translated and edited by Jonathan Mayne (Da Capo, 1964)

Budgen, Frank, *James Joyce and the Making of Ulysses* (H. Smith and R. Haas, 1934)

Gifford, Don, and Robert J. Seidman, *'Ulysses' Annotated: Notes for Joyce's Ulysses* (University of California Press, 1988)

Sirens – Sgt Joyce's Lonely Hearts Club Band

Eno, Brian, *A Year with Swollen Appendices* (Faber & Faber, 1996)

Cyclops – A Sneer and a Smile

Austen, Jane, *Emma* (Oxford World's Classics, 2008)

Shakespeare, William, *Henry V* (Oxford World's Classics, 1982)

Nausicaa

Aeschylus, *The Oresteia*, a new translation by Ted Hughes (Farrar, Straus and Giroux, 1999)

Alighieri, Dante, *The Divine Comedy*, vol. I: *Inferno*, translated, with an Introduction, Notes and Commentary by Mark Musa (Penguin Books, 2003)

Alighieri, Dante, *The Divine Comedy, Inferno 1: Italian Text and Translation*, translated, with a commentary, by Charles S. Singleton (Bollingen Series LXXX, Princeton University Press, 1970)

Benstock, Bernard, *Critical Essays on James Joyce's Ulysses* (G. K. Hall & Co., 1989)

Donne, John, *Selected Poetry and Prose*, edited by T. W. and R. J. Craik (Methuen, 1986)

Homer, *The Odyssey*, translated by Emily Wilson (W. W. Norton & Company, Inc., 2018)

Joyce, James, *A Portrait of the Artist as a Young Man* (Penguin Books, 1981)

Levi, Primo, cited in *The Penguin Book of Italian Short Stories*, edited, and with selected translations and an Introduction, by Jhumpa Lahiri (Penguin Classics, 2020)

Meyerhoff, Hans, *Time in Literature* (University of California Press, 1960)

Ovid, *Metamorphoses: A New Verse Translation*, translated by David Raeburn, with an Introduction by Dennis Feeney (Penguin Books, 2004)

Pliny the Elder, *Natural History* Vol. III, Libri VIII–XI, translated by H. Rackham (Harvard University Press, 1940; 1956)

Rose, H. J., *A Handbook of Greek Mythology* (E. P. Dutton & Co., Inc., 1959)

Shakespeare, William, *The Oxford Shakespeare: The Tragedy of Macbeth*, edited by Nicholas Brook (Oxford University Press, 1990)

Sophocles, *Sophocles I: Antigone, Oedipus the King, Oedipus at Colonus*, edited by David Greene and Richmond Lattimore, third edition, edited by Mark Griffith and Glenn W. Most (*Oedipus at Colonus* translated by Robert Fitzgerald, 1941) (The University of Chicago Press, 2013)

Statius, *Thebaid, Books 8–12, Achilleid*, edited and translated by D. R. Shackleton Bailey (Harvard University Press, 2003)

Virgil (P. Vergili Maronis), *Aeneidos, Libri VII–VIII*, edited by John D. Christie with a Commentary by C. J. Fordyce and Introduction by P. G. Walsh (Published for the University of Glasgow by the Oxford University Press, 1977)

___. *The Aeneid*, translated by Robert Fagles, with an Introduction by Bernard Knox (Viking, 2006)

Waugh, Evelyn, *Brideshead Revisited* (Little, Brown and Company, 1972)

Oxen of the Sun – Prescience and Parody

Homer, *The Odyssey* (Penguin, 2009)

Lawrence, K. R., *Who's Afraid of James Joyce?* (Oxford University Press, 2010)

Leveno K. J., F. G. Cunningham and J. A. Pritchard, 'Caesarean Section: An Answer to the House of Horne', *American Journal of Obstetrics and Gynecology*, vol. 153, no. 8, 1985

O'Driscoll K., M. Foley, D. MacDonald and J. Stronge, 'Cesarean Section and Perinatal Outcome: Response from the House of Horne', *American Journal of Obstetrics and Gynecology*, vol. 158, no. 3, 1988

O'Driscoll K., D. Meagher and M. Robson, *Active Management of Labour* (Mosby, 2004)

Schwarz, D. R., *Reading Joyce's Ulysses* (Macmillan, 1987)

Circe – Night-Rule in Nighttown

Anderson, Darran, *Imaginary Cities: A Tour of Dream Cities, Nightmare Cities, and Everywhere in Between* (Influx Press, 2015)

Carroll, Lewis, *Alice's Adventures in Wonderland* (Puffin, 1986)

Dante Alighieri, *The Divine Comedy* (Oxford, 2008)

Dickens, Charles, *A Christmas Carol* (Penguin, 2003)

Glück, Louise, 'Circe's Power', in *Meadowlands* (Carcanet, 1998)

Homer, *The Odyssey*, translated by Robert Fagles, with an Introduction by Bernard Knox (Penguin, 1996)

Lally, Caitriona, *Eggshells* (HarperCollins, 2018)

Lawlor, Andrea, *Paul Takes the Form of a Mortal Girl* (Picador, 2019)

Lewis, C. S., *The Lion, the Witch and the Wardrobe* (HarperCollins, 2012)

Miller, Madeline, *Circe* (Bloomsbury, 2019)

Ovid, *Metamorphoses*, translated by Mary M. Innes (Penguin, 1955)

Shakespeare, William, *Midsummer's Night Dream*, with an Introduction by Stanley Wells and Helen Hackett (Penguin, 2015)

Woolf, Virginia, *Orlando*, with an Introduction by Sandra M. Gilbert (Penguin, 1993)

Eumaeus – Leopold Bloom, Master-Economist

George, Henry, *Progress and Poverty* (Appleton, 1886)

Keynes, J. M., 'Alfred Marshall, 1842–1924', *The Economic Journal*, vol. 34, no. 135, September 1924, pp. 311–72

Kiberd, Declan, *Ulysses and Us. The Art of Everyday Living* (Faber, 2009)

Ithaca – Reading as the Police

Devlin, Kimberly, 'Bloom and the Police: Regulatory Vision and Visions in *Ulysses*', *Novel: A Forum on Fiction*, vol. 29, no. 1, Fall 1995, pp. 45–52. JSTOR, www. jstor.org/ stable/1345539

Duffy, Enda, *The Subaltern Ulysses* (University of Minnesota Press, 1994)

Ellmann, Richard, *James Joyce: New and Revised Edition* (Oxford University Press, 1982)

Joyce, James, *A Portrait of the Artist as a Young Man*, 1915, edited by Jeri Johnson (OUP, 2001)

___. *Dubliners*, 1914 (Viking, 1982)

___. *Occasional, Critical, and Political Writing*, edited by Kevin Barry and translated by Conor Deane (OUP, 2000)

McCourt, John, *The Years of Bloom: James Joyce and Trieste 1904–1920* (The Lilliput Press, 2000)

Stanzel, Franz K., 'Austria's Surveillance of Joyce in Pola, Trieste, and Zurich', *James Joyce Quarterly*, vol. 38, no. 3, Spring 2001, pp. 361–71. JSTOR, www.jstor.org/stable/25477813

Index

Characters in *Ulysses* are shown in *italics*. All places are in Dublin unless stated otherwise.

9/11 143
60 Minutes (CBS News) 134–5

Abbey Theatre 232
abstract concepts, as speaking
    characters 338–9
*Acid Communism (Unfinished
    Introduction)* (Fisher) 95–6, 99
Acts of Union (1800) 212, 220
Adam Court 173
Adelaide Road 211
advertisements 136, 139, 146, 149–50,
    160–1, 358–9
A.E. (George Russell, poet) 18, 171,
    175, 185
Aeneid (Virgil) 278–9, 281, 292
'Aeolus' (Ep 7) 133–51
Aeschylus, *Oresteia* 293
Agendath Netaim pamphlet 28, 362
agon, literary (conflict) 185, 190, 199
alcohol
    influence of 263
    journalism and 147–8
    algorithmic structure 89–93, 99, 104
Alice in Wonderland (Carroll) 340–1
Alloa, Emmanuel 61
*American Journal of Obstetrics and
    Gynaecology* 314
AML manual 313–14
Amsterdam 365–6
Anabasis (Xenophon) 9–11, 13

Anderson, Darran, *Imaginary Cities*
    336
Annals of Inisfallen, The 30
anti-Semitism 27–33, 37, 40, 260, 376,
    383–4, 387
Antient Concert Rooms 233
Anxiety of Influence, The (Bloom) 185
Aquinas, Thomas 17, 47, 62
Aristotle 17–20, 47, 49–50, 51, 62
    De Anima 18, 19, 50
    Metaphysics 271
    On Sense and Sensible Objects
        19–20
Arius 52
Artane Orphans 325
artist, as entrepreneur 350–5
Aryans, German 27–8
asylum seekers 31–3, 38–40, 42–3
Austen, Jane, *Emma* 262
Australia 38

Bakhtin, Mikhail 326
Balfour Declaration (1917) 136
Bank of Ireland 211, 212–13
Bannon, Alec 307–8
Barnacle, Nora *see* Joyce, Nora
Barney Kiernan's pub 253–67, 391
Barrington, Jonah 220
Barry, Mrs Yelverton 324
bats 271–85, 287–96
    definitions 274–5
Baudelaire, Charles 221–2

Bauman, Zygmunt 26
Beach, Sylvia 299–300
Beatles, The 234
Beaufoy, Mr Philip 84–5
Behan, Brendan 246
Bérard, Victor, *Les Navigations d'Ulysse* 13–14
Bergan, Alf 263
Berkeley, George 50, 51
Best, Richard 185
betrayal 7, 73, 83, 98, 196–7, 232, 244, 380, 392
Biddy the Clap 326
Bloom, Ellen (née Higgins) 48, 54
Bloom, Harold 185, 198
Bloom, Leopold
  imagined conversation with Mike Fitzgerald 155–82
  'Aeolus' 136, 138, 141, 142, 145–7, 149, 150
  'Calypso' 69, 73–85, 356–7, 358–9, 362
  'Circe' 194–5, 324–7, 329, 331–2, 334–44, 382
  'Cyclops' 253–4, 255, 257–8, 259–67, 387
  'Eumaeus' 199, 355–71
  'Hades' 109, 124–5, 126, 304
  'Ithaca' 375–91
  'Lestrygonians' 155–82, 225
  'Lotus-Eaters' 89–90, 92–3, 96–98, 99, 102–3, 104–5
  'Nausicaa' 271–6, 278, 279–80, 282–3, 286–91, 294
  'Nestor' 25, 26, 28–30, 32–3, 40–3
  'Oxen of the Sun' 300–4, 305, 307–10, 311, 312, 314
  'Proteus' 56, 59, 65
  'Scylla & Charybdis' 188–9, 196–7
  'Sirens' 235, 237
  'Wandering Rocks' 241
Bloom, Milly 84, 161–2, 224, 307–8

Bloom, Molly (Marion)
  imagined correspondence with Joyce 395–406
  'Aeolus' 146
  'Calypso' 75, 80, 83, 358
  'Circe' 338
  'Ithaca' 387, 391
  'Lestrygonians' 157, 161–2, 174, 177, 179
  'Lotus-Eaters' 98
  'Nausicaa' 290
  'Oxen of the Sun' 300–1, 302–3
  'Proteus' 56–7, 59–60, 65
  'Wandering Rocks' 218–19, 223, 241, 246–7, 250
Bloom, Rudolph (was Virag)
  'Hades' 125
  'Lestrygonians' 181
  'Nestor' 33
  'Oxen of the Sun' 304
  'Proteus' 48, 54
  'Sirens' 244
Bloom, Rudy 162, 300–1, 302, 303, 304, 344
Bloomsday 110, 347, 355
Bloomusalem 40–3, 336
blues, the 245–6
Boer War (1899–1902) 375
Böhme, Jacob 49
Boland, Colm 140
Borges, Jorge Luis
  observations 63–4, 79
  'Fragment on Joyce' 72
  'Kafka and His Precursors'. 197
  'The Maker' 192
  'Pierre Menard, Author of the Quixote' 189, 191–2, 197–8
  'Shakespeare's Memory' 198
  'Theme of the Traitor and the Hero'. 193–4
bourgeois outsider 363–6
Boylan, Blazes

'Circe' 342
'Eumaeus' 360
'Ithaca' 387, 391
'Lestrygonians' 157, 161, 177, 178
'Nausicaa' 291
'Oxen of the Sun' 302
'Sirens' 237, 246
'Wandering Rocks' 218, 224, 225
Brady, Conor 140, 145
Brayden, William 143–4
Breen, Mr Denis 163, 225, 256
Breen, Mrs Josie 162–3, 164, 338, 342
Brideshead Revisited (Waugh) 273
Britain 30, 36, 37, 136, 202, 255
brothels 324, 325, 327, 329–31, 335,
    340, 370, 386
Brown, Norman O. 100
Brown Thomas (fashion store) 173–4
Bruno, Giordano 94
Brunswick Street (now Pearse St) 233
Buddhism 97
Budgen, Frank 193, 210
Burke, Mr O'Madden 147
Burke's pub 254
Burren, Co. Clare 33
Burton Restaurant 174–6, 177
Butt Bridge 370
Byrne, Davy 177, 180

Caesar, Julius, Gallic Wars 10, 18
caesarean sections (CS) 313, 314, 315
Caffrey, Cissy 274, 289
Caffrey, Jacky 324
Callan, Nurse 309, 310, 312, 314
'Calypso' (Ep 4) 69–86, 356–7, 358,
    362
Canada 38
Canetti, Elias 90–1
Carey brothers 379
Carroll, Lewis, Alice in Wonderland
    340–1

cat-and-mouse analogy 79, 85, 91
Catholicism 144–5, 211–12, 311–12
    anti-Semitism 27, 29
    Britain and 136
    Catholic-run institutions 38
    converting from/to 30, 125, 172
cats 69, 74, 75, 85
Celtic Twilight, The (Yeats) 222
Census, Irish (1901) 333
centrist, radical 366–9
Cervantes, Miguel de, Don Quixote
    189, 197–8
Chamorro family 134
Charles the Bald, King 62–3
Cheng, Vincent 34–5
China 150
Christmas Carol, A (Dickens) 329
Cibber, Susannah 232
cicadas 295–6
cinemas 348–55, 371
'Circe' (Ep 15) 79, 81, 194–5, 321–44,
    382
Circe (Miller) 324, 325
'Circe's Power' (Glück) 323, 325
citizen economist 358–62
Citizen, The 254, 255–63, 265, 266,
    383–4, 391
Citron 362, 363
Citywest 135, 137, 139, 148
Clancy Brothers 244
Clingan, Willy 140
Clinton, Bill 343
Cohen, Bella 329–30
    Cohen, Bella
    'Circe' 324, 325, 329, 331, 341, 386
    'Ithaca' 387, 391
Cohen, Stanley 37
Collins, Wilkie 223
colonialism 25, 36–40, 186, 190, 193,
    207–8, 210–15, 219, 221, 226–7
Colum, Padraic 7, 191

Commons Restaurant, Newman House 155, 178
compound nouns 336–7
Condell, Sonny 249
Conmee, Revd John 93, 215–18, 224–5, 226
Connellan, Revd Thomas 180
Conroy, Father 271
Corbin, Henry 103
Cork 30
Costello, Dr Punch 307, 310
Cowen, Brian 142
Crane Bag, The (journal) 63
Cranly 188
Crawford, Myles 140, 141–4, 146, 147, 149, 150–1
Creagh, John 37
Criminal Law Amendment Act (1935) 311
Crimmins, Mr 220
Crofton, J. T. A. 255, 264
'The Croppy Boy' (Clancy Brothers) 244
'The Croppy Boy' (Malone) 243–4
Cumann na mBan 310
Cunningham, Martin 255, 262, 376, 377, 383–4, 391
Cunty Kate 326
Cusack, Michael 253
'Cyclops' (Ep 12) 253–67, 387

Dan Lowry's Music Hall 232
Dante, *Divine Comedy* 60, 190, 191, 192–3, 278
Inferno 278, 283–4, 329
David (Hades) 123
Davy Byrne's pub 254
Dawson, 'Doughy Dan' 146
Dawson Street 180
De Anima (Aristotle) 18, 19, 50
de Villepin, Dominique 146

Dead Sea analogy 82, 98, 99
'The Dead' (*Dubliners*, Joyce) 77, 243
Deane, Sir Thomas 155, 182
Deasy, Garrett 25, 29–31, 48, 71, 142, 211–12
death 109–30
Decay of Lying, The (Wilde) 194
Dedalus, Dilly 158, 214, 219–20, 223, 225
Dedalus, Mary (May) 70, 322
Dedalus, Simon 126, 146, 147, 187, 219–20, 237
Dedalus, Stephen
comparison with *Bloom* 69–75, 77, 81–2, 84
in *Portrait of the Artist* 276, 292
'Aeolus' 133, 136, 140, 142, 151
'Circe' 382
'Cyclops' 259
'Eumaeus' 199, 347, 357, 364, 367, 369–71
'Ithaca' 385, 388, 389
'Nestor' 18, 29, 70–1, 211–12
'Oxen of the Sun' 300, 303–5, 307, 308, 311
'Proteus' 48–62, 64–5
'Scylla & Charybdis' 185–202
'Telemachus' 9, 11, 16, 19–21
'Wandering Rocks' 221–3
denial 37–40
Deutscher, Isaac 25
Devlin, K. J. 378
Dick, Philip K. 100
Dickens, Charles, *A Christmas Carol* 329
digital voodoo 89–91, 98, 99, 103–4
Dignam, Mrs 262, 338
Dignam, Paddy 110, 216, 244, 262, 263, 327
Dignam, Patrick 216, 226
Dillon, John 7
Dillon, Mat 303

Dillon, Myles 7
Direct Provision (DP) centres 32, 38–9
disavowal, of race 37–40
Disraeli, Benjamin 34
diversity 207–8, 368–9
Divine Comedy (Dante) 191, 192–3, 278, 329
Dixon 310
Dlugacz 360, 362, 363
Dlugacz, Moses 362
D'Olier Street 135
Don Quixote (Cervantes) 189, 197–8
Donne, John, Holy Sonnet XIV 292
Donohoe's pub 266
Doors of Perception, The (Huxley) 94
Doran, Bob 173, 254, 263
Dorset Street 360
Dos Passos, John 290
Douce, Miss 214, 236–7
Doyle, Roddy, *Guess Who's Coming for the Dinner* 41
Driscoll, Mary 342, 343
Dublin 16, 40–1, 97, 208–27
Dublin Castle 376, 380, 391
Dubliners (Joyce) 77, 299, 353, 380, 383
Dudley, Lady 214
Dudley, William Humble Ward, 2nd Earl of 213–14, 215, 216, 221
Duke Lane 180
Duke Street 165, 174
Dún Laoghaire 233
Dunne, Miss 223–4
Duns Scotus, John 64

Easter Rising (1916) 221, 226, 305, 310, 375
Eblana Theatre 233
'Ecce Puer' (Joyce) 64
Eccles Street 218, 358
echolalia/echolocation 288–9

economy/economists 32, 256–7, 353, 355–66
Edward VII, King 327
Edwards, Hilton 232
Egan, Kevin 48
Eggshells (Lally) 321, 327–8, 339
Eglinton, John 185, 187, 188, 190, 196
Eliot, T. S., 'Tradition and the Individual Talent' 197, 302
Ellmann, Richard, *Ulysses on the Liffey* 185, 190–1, 193, 392
Emma (Austen) 262
Emmet, Robert 220, 245
Encounters: How Racism Came to Ireland (Rolston and Shannon) 34
Eno, Brian 236
entrepreneur, artist as 369–71
Ephron, Nora 151
Epic of Gilgamesh 13
Eriugena, John Scotus, *On the Division of Nature* 62–4
EU (European Union) 32–3, 142
'Eumaeus' (Ep 16) 188, 199, 347–71
Evening Telegraph 139, 142, 351

Family Planning Association, Irish 311–12
farce, bedroom 83
Farrell, Cashel Boyle O'Connor Fitzmaurice Tisdall 163
Faulkner, Sir Frederick 181
'Fenianism' (Joyce) 380
Fergus of Loan 63
Ferry, Bryan 236
Field, John 231
Finnegans Wake
  characters in 11–12, 14, 43
  H. C. Earwicker 35, 64, 100–1, 380
  'intermisunderstanding minds' 61
  language of 8, 11–12, 97, 195–6

O'Hehir–Dillon *Lexicon* 21
psychedelic counterculture 100–2
reading 7
First World War 89, 203, 290, 375, 381
Fishamble Street 232
Fisher, Mark, *Acid Communism (Unfinished Introduction)* 95–6, 99
Fitzgerald, Anne 171
FitzGerald, Edward 220
Fitzgerald family 211, 212
Fitzgerald, Mike 155–82
FitzGerald, Thomas (Silken Thomas) 212
Fitzgerald, Tom 162, 171
Fitzgerald's pub 155
FitzPatrick, Colm 137–9, 148, 149
Fleet Street 135–6
Flynn, Nosey 176, 177, 178
Focus Theatre 233
Forty Foot 233
Fortycoats & Co. 327
Fottrell, George 341
'Fragment on Joyce' (Borges) 72
France 37, 142
Francie Con Joe (Hades) 116, 117
Francis Street 231
Franks, Dr Hyman 160–1
Freeman's Journal, The 139, 143–4
Freud, Sigmund 39, 95, 100, 326, 361
Friel, Brian, *Translations* 191

G-men (Dublin Metropolitan Police) 168, 169
Gaelic language 191
Gageby, Douglas 142, 145
Gaiety Theatre 234
Gallaher, Fred 142, 143
Gallaher, Ignatius 142
Gate Theatre 232
Geminiani, Franceso 231

gender-bending 97, 293, 322, 337–8
General Post Office 226–7
George, Henry, *Poverty and Progress* 359
George's Street 165
Gifford, Don, *Ulysses Annotated* 211
Glasnevin 110, 124
Glück, Louise, 'Circe's Power' 323, 325
Goethe, Johann Wolfgang von 185–6
Gogarty, Oliver St. John 7, 9, 11
Goldberg, David Theo 35
'golden-mouth' (epithet) 15
Goulding, Richie and Sally 52
'Grace' (*Dubliners*, Joyce) 383
Grafton Street 173
Great Hunger 159, 168, 172
Great Music Hall 232
Greek language 8–10, 15–16, 191
Greek philosophy 17–21
Gregory, Lady 232
Grey, Katherine 180
Griffith, Arthur 27, 29, 262
Grynberg, Fabian 122–4, 126, 127–8
Grynberg family 110, 127–8
Guess Who's Coming for the Dinner (Doyle) 41
Guinness Brewery 160
Gulliver's Travels (Swift) 194

'Hades' (Ep 6) 109–30, 216, 303, 304
haecceity 64
Haines 16–17, 70, 185, 186, 213, 215
Hamlet (Shakespeare) 56, 102, 185–9, 199
Handel, George Frideric 232
Hanlon, Micky 179
Harrington, Lord Mayor 332
Heaney, Seamus 63
Helen of Troy 196
hellish links 328–9

Henry V (Shakespeare) 200, 260
Hibernensis, Martin 63
Higgins, Francis 144
Higgins, Zoe 341
Holles Street 163, 299, 306, 310
Holocaust 31
home rule, Irish 286, 378, 389
Homer, *Odyssey* 13–14, 189–92, 199,
    209, 277, 286, 305–6, 322
Horne, Sir Andrew 307, 311
House of Parliament, Irish 166, 212
How the Irish Became White
    (Ignatiev) 37
Howth Head 60, 179, 233
Hugh (Hades) 115–18
Hughes, Ted 293
humour 64–5, 244–5, 264
Hungarian refugees 25, 31, 32–3
Huxley, Aldous, *The Doors of
    Perception* 94
Hynes, Joe 48, 54, 255, 259, 263, 264

Ignatiev, Noel, *How the Irish Became
    White* 37
Imaginary Cities (Anderson) 336
imagination 102–5
In The Track of the Sun (Thompson)
    79
inanimate objects, as speaking
    characters 338–9
income, basic 366–7
Inferno (*Divine Comedy*, Dante) 278,
    283–4, 329
Invincibles, Irish National 144, 379
Ireland
    asylum seekers 31–3, 38–40, 42–3
    colonialism 36
    exceptionalism 26–7
    identity 257–8
    institution regimes 38
    post-colonialism 35–6, 38

    refugees in 25–6, 31–3
*Ireland, Colonialism and the
    Unfinished Revolution* (McVeigh
    and Rolston) 38
'Ireland, Island of Saints and Sages'
    (Joyce lecture) 25
Irish Dáil 311
Irish Field (newspaper) 164
Irish Free State 31, 187, 227, 310, 311
Irish Republican Brotherhood 144,
    168–9
Irish Sea 347
Irish Times, The 133, 134, 135–50
irony 14, 15, 53, 62–4, 71, 262
Irving, Henry 232
Island Street 220
Isle of Man 150
Israel 26, 28, 136, 362
Italian language 8, 9, 190, 192, 284
'Ithaca' (Ep 17) 375–92
It's a Wonderful Life (film) 329

Jacobs, Jane 368
James Joyce Tower and Museum. 155
James's Street 220
Jews and Judaism 25–31, 34, 40–2,
    123–6, 211–12, 265, 363–5
wandering Jew(s) 26, 82, 110–11, 192,
    383
Jolas, Maria 61
journalists 135–42, 146, 148–51
Joyce family 333, 348
Joyce, James
    Works by
    Dubliners 77, 299, 353, 380, 383
    'Ecce Puer' 64
    'Fenianism' 380
    *Portrait of the Artist as a Young
    Man, A* 55, 86, 189, 193, 276–8,
    380
    Work in Progress 79

see also *Finnegans Wake*
Joyce, Nora (née Barnacle) (wife) 29,
185, 334, 352, 353
Joyce, Stanislaus (brother) 8, 72, 81,
237
joyceproject.com 80, 83
'Joyce's Agon with Shakespeare'
(Bloom) 185
Julius Caesar (Shakespeare) 193
Jung, Carl 95

'Kafka and His Precursors' (Borges)
197
Kearney, Richard, *Touch: Recovering
our Most Vital Sense* 47, 60
Kearns, Anne 133
Kelleher, Corny 375, 379, 381–2, 391
Kelly (Hades) 114
Kennedy, Miss 214, 236–7, 239
Kenner, Hugh 85, 291
Kernan, Tom 220–1
ketamine 99
Keyes, Alexander 136, 150
Keynes, John Maynard 356
Kiberd, Declan, *Ulysses and Us* 47, 61,
134, 370
Kildare rebellion (1534–5) 212
Kildare Street 157, 182
King, Stephen, *Pet Sematary* 344
Knockalisheen Camp, Co. Clare 32–3
Kolkata, India 207–9
Korda, Alexander, *Lady Hamilton* 133

La Prensa newspaper 134–5
Lady Hamilton (Korda) 133
Lally, Caitriona, *Eggshells* 321, 327–8,
339
Lambert, Ned 146, 147, 210–13, 215,
264
Lambert Puppet Theatre 233

landlordism 360
Lando, Barry 134–5
language
failing 342–3
of *Finnegans Wake* 8, 11–12, 97,
195–6
fun with 343
see also individual languages
Largymore, Killybegs 112
Latin language 8, 9, 283–4
Lawlor, Andrea, *Paul Takes the Form
of a Mortal Girl* 338
Le Bon Crubeen restaurant 331
Leary, Timothy 100
lectures, Joyce 25, 34, 36
Lemon, Graham 157
Lenehan, Matt 146, 147
Lentin, Alana 36
Lentin, Kalman Solomon 30
Lentin, Louis 26, 29
Leopardi, Giacomo, 'To Silvia' 76
'Lestrygonians' (Ep 8) 79, 155–82,
225
Leveno, Prof Ken 314
Leventhal, A. J. 110
Lewis C.S., *The Lion, the Witch and
the Wardrobe* 327
Liberties, The 231, 232
Liffey, River 55, 155, 160
Lilly, John C. 98–9, 100
Limerick 29, 30, 37
*Lion, the Witch and the Wardrobe,
The* (Lewis) 327
lists 334, 335, 388–9
Little Britain Street 253, 258
Little Green Street 266
Little Jerusalem 41, 363
Little Review magazine 189
Livi, Primo, 'Quaestio de Centauris'
280–1
Livorni, Ernesto 61
Lloyd George, David 141

'Lotus-Eaters' (Ep 5) 89–105
Lourdes water 133
Love, Revd Hugh C. 211, 214
Lower Tyrone Street 333
LSD 99, 100
Lycidas (Milton) 18
Lynch, David 325
Lynott, Philip 240
Lyster, Mr 185–6

McAleese, Mary 133
McAuley's pub 359
Macbeth (Shakespeare) 193, 291
MacCabe, Florence 51
McCool, Finn 12–13
MacDowell, Gerty 271–5
    'Calypso' 81
    'Nausicaa' 279, 280, 282, 287,
        288–9, 290–1, 294
    'Wandering Rocks' 214
McDowell, Thomas Bleakley 143
McEldowney, Eugene 140
McGahern, John 130
machines 134–5
MacHugh, Professor 136, 140, 141,
    144, 146, 147, 149
Mack, Eliza 333
McKenna, Terence 100
MacLiammoir, Michael 232
McLuhan, Marshall 100
McVeigh, Robbie, Ireland,
    Colonialism and the Unfinished
    Revolution 36, 37, 38
Maggie Ann (Hades) 114–18
Maginni, Denis J. 162
Maiden's rock 55–6
maids 80–1
Malahide Road 216, 225
Malone, Carroll, 'The Croppy Boy'
    243–4

March Up Country, The (study of
    Xenophon's Anabasis) 9–10
Marr, Wilhelm 27
Marsh's Library 49, 52
Martello Tower, Sandycove 7, 10,
    16–17, 54, 233
Mastiansky 363
masturbation 81, 272, 335
Meehan, Paula 248–9
Mennipean Satires (Varro) 279
Metamorphoses (Ovid) 278, 284–5,
    286, 322
metamorphosis 97, 284, 295
Metaphysics 19, 62
metempsychosis 58, 59, 83, 276, 281
Meyerhoff, Hans 295
Mfaco, Bulelani 42
Mickey (Hades) 118–19
Midsummer Night's Dream, A
    (Shakespeare) 323, 325, 326, 327,
    328
Miller, Madeline, Circe 324, 325
Milton, John 190, 192–3
    Lycidas 18
    Paradise Lost 187, 188, 222, 328
mirrors 194–5
Molesworth Street 180
monoculturalism 33–4, 36–7
Monto (red light district) 321–44
Moon and the Bonfires, The (Pavese)
    85–6
Mooney's (pub) 147
Moore, Thomas (Tommy) 166–7, 189
Morrissey (Hades) 113–16, 118, 119,
    126, 127
Morrissey (singer) 238
Mother and Baby Homes report
    (2021) 39
Movement of Asylum Seekers in
    Ireland (MASI) 42
Mulligan, Buck
    'Calypso' 70, 71

'Eumaeus' 347
'Oxen of the Sun' 307–8
'Proteus' 48, 54, 56
'Scylla and Charybdis' 185–6
'Telemachus' 9, 11, 13, 16–17, 185,
    191, 222
Murray, Red 137
music 234–6, 238–9, 243–50
music halls 232, 247

Nagle, Susy 224
National Library of Ireland 157, 165,
    182, 185
National Maternity Hospital (NMH)
    299, 306–7, 313–15, 314
Natural History (Pliny the Elder) 281
'Nausicaa' (Ep 13) 271–96
Navigations d'Ulysse, Les (Bérard) 13
Nazi era 26, 28, 31
Neasa (Hades) 109, 111, 119, 120–1
Nelson, Horatio 133
'Nestor' (Ep 2) 18, 25–43, 70–1, 142,
    211–12
Netherlands, the 365–6
New Jerusalem see Bloomusalem
Newcomen Bridge 217
Newman, Alec 148
Nicolas II, Czar 141–2
Nighttown 321–44, 370
'the Nodder' (Hades) 114
North Circular Road 217
North Richmond Street 287
Nouvelle Révue Française journal 14
Nowlan, Dr David 140

O'Brien, Conor 248
O'Carolan, Turlough 231
O'Casey, Sean 232
O'Clery, Conor 143
O'Connell Bridge 160, 225

O'Connell Street 220
Odyssey (Homer) 13–14, 150, 189–
    92, 199, 209, 277, 305–6, 322
Oedipus at Colonus (Sophocles) 293
O'Farrell, Elizabeth 310
O'Hare, Dr 309
O'Hehir, Brendan 7–8
O'Laoghaire, Patrick 248
Old Monks 145
Olympia Theatre 232
O'Molloy, J. J. 141, 148, 150, 255,
    343
'omphalos' (navel) 16–17
On Sense and Sensible Objects
    (Aristotle) 19–20
On the Division of Nature (Eriugena)
    63–4
Oram, Hugh 148
Orbán, Viktor 150
Oresteia (Aeschylus) 293
Orlando (Woolf) 337–8
Ormond Hotel 214, 236–7, 254
O'Rourke, Fran 61
O'Rourke, Larry 358–9, 361
O'Sullivan, Camille 248
Ovid, Metamorphoses 278, 284–5,
    286, 322
'Oxen of the Sun' (Ep 14) 197, 199,
    225, 299–317
Oxford English Dictionary (OED)
    275

Paddy Sean (Hades) 124
Palestine 26, 28, 136, 362
Paradise Lost (Milton) 187, 188, 222,
    328
Paris 7, 14, 19, 47, 53–4, 142, 305
Parnell, Charles Stewart 7, 13
Parnell, John Howard 171
Paul Takes the Form of a Mortal Girl
    (Lawlor) 338

Pavese, Cesare, *The Moon and the Bonfires* 85–6
Pearse Street 233
Pearse, Willie 233
'Penelope' (Ep 18) 395–406
Pet Sematary (King) 344
phallic symbolism 93, 105, 274
philosophy 17, 47–65
Phoenix Park 164, 169, 214, 380
Phoenix Park murders (1882) 143, 144, 386
Picture of Dorian Gray, The (Wilde) 194
'Pierre Menard, Author of the Quixote' (Borges) 189, 191–2, 197–8
pigs/piggishness 322–5, 331, 335, 340, 341
Plato 17, 18, 185–6
Pliny the Elder, (*Natural History*) 281
Plunkett, Joseph Mary 233
Poddle, River 214
Pogues, The 247–8
Poland 110–11, 127
portals 321, 327–8, 340
Portrait of the Artist as a Young Man, A (Joyce) 55, 86, 189, 193, 276–8, 380
potato(es) 78, 79–80, 158, 159, 325–6
Potter, Fred 141–2
Pound, Ezra 63
poverty 159–60, 164–5, 217
Poverty and Progress (George) 359
Power, Jack 91, 126
Protestantism 34, 125, 144–5, 172, 180
'Proteus' (Ep 3) 14, 19, 47–65
psychedelic culture 94, 96–100
Purefoy, Mina
 'Lestrygonians' 163, 165
 'Oxen of the Sun' 299–301, 310, 312–13, 314, 317

Purefoy, Richard Dancer 301
Pyrrhus 18

'Quaestio de Centauris' (Livo) 280–1
Quigley, Nurse 307

R&B scene 248
Rabaiotti, Antonio 331
race and racism 25–30, 33–43
Radiators, The, *Ghostown* 247
radical centrist 366–9
al-Raschid, Haroun 56
Rebellion, Irish (1798) 220, 244
religion 25–33, 51–3, 91, 93, 102, 126–7, 158
 See also individual religions
Richard II (Shakespeare) 187, 200
Richardson, Sorcha 248
Robinson, Mary 145
Rochford, Tom 214
Rolston, Bill 34, 38
Rose, H. J. 293
Ryan, Philip 247

St Mary's Abbey 211–12
Salvation Army 172
Sandinista revolution 134–5
Sandymount Strand 19, 47–57, 58–9, 60
scholars, Irish 62–3
Scotus, Sedulius 63
'Scylla & Charybdis' (Ep 9) 185–203
Seidman, Robert J., *Ulysses Annotated* 211
'The Selfish Giant' (Wilde)
Senn, Fritz 291
senses 49–50, 51, 286–7
sex 69, 81, 93, 273–80, 334–5
Sexton, Walter 171

Shakespeare & Company Bookshop, Paris 299
Shakespeare, William 185–90, 195–202
  Hamlet 56, 102, 194, 199
  Henry V 200, 260
  Julius Caesar 193
  Macbeth 193, 291
  A Midsummer Night's Dream 323, 325, 326, 327, 328
  Richard II 187, 200
  The Tempest 58–9, 194
Shannon, Michael, Encounters: How Racism Came to Ireland 34
Shatter, Alan 40
Shaw, George Bernard 232
Sheehy, Bessie 224, 225
signatures, reading 20–1, 48–50, 52–5, 57, 58
Simmel, Georg 110
Singleton, Charles 284
Sinn Féin 16, 169, 262, 383
'Sirens' (Ep 11) 231–50, 303
Skeffington, Francis Sheehy 305
Skibbereen Eagle, The (newspaper) 141–2
Smith, Bessie, 'Sugar in my Bowl' 247
Smock Alley Theatre 231–2
smoking, journalism and 149
Smyllie, Bertie 141, 145, 148
snacks 339–40
Socrates 358
Sophocles, Oedipus at Colonus 293
'sound' 242–3
Soviet Union 143, 368
Spain 365–6
Spinoza, Baruch 94
'spoken word' scene 248
Stephens, James 169, 380
Stoker, Bram 232
streets, Dublin 329–33
'Sugar in my Bowl' (Smith) 247

surveillance
  readers' 385–90
  subplot 375–92
Swift, Jonathan (Dean Swift), Gulliver's Travels 53, 194, 231
Synge, J. M., The Tinker's Wedding 43, 232, 236

Tara Street 139–40, 148
Taylor, Harriet 109, 110, 113, 122–4, 127, 128–9
Taylor, John F. 136, 144
technology 135, 138–9, 217, 226, 348–9, 367–8
'Telemachus' (Ep 1) 7–21
Tempest, The (Shakespeare) 58–9, 194
'The Maker' (Borges) 192
theatres 231–4, 247, 249
Thebaid (Statius) 278
'Theme of the Traitor and the Hero' (Borges) 193–4
Thomas Street 220
Thomists see Aquinas, Thomas
Thompson, Frederick Diodati, In The Track of the Sun 79
three, rule of 285, 293, 296
Time magazine 147
Tinker's Wedding, The (Synge) 43
Titbits (magazine) 84
Tivoli Theatre 231
'To Silvia' (Leopardi) 76
Touch: Recovering our Most Vital Sense (Kearney) 47, 60
'Tradition and the Individual Talent' (Eliot) 197
trams 214, 217, 226, 331
Translations (Friel) 191
Travellers, Irish 37, 43
Trieste, Italy 348–50, 355, 362, 380–1
Trinity College 9, 35, 144, 166
'Two Gallants' (Dubliners, Joyce) 380

Ulysses Annotated (Gifford and
    Seidman) 211
Ulysses on the Liffey (Ellmann) 185,
    190–1, 193
United Irishman (newspaper) 27
United States 37
University College Dublin (UCD) 155,
    249

van Caspel, Paul 291
Varro, *Mennipean Satires* 279
vegetarianism 169, 171, 175, 177
Victoria, Queen 215
Virag, Lipoti 327
Virgil, *Aeneid* 278–9, 281, 292
Volta cinemas 348–55, 371

Walker's Pronouncing Dictionary 274
Wallace, Mike 135
'Wandering Rocks' (Ep 10) 207–27,
    241, 246–7, 250, 381
War of Independence (1919–21) 375
Waugh, Evelyn, *Brideshead Revisited*
    273

Weaver, Harriet 8
Western Canon, The (Bloom) 185, 198
Westmoreland Street 135, 160
Wilde, Oscar 191, 196
    The Decay of Lying 194
    The Picture of Dorian Gray 194
    'The Selfish Giant' 233
will-o'-the-wisp 328
Wilson, Robert Anton 100
Wisdom Hely's (stationers) 161
Wolfe, Patrick 36
Woolf, Virginia, *Orlando* 191, 337
Work in Progress (Joyce) 79

Xenophon, *Anabasis* 9–11, 13, 347

Yeats, W. B., *The Celtic Twilight* 18,
    187, 222, 232, 267

Zappa, Frank 236
Zgierz, Poland 122, 124, 127, 129
Zionism 28, 362
Zwikielski family 110